'This book presents the entire spectrum of empirical coaching research to date and depicts an almost complete status quo of coaching research.

The book is therefore suitable for researchers to identify the gaps that coaching research has not yet addressed and for practitioners of any school and any methodological background who either want to read up on the subject of effectiveness or are motivated to gain inspiration on how to enrich their coaching practice with evidence-based elements and 'magic ingredients' that help their clients the most.

I am convinced that this book will be a future standard reference for coaching researchers and practitioners interested in evidence-based coaching and, despite the title, definitely is not limited to executive coaching.'

— Dr Katharina Ebner, Senior Lecturer, Friedrich-Alexander-Universität Erlangen-Nürnberg, Germany

What Works in Executive Coaching

This book reviews the full coaching outcome research literature to examine the arguments and evidence behind the use of executive coaching. Erik de Haan presents the definitive guide to what works in coaching and what changes coaching brings about, both for individual coaches and for organisations and commissioners.

Accessibly written and based on contemporary quantitative research into coaching effectiveness, this book considers whether we know that coaching works, and, if so, whom it works for, and what it offers to those involved. *What Works in Executive Coaching* considers the entire body of academic literature on quantitative research in executive and workplace coaching, assessing the significant results and explaining how to apply them. Each chapter contains direct applications to coaching practice and clearly evaluates the evidence, defining what really works in executive coaching.

Alongside its companion volume *Critical Moments in Executive Coaching*, this book is an essential guide to evidence-based effectiveness in coaching. It will be a key text for all coaching practitioners, including those in training.

Erik de Haan studied Theoretical Physics and undertook his PhD in Psychophysics. He is Director of the Ashridge Centre for Coaching at Hult International Business School, UK, and Professor of Organisation Development at the VU University in Amsterdam, the Netherlands. He is the programme leader of Ashridge's MSc in Executive Coaching and PG Diploma in Organisational Supervision. He has published more than 200 professional and research articles and 14 books, covering his expertise as an organisational consultant, therapist, and executive coach.

What Works in Executive Coaching

Understanding Outcomes Through Quantitative Research and Practice-Based Evidence

Erik de Haan

LONDON AND NEW YORK

First published 2021
by Routledge
2 Park Square, Milton Park, Abingdon, Oxon OX14 4RN

and by Routledge
605 Third Avenue, New York, NY 10017

Routledge is an imprint of the Taylor & Francis Group, an informa business

Copyright © 2021 Erik de Haan

The right of Erik de Haan to be identified as author of this work has been asserted by him in accordance with sections 77 and 78 of the Copyright, Designs and Patents Act 1988.

All rights reserved. No part of this book may be reprinted or reproduced or utilised in any form or by any electronic, mechanical, or other means, now known or hereafter invented, including photocopying and recording, or in any information storage or retrieval system, without permission in writing from the publishers.

Trademark notice: Product or corporate names may be trademarks or registered trademarks, and are used only for identification and explanation without intent to infringe.

Extract from Little Gidding by T. S. Eliot, as printed in Four Quartets (1942) appears here by kind permission of Faber and Faber Ltd.

British Library Cataloguing-in-Publication Data
A catalogue record for this book is available from the British Library

Library of Congress Cataloging-in-Publication Data
A catalog record for this book has been requested

ISBN 13: 978-0-367-64942-5 (hbk)
ISBN 13: 978-0-367-64943-2 (pbk)

Typeset in Sabon
by Apex CoVantage, LLC

To my friend Tony Grant, leader in quantitative research in coaching, who left us too soon

We shall not cease from exploration
And the end of all our exploring
Will be to arrive where we started
And know the place for the first time.

T.S. Eliot, Little Gidding, 1942

Contents

Highlights of the book   xv

Introduction   1

An interlude before Chapter 1   11

1 Does executive coaching work? Is coaching worth the effort?   13
   Part A: some controversies 14
     Controversy 1: how universal and generalisable are the results? 14
     Controversy 2: choice-supportive biases skewing the results towards false positives 15
     Controversy 3: if the same people are asked to measure all variables, biases will result 17
     Controversy 4: the Hawthorne effect 17
     Controversy 5: realistic settings do not satisfy lab research conditions 18
     Controversy 6: the diminishing power of statistical tests on the same data 19
     Controversy 7: nonattendance of participants in coaching and in research 20
     Controversy 8: nonrepresentative samples 20
     Controversy 9: coaching is not very sharply defined 21
   Part B: how to establish whether coaching works 22
   Part C: overview of outcomes of coaching research with randomised control groups 25
     1 Randomised controlled experiments in health coaching 25
     2 Randomised controlled experiments in workplace coaching 28
     3 Limitations of past research 35
   Part D: what it means for coaching practice 36

An interlude before Chapter 2   **39**

2   What works in executive coaching? What makes coaching really worthwhile?   **41**
   Part A: some controversies 41
     Controversy 1: what to do with studies of a different standard than RCTs 42
     Controversy 2: the technique versus common-factors debate 43
     Controversy 3: difficult to compare different studies when they use different constructs 44
     Controversy 4: where does 'technique' end and do 'common factors' begin? 45
   Part B: how to establish the 'active ingredients' 46
   Part C: overview of more evidence with an eye for possible active ingredients of coaching 49
     1 *Overview of coaching outcome research I: evaluation or field studies* 50
     2 *Overview of coaching outcome research II: incorporating objective outcome variables* 52
     3 *Manager-as-coach research with objective outcome variables* 54
     4 *Overview of coaching outcome research III: employing control groups* 56
     5 *Overview of coaching research which compares conditions* 61
     6 *Overview of coaching research which compares techniques of coaching* 67
     7 *Overview of coaching research which compares virtual and face-to-face coaching* 72
   Part D: what it means for coaching practice 73

An interlude before Chapter 3   **85**

3   The coaching relationship as 'best predictor'? How does the working alliance help to achieve outcomes?   **87**
   Part A: some controversies 88
     Controversy 1: does the 'medical model' apply? 90
     Controversy 2: does the 'therapy model' apply? 90
     Controversy 3: causality is still open to debate 91
     Controversy 4: the puzzle of 'the' relationship 91
     Controversy 5: what is the core of 'the' relationship? 92
     Controversy 6: how to optimise the relationship factor 92
   Part B: what we need to know about this 'best predictor' 93

Part C: overview of coaching relationship outcome research 95
   1 A brief review of research on the coaching relationship 95
   2 A brief review of relevant mentoring outcome research 95
   3 Longitudinal research on the coaching relationship 96
   4 An interpretation of these findings 98
   5 Future research: time to think differently about active ingredients 99
Part D: what it means for coaching practice 100

An interlude before Chapter 4   103

4 Which outcomes does coaching actually deliver? What does executive coaching work on?   **105**
Part A: some controversies 106
   Controversy 1: very high diversity of study methods 106
   Controversy 2: some contradictory findings 107
   Controversy 3: the possibility of moderation 108
   Controversy 4: it's hard to see the wood for the trees, because of many weak results 108
Part B: how to establish different coaching outcomes 109
Part C: overview of what we know about outcome measures 113
   1 Changes to objective measures 114
   2 Changes to multi-source performance measures 116
   3 Changes to self-rated personality measures 118
   4 Changes to self-rated preparedness or well-being measures 119
   5 Changes to self-rated goal-attainment measures 121
   6 Changes for the coach rather than the coachee 121
Part D: what it means for coaching practice 122

An interlude before Chapter 5   127

5 What perceptual biases may be at play? Can we trust a coach's perceptions of coaching?   **131**
Part A: some controversies 131
   Controversy 1: what is so bad about the biases in self-scores? 133
   Controversy 2: what is so bad about using self-scores for research? 133
   Controversy 3: is the distinction between self- and other-scores not artificial? 133
Part B: how to establish coaching self-perception outcomes 134
   1 Research showing coaching changes personal ratings of performance 134

    2 *Research showing the coach's mindset about change is an important predictor of outcomes* 134
    3 *Research showing that mindsets of coach and coachee about change strengthen one another* 135
    4 *Research showing that coaches develop perceptual biases in looking at their own skills* 135
  Part C: overview of what we know about perceptual biases in coaches about their own coaching 136
    1 *A brief review of research on coaching interventions* 136
    2 *Research on coaching interventions using the Coaching Behaviours Questionnaire* 138
    3 *Significant differences found for gender, age, job, and nationality of the coach* 140
    4 *An interpretation of these findings* 142
  Part D: what it means for coaching practice 144

An interlude before Chapter 6   147

6 **What about negative side effects of coaching? Are there risks? Can coaching do harm?**   151
  Part A: some controversies 152
    Controversy 1: can we actually treat 'negative' outcomes separate from 'positive' ones? 152
    Controversy 2: is there an assumption that reported experiences are significant outcomes? 153
    Controversy 3: there seems to be a difference between the coaching and mentoring literature 154
  Part B: how to establish negative side effects of coaching 155
  Part C: overview of what we know about side effects 157
  Part D: what it means for coaching practice 160
    1 *What do coaches need to know about negative (side) effects in coaching?* 160
    2 *What expert advice can we give to coaches who want to do quantitative research?* 161
    3 *What moral advice can we give to coaches who want to do quantitative research?* 162

  References   165
  Subject index   180
  Author index   181

Highlights of the book

- The *definitive* guide about what works in coaching and what changes coaching brings about
- The coaching 'evidence base' made accessible without formulas, statistics, and nearly no numbers
- Containing a section in every chapter about what it all means for coaching practice:
  - What it means for your clients if you are a coach
  - What it means for your organisation if you are a commissioner of coaching
  - Do we know coaching works? (the answer: 'yes, probably')
  - If coaching works, for whom does it work?
  - If coaching works, what does it give to coachees, their reports, and their organisations?
  - For your coaching to work, what do you need to emphasize in your coaching conversations?
- Including some early explorations of negative side effects of coaching

Introduction

This book captures our best answers to the question 'What works in executive coaching?' at the time of writing. I analyse all findings about effectiveness and outcome in executive and workplace coaching, by looking at three core questions: can we demonstrate *effectiveness*? Do we know the *circumstances* in which coaching is (most) effective? Do we know the *kind* of effectiveness that coaching has, i.e. the outcomes or impact that coaching tends to have, e.g. on the coachee and more widely on organisations?

It is ironic that virtually every coaching research article begins with the observation that despite the rapid growth in application, coaching has essentially been under-researched and that we know very little about its effectiveness. However, this is no longer true! The last 15 years have seen a veritable explosion of coaching research, and it has now become very easy to find hundreds of original, good-quality research articles with interesting experiments and significant findings. If we compare this with the larger field that coaching is a part of: leadership and organisation development, then we realise that coaching has a much stronger evidence base than its first cousins and may even begin to inform those wider professions and lend them the beginnings of an understanding whether, how, and towards what they may contribute to today's organisations.

I have endeavoured to capture the entire workplace and executive coaching literature to date. In my keenness to include the broadest range of quantitatively rigorous, valid research I went slightly outside the domain of executive coaching per se. Not so much into psychotherapy outcome research, which I have done already in *Relational Coaching* (De Haan, 2008) and which has since been summarised by many others. This time I broadened out to other organisational interventions with some similarity to executive coaching, which have been equally well researched. Managerial and life coaching, mentoring, multi-source feedback, and corporate training all have some good evidence behind them. In this book I make fairly extensive excursions in those other directions: the impressive number of *health-coaching* randomised controlled trials (in Chapter 1), the *management-coaching* ('manager as coach') outcome literature (in Chapter 2), and the *mentoring* outcome literature (in Chapter 3); moreover, some effectiveness studies of 360-degree feedback and training or instruction are also mentioned, e.g. when the word 'coaching' was used in that research. All in all, I have selected well over 200 original empirical studies all using valid statistical analysis. I believe I have surveyed this database from a wider perspective – the perspective of what it all means and how it can inform our coaching – for the first time.

I am conscious that there are many more coaching articles than I have brought together here, that offer definitions and experiences of coaching, and I summarise a smaller cross-section of these articles. I am also aware that there are thousands more 'practitioner articles' that offer views and opinions about coaching trends. Trying to bring all of those into this overview would have been ponderous and something of a distraction since neither of these large classes of coaching articles offers any new statistical evidence. The only class of articles that are not covered by this book but are nevertheless worth reading because they bring in evidence of a different kind, are the over 100 *qualitative* articles in coaching, which I have analysed separately, in De Haan, 2019a, 2019b.

In this way, the book neatly complements the companion volume *Critical Moments in Executive Coaching* (De Haan, 2019a), where around 100 original qualitative research studies in coaching are summarised and analysed to extract their advice for practicing coaches. Here, I hope to do the same for quantitative research, where we have around three times as large a research base, leading to many more findings with advice for coaches. Whilst in the earlier book coaches can recognise themselves in all the cases and field studies but are never quite sure what recommendations to take from those cases, in this book coaches will occasionally struggle to see how the rather general and abstract knowledge can be useful for their own practice and clients, even if this time the advice is clear, unambiguous, and backed up by numbers, even by 'evidence' (evidence usually consisting of significant effects or demonstrably likely null results). Very few of the studies that went into *Critical Moments in Executive Coaching* are used again in this book: only those that were able to assemble many hundreds of qualitative 'data points' that then could be reaped in terms of general, quantifiable conclusions and 'evidence' statements.

I think this book will be controversial and should be controversial, just as all quantitative research is and has to be controversial, until such a time that we have emerging, broad agreement about findings, like in the much larger and established research bases of medicine and the natural sciences – albeit that the most advanced research in those fields will be equally competitive, controversial, and polemic as it is for us in executive coaching. I will shed a light on controversy at the beginning of every chapter, highlighting at least three areas each chapter where there is disputation, controversy, or dogmatic squabbling. Feelings may run high and convictions may run deep. I personally love this aspect of research; it gives a great passion and liveliness to what are essentially cold numbers about no one in particular. What I have tried to do with these passions is mainly to be as explicit about them as I could, including about my own. I am a physicist by background, so I have a basic trust in statistics to ultimately lead us beyond controversy, and I am also a 'psychoanalytical' psychotherapist and a 'relational' coach which may mean that I have more faith in some approaches than in others; although ultimately I have the most faith in 'having faith' (i.e. the powerful 'allegiance' to your own approach, whichever it is) than in any particular creed or methodology of coaching.

I give most space to what are objectively more rigorous, larger-scale, and more significant studies; to highly original yet thorough methodologies; and to counterexamples. Less rigorous studies only get a brief mention or do not figure at all in this book, e.g. if they are very small scale and do not make use of control groups. The choice regarding how much space to give any single study was often a difficult one, and it was usually made on the basis of how unique the study was, whether it was a single counter-example to a series of other articles that had demonstrated a significant relationship, or whether it was another supportive source for a fairly well-established result. I had to make these decisions in order to keep the book easily readable and not too unwieldy. Moreover, it would have felt distinctly unfair and unscientific if much less rigorous studies would have been given equal space and attention in the book. I do realise though that in the end this remains a highly subjective choice and that I can be accused of partisanship, bias, favouritism, perhaps blind admiration or conversely, exaggerated scepsis and doubt. One thing I learned in science is that we all have our biases.

Notwithstanding my biases, I tried to select objectively and summarise frankly and to the best of my ability, on the basis of merit within the context of all coaching outcome studies, and without taking into consideration the personal reputations of, let alone my personal acquaintances with any of the authors. The tremendous risk of false positives in executive-coaching research (which will be argued in Chapter 1) has also been explored by Grover and Furnham (2016) in their review of coaching outcome research. I am glad to say that my choices and summaries overlap with their risk estimates, i.e. I have mostly based my conclusions on their 'low-risk' papers and others such, which I have found independently.

It is surprising that some of the best, most credible, and most rigorous studies (Duijts *et al.*, 2008; Liu & Batt, 2010, just to name a few), are actually amongst the least-known and least quoted in the coaching research literature, and have often been overlooked in review studies and meta-analyses. I do not know if this is because they were published slightly outside the typical 'coaching' journals or for other reasons.

Let me mention a few of my convictions when it comes to 'doing' the research and 'publishing' it that have played on my mind as I was writing this book. They made it harder in some cases to come to a valid and reasonably objective summary of certain contributions. Firstly, I have encountered the problem of publishing several seemingly original articles which nevertheless refer to the same dataset, a practice sometimes called 'data slicing.' Moen and Skaalvik's dataset can be found four times in peer-reviewed journals, headed up by different co-authors, so it takes a while to realise that they are all essentially the same experiment. And there are other examples of single studies reported over a series of articles, e.g. the works mentioned with first author Bozer, Baron and MacKie in this book. Secondly, I have come across the related problem of original research papers which include older datasets that had already been published. The Zimmermann and Antoni and the Kauffeld *et al.* references are just some examples of this phenomenon, where we are left in the dark as to what proportion of the findings is based on new data collected specifically for the particular article. In such cases, where conclusions based on only the new data might be contradictory or insignificant on their own, the studies may artificially boost significance or gloss over other differences within their spread-out data. It has been impossible to check if later measurements and additions are dependent upon the earlier reported significances.

I know that in some cases in the book (e.g. Teemant, 2014; Vande Walle *et al.*, 2020) the interventions which were being called 'coaching' were perhaps better described as 'instruction' or 'mentoring,' i.e. a rather different intervention that has actually been demonstrated to have different effects (see, e.g., Sun *et al.*, 2013; Hui *et al.*, 2013; Deane *et al.*, 2014, for articles comparing coaching and instruction). I believe it is still too early to separate out from the coaching outcome literature all directive, educational, and instructional interventions which still go by the name of 'coaching,' so I have kept all of those in with a warning to the reader.

Does this book now summarise the whole quantitative research literature in coaching? We will never know. Even if it does, it will probably be incomplete in only a few months' time. Moreover, I do know that a certain type of article, the fairly typical pre- and post-measurement evaluative field study without a control group (i.e. what is often called a 'within-subjects analysis'), with only self-reported variables, has not been completely represented. After reading maybe a hundred of these papers, I decided to keep just a few of the best ones in, add the ones that are most often quoted, and then close the shop for all the others. I regret therefore that I could not incorporate many local samples in this category, from different geographies and organisations. I have also checked but then disregarded many studies with tiny sample sizes, where the outcomes reported could just as well be a chance occurrence in such a small population.[1] In fact, if there were one way in which we can improve coaching outcome research for the future, then it would be simply by increasing our sample sizes: we could forestall so many (unfortunately there are many!) false positives or studies where only the inherently biased 'self-scores' reach statistical significance.

In order to make all the studies in this book easiest to compare I have converted all reported effects (in η-squares, F's, proportions of explained variability, correlation coefficients, β-coefficients, success rates, odds ratios, etcetera) to the standard 'effect size' δ. It may be good to be reminded that generally a range of δ up to 0.1 is considered 'no effect' (although many cancer treatments are still based on such low δ's and do save many lives!), then from 0.1 to 0.4 δ signifies a small effect, then from 0.4 to 0.7 an intermediate effect, and any δ above 0.7 is termed a large effect (Cohen, 1988), just because the difference (delta, δ) between the distributions (e.g. involving 'coaching' and 'no coaching') is getting progressively larger.

No introduction to a research analysis book would be complete without a word of 'kudos' to all the many coaching researchers who have been so dedicated and thorough to bring their experiments to an end and stick with the ups and downs of the editorial process. They are applying huge efforts to produce those deltas and other hunches, often in their spare time and weekends. It is high time we dedicate a book to the fruits of these quantitative coaching researchers. I think it is safe to say that they are the most courageous, serious, and hardworking in our wider profession:

> *Courageous* because they dare to challenge and explore with an open mind the time-honoured truths in the profession, or at least, when their strong beliefs and opinions are underpinning their commitment as researchers, they dare to put their own fond ideas to the test, where there is always a chance they will have to reconsider them. Researchers open themselves up to doubt, and coaches know from experience how important the courage to doubt is in coaching conversations too (De Haan, 2008).
>
> *Serious* because they will only listen to empirical findings and to arguments that can be backed up by data and valid information. And they will consider those arguments and views critically, so as to investigate whether different conclusions can be based on the same data.

And *hardworking* because they stick with their research designs and bring them all the way to publication (in most cases). From my early days when I was a full-time researcher I can calculate the time it has cost me to produce one peer-reviewed paper: I wrote four articles in a little over four years (1990–1994), i.e. I expended at least 1,600, possibly 2,000 hours per article. Compare that with an opinion piece that most of us can write in a day, something of the scope of this Introduction: just ten hours and therefore only half a percent of the time it would take to undertake a proper scientific investigation. I know this number of hours per scientific publication drops over the years, and for me it has made a real difference that I now have generous support in the areas of library services (thank you so much Rachel Piper and Claire Shaw), data administration (thank you again Audrey Vandenborne, Sue Gammons, and Judy Curd) and statistical analysis (thank you profoundly Viktor Nilsson and Nadine Page). Nevertheless, I would estimate it is still many hundreds of hours of work for every single article, and such hours need to be multiplied by close to the number of authors above an empirical article.

We as practicing coaches need to make use of what these industrious and conscientious researchers bring us, if only because it is the single verifiable and objective source of 'hard' data that we can glean about our own hunches, doubts, contracts, offers of help, and sessions of coaching – the only compass that can tell us if what we are doing now, bringing the best of our judgement, will make sense, add value, acquire meaning, or develop an organisation that hires us.

Even after a few hundred rigorous empirical research studies in coaching, i.e. possibly millions of hours of work for all the researchers involved, there are still so many unanswered questions, new untested hypotheses that the research has generated, and uncharted territories: the coming years in this profession will be no less fascinating than the busy decade behind.

In this book I will analyse all findings pertaining to effectiveness and outcome by looking at three core review questions: (1) Can we demonstrate effectiveness? (2) Do we know the circumstances in which coaching is (most) effective? (3) Do we know the kind of effectiveness that coaching has, i.e. the impact that coaching tends to have? The six chapters of this book analyse a comprehensive coaching research literature with those three review questions in mind. Chapters 1, 2, and 4 summarise the full evidence base in terms of the three review questions:

1. whether coaching works (Chapter 1)
2. which contents or aspects of coaching work (Chapter 2)
3. towards what kinds of changes coaching works (Chapter 4)

Or, to put it still more concisely, whether it works Chapter 1, how it works Chapter 2, and for whom it works Chapter 4.

The other three chapters are more narrowly focused. They deal with three contentious issues in the field: whether the coaching relationship is the 'best predictor' of the coaching outcomes that we have, as some say (Chapter 3), how self-perceptions and biases distort the coaching results yet at the same time help the coach to do good work (Chapter 5), and whether there are any contraindications or negative side effects of coaching that need to be taken into account (Chapter 6).

I believe that this larger overview can do more than simply provide executive coaches with the latest information on 'what works' in their field. The results as summarised here may be the best guidance on objective outcomes that we can provide in adjacent fields as well. Team coaching, organisation-development consulting, process consultation, even expert consulting – they all have a lot less research behind them than (executive) coaching. They are, however, equally conversational in nature, so one would expect similar factors to be evidenced when rigorous research could be done in those fields. In fact, for group and team coaching one might expect slightly higher effectiveness than for individual coaching, because such has been found in the adjacent field of psychotherapy (Yalom & Leszcz, 2005).

If you want to quickly find out about the effectiveness of coaching and about what science has to say about what works and for whom and what it delivers, this can all be done in five minutes, by reading the special *one-page summaries* at the end of each of the six chapters. I dare say they tell you all a coach needs to remember from what quantitative research has demonstrated.

Every chapter is also preceded by a short 'case vignette' from my own coaching practice, anonymised in the usual way (they are mostly amalgamations of different client assignments, and in those instances where they are based on specific work, I have asked the main client for permission to publish in this anonymised form). The case material is not intended to demonstrate anything that is argued within the chapter. It is only to make sure that we do not lose sight of the work itself, the beauty of coaching. In other words, these 'interludes' are intended as gentle reminders of what coaching is about and what knotty issues and complexities coaches face that will have to be entirely overlooked by the data gatherers of quantitative research. Inescapably, all of this content in coaching conversations gets skimmed over to collect the one or two data points that the quantitative researcher needs, which is why it is so hard for some of us coaches to understand that the fruits of research still have an important bearing on practice. All statistically significant trends amongst research variables play a hidden role in every coaching case, almost like the individual subconscious, guiding and moulding the work in the background, striking us like the sudden appearance of a *deus ex machina*, or accompanying us like a *guardian angel* – and so it might really pay off to know about them.

Finally, here is what I would personally really like to know *next* about coaching – all are areas that have never been researched as far as I know but that are amenable to quantitative research. With some effort we could begin to test these assertions:

- The importance of allowing the client to take charge (**nondirectiveness**)
- The importance of **relational** work with clients including here-and-now hypotheses
- The importance of a conducive organisational environment for coaching
- And conversely, the impact of coaching on **third parties** in the organisation
- The importance of coaching with a truly **open mind** ('without memory or desire')
- The importance of the very **beginning** of the session for our understanding
- The importance of ruptures and **staying with ruptures**
- The importance of completing a **qualification or accreditation** as a coach
- The unimportance of **experience** for the effectiveness of a coach

I would like to profusely thank a few very kind people. Claire Shaw, Lisette Tepe, and Rachel Piper of the VU and Hult Ashridge university libraries: without your ability to trace and source all those quantitative studies – even the original, unpublished ones in PhD dissertations, this book would never have come into existence. My father, Laurens de Haan, who is emeritus professor of statistics, read the manuscript and offered very valuable advice. My colleague David Birch improved the style of the introduction. Arend van Dam drew the cartoons at the beginning of each chapter.

Last but not least I would like to thank the amazing co-authors that have helped with the outcome studies that I am reporting on again in this book: David Birch, Sally Bonneywell, Yvonne Burger, Vicki Culpin, Judy Curd, Anna Duckworth, Per-Olof Eriksson, Tony Grant, David Gray, Claire Jones, Joanna Molyn, and Viktor Nilsson.

After completing the book, I asked seven fellow researchers in the coaching professions to check my data and interpretations, and to come up with a few sentences to describe the book. Here are the conclusions they came to upon reading the book:

> This is a great contribution to the practice and science of coaching. I find the controversy issues raised at the opening of each chapter very useful and essential as they provide us with a more balanced perspective of the story that is being told in each chapter. I also greatly value the guidelines for both practitioners and researchers to better assess and interpret coaching research findings and ultimately become more informed consumers of coaching research. This book celebrates the exciting journey of discovery that workplace coaching scholars have achieved to date and on the same breath highlights areas that need to be further addressed.
> – Gil Bozer, PhD, Sr Lecturer of Coaching,
> Sapir Academic College, Israel

> This book will be an instant classic! It can advance coaching research in many ways. Not only does it provide a comprehensive review of the literature to date, it also reviews this literature in an open, critical, courageous, and creative way. The book goes beyond summarizing the results and pointing out directions for future research. It challenges your way of thinking about (executive) coaching, about what effectiveness means, about how we can and should measure it, and about how we should continue to build an evidence base for (executive) coaching. This book should be on the reading list for everyone who is professionally involved in coaching in any way.
> – Dr. Tim Theeboom, Sr Lecturer at Center for Coaching,
> VU University, Amsterdam, The Netherlands

> I found this book extremely interesting, very well written and actually a pleasure to read. I loved the vignettes at the beginning of each chapter: they fit very well. I also appreciated that every chapter starts with the controversies – as a way to acknowledge the issues even before the successes of coaching, which is rare compared to a lot of uncritical enthusiasm that coaching often elicits. All effect sizes are made comparable by transforming them into standard delta's. At the end of the book there is an impeccable guide for good (ethical) research. Thank you for

a very fine book that is rigorous, scholarly and solid but speaks to a very broad audience.
– Silvia Dello Russo, Associate Professor,
Toulouse Business School, France

This is a wonderfully interesting book that helps clearing up lots of enquiries, rumours and controversy about coaching. Unlike many other practitioner books, you base your discussion on a solid and comprehensive review of prior research studies. More importantly, you provide a wider and more inclusive view about coaching that will benefit researchers and practitioners alike.
– Dr Ray Hui, Assistant Professor, NUCB Business School,
Nagoya University of Commerce and Business, Japan

Thank you for the opportunity to read your new book which builds bridges and at the same time offers both interesting controversies and new impulses. I love the way you write: well understandable; reflective; tying all these loose ends in coaching research; and interesting for both practitioners and researchers. Only someone with rich practical and scientific experience could have written such a book! And what an impressive task to gather and analyze all those research articles. I particularly enjoyed and was challenged by your thoughts regarding the research on the working alliance. I realized I now may have to abandon well known, comfortable, widely shared perspectives on the working alliance. I am not sure if I have already 'bought in' but your thoughts stimulate me to think again about the complex relational dynamics that take place between coaches and clients.
– Professor Patrizia Ianiro-Dahm, University of
Applied Sciences Bonn-Rhein-Sieg, Germany

Navigating the field of coaching has always been a challenge. Twenty years ago, the salient questions were, *What is it really? Who should I use?* and *Where's the research?* Two decades on, the emergence of a decent and growing evidence-base has created other navigational challenges, with stakeholders left to wonder, *What sort of evidence is best?* and *What can be said to work?* In this book vital navigational assistance is provided, by addressing these and many other questions. Importantly, I like that the book provides an eminently clear expression of the factors that contribute to quality in quantitative research in coaching, and overviews the intricacies of research in a way that is accessible and should increase the research literacy of readers. What I especially appreciated was the view that good quality coaching research is bloody hard to do; something that (I suspect) is not so well appreciated. Particularly the sort of research that is more valuable: designs that have some ecological validity to them and resemble what happens in the real world. So much of what you say is not just relevant for practitioners and the purchasers of coaching, but also for researchers, who can sometimes become blinkered in their work and benefit from helpful reminders.
– Dr. Gordon Spence, Senior Lecturer, Sydney Business School,
University of Wollongong, Australia

London, Erik de Haan, July 2020

Note

1 To be more precise in terms of the selection criteria in this book, I accepted *all* original empirical articles in all languages, which had dependent variables (coaching outcomes) and at least a sample size of $N > 20$ which included a comparison group or a comparison condition, i.e. no pre-/post-studies without comparisons of which there are very many, but arguably they cannot demonstrate much. Although 99% of the studies selected were peer reviewed and published as dissertations or journal articles, I did also accept unpublished studies where I could find them.

An interlude before Chapter 1

Before writing about outcomes and coaching let me come clean about my own most memorable outcomes as a coach. They have mostly taken place in 'remedial' work, where after all making a measurable difference is an essential part of the coaching contract. I have worked with a few clients under pressure of losing the board or of losing their jobs, and effectiveness was always more critical and apparent in those 'remedial' contracts. In fact, high effectiveness could be demonstrated by just keeping the job my client was in. The 'remedial' clients usually needed to change something about their behaviour as perceived by their teams and bosses. They were told either to deliver more promptly, to be less critical or aggressive in the workplace, to become 'pro-active' or 'strategic' in their contributions,[1] or simply to be more available and helpful to their colleagues – and sometimes all four of those.

Jacob was one of these clients.

The very first 'chemistry' meeting with him already went very well – unusual for me since I am usually seen as too serious or too challenging in chemistry meetings. Here I was chosen from a competitive field. Jacob phoned me up and said,

> You observed so many things that made me think; so, in the past week I have spent a lot more time thinking through my questions for coaching. When you asked me the question 'what is this worth for you?' I realised I had never asked that question myself. And I had to conclude that so far, I have been able to get away with *not* changing, so it probably wasn't worth enough for me up to this point. That question really made me reflect.

I met Jacob's boss next and heard a litany of problems and also, between the lines, that the boss's preference was to fire him but he felt he could not do that without the full consent of the Canadian holding company. Coaching for Jacob seemed very much a 'second best' solution. Then the three of us met and Jacob made clear that he wanted to take this option seriously and not with the irony and even cynicism that he was known for in the workplace. He realised that he had let things slip and that most of his relationships with his direct reports could be improved. I interviewed the direct reports and several of the other board members, after which we had a very sobering first coaching session, where we managed to go over many of the hopes, expectations, and even 'demands' regarding this executive coaching contract on the part of Jacob's colleagues and direct reports. His boss had even requested two further conversations with me telling me all the many things that he had picked up from staff and that he had mostly never told Jacob himself. I had let everyone know that I would be open with Jacob about their grievances, and I was. From the start Jacob seemed to be listening attentively and although he defended himself occasionally, he did confirm that he 'was not good at reading people,' that he 'was not very polite and could be challenging of others,' that he 'always took the direct route to his goal,' and that people found his behaviour sometimes upsetting, so he must have 'annoyed' several of his Board colleagues with, for example, blunt ideas for improvement in their departments. By the time we had worked together for some four sessions, Jacob told me that one of his direct reports was occasionally saying 'thank you' to him for positive changes made – but that she had cheekily phrased it as 'thank you Erik' to him, remembering me from the interview she had had with me. I could not think of a better outcome of our coaching work than that a direct report of Jacob sincerely thanked me through him in this manner.

After some eight sessions of coaching his boss the CEO agreed that Jacob had turned around completely and had really seen the benefit of contributing in a more thoughtful and less challenging way, to such an extent that the CEO in his final triangular meeting with us, before the final coaching session, said, 'I don't think I could have undertaken something like this myself. It would feel like too much of a humiliation to me. But you, Jacob, grasped the nettle admirably and are now experienced very differently by your Board colleagues.'

Even after such a speech I tend to remain cautious and pessimistic. And in fact with this particular client, when I met his HR Director on an unrelated assignment nearly a year later, he sighed and said that Jacob was just 'the wrong person on the job' and that the coaching had probably come too late to do anything for him. I was left wondering whether these were just two different opinions representing different perspectives within the wider executive team, or whether there had been a reversal of all that great progress that we were celebrating towards our final session. I shall never know.

As Raymond Corsini beautifully illustrates in the introduction of his book on current psychotherapies, important outcomes can often be found in marginal moments or unexpected places. Think of the coach who picked up from an initial conversation with the commissioner that her new client was described as an 'unguided missile.' Then she noticed that the client turned out quite intense in the conversations, with little focus, so she mentioned the feedback she had heard, gently inquiring into the client's working style. And made a link to something the client had brought to the session about their children being very unfocused and having some concentration problems. The client became thoughtful, went away, spoke with friends, went to the general practitioner, did a test for ADHD, had a high score, and eventually came up with a diagnosis and prescription for the children which vastly improved their results and behaviour at primary school. This is just one example of the major, unintended positive benefits that simple coaching interventions can sometimes have.

Note

1 This can be a real killer for executives: asking someone to be more 'strategic' or 'proactive.' It means asking them at the same time to obey you and follow your lead, and to be more spontaneous and follow their own best insight. It will be impossible to satisfy the internal contradictions in that request so that usually the coachee gets stuck in what is technically called a 'paradoxical injunction,' an instruction to do something that is rendered impossible by the instruction itself.

Chapter 1

Does executive coaching work? Is coaching worth the effort?

In this first chapter we will look both at the practice of doing quantitative research in coaching, and at the findings of quantitative research in coaching up to this point, after exactly 30 years of empirical research in workplace and executive coaching (since Miller, 1990). We will discover, through the lens of some 35 Randomised Controlled Trials (RCTs), that we can now be fairly certain that executive coaching does make a significant difference, that it is likely to be an effective intervention which after some six sessions builds to an effect size δ around 0.6. This means that coachees would be better off on average than about 72% of the control group that has not received coaching over the same period (De Haan *et al.*, 2019).

Part A: some controversies

Quantitative research is about the pursuit of 'truth,' so its methods and findings are understandably hotly debated. And in accordance with our troubled times, there is quite a bit of 'fake news' around, including a disturbing number of 'alternative facts.' Some researchers are better able to market their 'truths' than others, which leads to a skewed reception of their findings. Some researchers are more modest and circumspect than others, in reporting only what they can truly demonstrate in their sample. Some researchers have a better understanding than others of the statistical power (or lack of it) in their findings. All of this affects their ability to report on the 'truth' of their experiment and to limit themselves to the truth only. In my view, we as readers of research reports should try to modestly inquire into, check, and newly establish in our minds the facts behind the main messages of scientific articles. We as readers need to be open and curious, yet also alert and slightly suspicious with every new research publication. We need to keep relying on and making use of fine research traditions such as 'peer reviews' and the testing of experiments by replicating them under slightly changed conditions.

Controversy 1: how universal and generalisable are the results?

Where qualitative research is essentially narrative and tells a story about a coaching relationship which is highly personal and unique (see, for a recent summary of the qualitative research tradition in coaching, De Haan, 2019b), quantitative research is all about *generalisability*. In other words, will we find the same effects if we repeat the study with a new sample? Could this result be universal? That is, could it be relevant and true in the vast array of all similar situations? Could this coaching research that I am reading about now therefore be relevant for me and my coachees: now, tomorrow, and onwards?

Any quantitative results that are worth noticing have to be 'significant,' so they have to stand out clearly above the background noise and the diversity within the sample, which gives them a decent probability to occur again in any similar samples worldwide. Significant results have the potential to be replicated (with a small likelihood that they will be falsified) by other researchers, so they gradually become respected 'truths' for the whole profession, and remain generalisable over time (which means that they provide a reliable prediction for the future) and space (namely to any coaching conversation in any country or culture that is assumed to be similar enough to one of the samples where the result has already been demonstrated). The fact that quantitative results have this potential of being true anywhere and at any time makes them so powerful and so hotly debated, and frankly, so *controversial* as well. Unless of course they are demonstrated with at least 'five sigma accuracy.' Five sigma accuracy means that we can trust that the result is true for this population with a probability of 99.99997% and so we know that this is generalisable to hundreds of thousands of similar populations. Five sigma accuracy is very rarely achieved in the social sciences.[1] This means that there is always some interesting and possibly unsettling room for doubt and debate. Most results in the social sciences are reported with 95% ($p < 0.05$) or 99% ($p < 0.01$) accuracy; i.e. two or three sigma only. Lower accuracies give at least a one-in-twenty chance that the result was a fluke, so they will not be recognised in the research literature, nor in this book.

In every chapter of this book I will first report on the controversies before reporting on the results, to underline that all results that I write about are still open to debate, and that no findings are above or beyond debate at this point in time. The strongest finding at the moment is that coaching seems to be an effective intervention, but even this is only known from just over 30 small-scale experiments and never with an accuracy greater than $p < 0.01$, so still a one-in-a-hundred chance (or perhaps one thirtieth of a one-in-a-hundred chance) that we are mistaken to assume such effectiveness and a much bigger chance that we are actually over-estimating coaching effectiveness, i.e. that there is an effect but not such a large one.

Historically, there have always been powerful voices to say that the helping professions are *not* effective at all, the most famous of which comes from Professor Hans Eysenck, who was a leading psychologist in the twentieth century. To be fair to him his doubts were expressed when we still had very little evidence (Eysenck, 1952), and moreover, he had many other unsubstantiated, non-mainstream views, e.g. the conviction that parapsychology and astrology were indeed empirically supported. It is nevertheless easy to find many articles online that argue that coaching is not effective, or that particular approaches to coaching are not effective, or that there are real dangers in the hiring of coaches (see, e.g., Berglas, 2002; Nowack, 2003; Briner, 2012); however, it is harder to find peer-reviewed, academic articles nowadays, that argue against the (general) effectiveness of coaching, mentoring, counselling, and psychotherapy. The accumulated evidence over decades of doing research is simply too hard to argue against. Still, in the interest of protecting the quality of our generalisable results, it *must* be argued against, again and again.

Controversy 2: choice-supportive biases skewing the results towards false positives

One deeper problem – and controversy – with coaching outcome research, something we will encounter in the description of the research done to date, is that most variables in most of the research experiments were self-scored. From a scientific (i.e. quantitative-research) point of view, the coachee and the coach are the least appropriate people to ask whether coaching was effective or not. After all, they already have a biased view of and a stake in the matter, so they are expected to suffer 'choice-supportive' biases. A coach has spent many hours learning about coaching, and both coach and coachee have spent many hours together in their sessions. So, they are already 'wedded' to the coaching by the simple act of spending time and energy and money on it, and thus arguably preferring it to something else that they equally could spend their resources on. So, from a standpoint of post-hoc rationalisation, coach and coachee will have a positive view of coaching and may attribute their luck or their career success, e.g. wise decisions or promotions, to the coaching sessions, even if that link is rather tenuous and one cannot (by definition) know what would have happened if the sessions had not taken place. This positive view of those who have already invested in coaching does not mean that coaching is effective in an 'objective' way, i.e. for a general target group which includes colleagues and clients of the coachees, or from the viewpoint of others in the organisation of the coachee.

More than just developing a positive bias by spending time on the intervention, there may be other reasons for positive scores that are not related to 'effectiveness' as we would define it (i.e. effectiveness in helping to achieve goals, to overcome obstacles, and to become more competent and successful in the work role). Coaches give their coachee full and undivided attention and try to help them during the conversations (following from the idea of a 'helping conversation'). That does not just sway the coach towards a positive view of his or her own profession, through the dynamics of 'hope' and 'charity' or even simply because naturally they try to be positive to the coachee; but it will also sway the coachee towards experiencing coaching as positive. It is completely natural for the coachee to think, 'Here is someone who takes time for me, who listens to me, tries to help me, someone that must be a valuable resource, even if just because I know that my organisation is paying good money to hire them,' etcetera. Therefore, coaching sessions not only feel good and precious, but they also come with an aura of being good and valuable. Increasingly, coaching has become a veritable status symbol in organisations; I have written about this under the caption 'Coaching – from stigma to status' (De Haan, 2005). This positive connotation emerges independently from any good ideas or new decisions being developed in the sessions, let alone performance being enhanced or contractual objectives being achieved. Finally, there may be so-called 'gamma' change where the coachee (through coaching) becomes more familiar with one of the concepts on the questionnaire, such as 'resilience' or 'leadership,' so that a higher score is produced on the second, post-coaching questionnaire, even if there was no actual change in, say, the coachee's resilience or leadership abilities.

Unfortunately, and similar to other disciplines, most other people who tend to be involved with the research also already have a stake in coaching, in such a way that they are already positively disposed before they give their contribution to the research. Firstly, of course, the researchers themselves: the overwhelming majority of researchers tend to be coaching professionals, so again they have spent time and money to qualify and will have developed a positive attitude towards coaching, which they take into their work as a coaching researcher. In my experience, even when researchers are not trained coaches, most of them do seem to have a positive regard for coaching when commencing their research. Otherwise, they might have chosen a different topic. Next, the managers and organisational sponsors of the coachee: they make a positive choice for coaching at the outset of the coaching programme, i.e. well before the research begins. So, if those managers or sponsors are later asked for information about how their reports and colleagues are doing, they will be more positively than negatively disposed, regardless of any positive outcomes of coaching that they can notice. All these positive predispositions towards coaching will have measurably contributed to the results of the quantitative research base in coaching, which is one of the reasons we need so many measurements and will need to establish 'effectiveness' from very many angles.

The final group of those who may be biased when contributing to the research are the editors and reviewers of professional journals. They will be reading and judging the material because it is 'their area of expertise' and that again will more often than not mean that they have invested in becoming a coach or a coaching researcher, or at least are a benign 'fellow traveller' of the helping professions, and will have developed a generally positive attitude towards coaching alongside preparing themselves for their editorial roles. One example of how biases may play out is the suppression of 'null results,' the tendency not to publish studies which show no significant results. There is evidence that authors and editors may conspire in keeping such results hidden in the researchers' file drawers rather than getting it published (Franco et al., 2014).

Controversy 3: if the same people are asked to measure all variables, biases will result

Another controversy or issue with modern quantitative research in the helping professions is so-called 'same-source bias,' the difficulty of comparing data which comes from the same source; for example, as in most instances of coaching research, from the coachee. Coachees are often asked to do more than just give biographical data and complete a questionnaire on the outcome of coaching; more often than not the same coachees are asked to score the other, so called 'independent' variables as well. In that case the coachee might be asked about his/her personality, through a validated psychometric, or about her resilience, well-being, outcome expectations, etcetera. If these variables are then treated as independent, a proven outcome of coaching would be determined by the coachees' resilience, say, significantly predicting their (self-scored) outcomes. The problem with this 'same-source' or 'common-methods' bias is that every coachee will have some propensity to score higher (or lower) than the average person in the sample on *all* questionnaires, which leads these different variables to *correlate*, even though they are thought to be independent. The coachee's mood or general optimism (or lack of it) may also influence the scores and create spurious correlations in this way. To put it succinctly, just their personal bias, whatever it is, when responding to a questionnaire (any questionnaire!) will lead to a demonstrable 'outcome' of coaching. This type of correlation would have in fact nothing to do with the coaching, only with response patterns in answering questionnaires that we all have; nevertheless it would contribute to a measurable 'positive effect' of coaching.

Even if one could correct for scoring biases (something that is conceivable but very hard to do except approximately – and has not been done in most of the articles summarised in this book which are bound to suffer from same-source biases), there may be other factors that are not really to do with coaching and that may distort the findings, usually in the direction of the risk of finding 'false positives.' These are significant indications for the effectiveness of coaching demonstrated by the research, which should actually be attributed to other aspects, e.g. the coaching is pleasant or enjoyable, or seems worthwhile; that does not mean that it is actually effective. For effectiveness one would need the coachee to move on their goals, become a more skilled or resilient communicator or a more effective leader. If one only asks the coachee to rate such aspects and he or she has a positive experience in coaching, then out of that general 'good feeling' about coaching s/he may score his or her own effectiveness higher, even though there is no objective evidence for change (which would be: better work results, or colleagues and direct reports experiencing positive changes in collaboration with the coachee).

Controversy 4: the Hawthorne effect

Another fascinating source of bias comes from the research protocol and the researchers themselves. Often in the research design questionnaires arrive before and after coaching, or after every coaching session, asking about a certain phenomenon such as, say, the performance or productivity of the coachee. One example of this is given by 360-degree feedback instruments which are repeated before and after coaching, producing a helpful and relatively objective estimate of the performance of the coachee. It has been shown that the repetition of the measurement alone can lead us to expect a growth of the measured phenomenon upon second (third, fourth, etc.) asking. In other words, we can expect an amplification of performance or productivity in the eyes of direct colleagues, direct reports, line managers, and clients of the coachee, simply because the question is being asked more than once. This is the so-called Hawthorne effect, named after the Hawthorne Works plant and discovered by Henry Landsberger in 1958. It is essentially a motivational effect due to the interest being shown by the research protocol in the subjects of the research. The way to avoid the Hawthorne effect is to have a control group which answers the same questionnaires or surveys at exactly the same time points.

So far, I have summarised some of the issues with statistics, with sources of information, and with using the same source of information several times over in data collection (leading to built-in correlations which are nothing to do with the topic being studied). In traditional social, psychological, and particularly medical research, the standard answer to all these difficulties has been to create a 'double-blind randomised controlled trial' (db-RCT) or something as close as possible. In research in the helping conversations, the 'double blind' is unfortunately not possible, because neither party can be entirely blind to the treatment. Both parties know whether they are in a helping conversation or not. Unless the helper secretly tries to 'just chat' or not to be helpful, in which case this would be the control condition in a 'single blind' experiment. However, that has obviously its own difficulties because of the inauthenticity of those conversations and the fact that they will not be neutral, because of the mere fact of spending time together.

In coaching (and all other domains of helping conversations) the so-called 'gold standard' is the nonblinded randomised controlled trial (RCT), where two groups are being followed at the same time; one receiving the intervention (coaching) and the other in exactly the same circumstances, but without the intervention. RCTs are the best research tools that we have: we make the experience in both groups equal *except for* the intervention (the intervention then normally consists of a normal coaching contract of a distinct number of sessions; or even, in some cases, a few additional coaching sessions only for the intervention group – see e.g. Niglio de Figueiredo *et al.*, 2018). RCTs in realistic settings are rare because they are very hard to organise and get permissions for from the organisations where the coachees work. Most RCTs are therefore experiments set up by the researcher, amongst paid subjects, usually students who receive credit points or a small payment for participating. One can then argue the 'realism' of the RCT, e.g. the participants have no jobs, no power in the job, no leadership experience, which is all very different from coaching for executives.

Controversy 5: realistic settings do not satisfy lab research conditions

Even with the use of realistic RCTs there are still many other challenges for researchers of coaching effectiveness. Let us look into some of the most common ones that are recognised in the literature. Firstly, a big problem, also in coaching research, is that of a lack of randomisation. In realistic settings, i.e. when studying coaching in working organisations and institutions, it is very hard to get a truly randomised allocation to intervention and control group. Those managers or leaders that want coaching, want it now. Other, 'equivalent' managers can be found who do not want coaching now, and they can be asked to form a control group, but they now systematically differ from the intervention group, e.g. in their motivation to be coached. The very fact that they did not apply to be coached may indicate that they will give scores that are more negative about, say, their personal change or self-improvement through coaching. In any case, they are not a fair comparison group to the ones that are being coached: they have not volunteered to be coached which makes them different. I have decided to take nonrandomised control groups out of this chapter and stick with the 'gold standard' of RCTs in this first chapter which is about demonstrating effectiveness.

Another issue that we see in the literature with control groups is that the sizes of target and control group are very different, simply because in industry settings it is easier to find larger numbers of people to complete a questionnaire than it is to find people who want to complete it *and* be coached. Different sizes of groups can also create selection biases and statistical challenges.

Other issues that all researchers encounter are those of 'nested' groups, due to the fact that several coachees may have something in common. They may have the same line manager, or they have the same coach in the trial. That might skew the scores from those subgroups, particularly if the coach or manager is a statistical outlier. The same might be true of course with samples nested in just one organisation, just one work role (e.g. all engineers), or specific geographies and industry sectors. In all of these cases one can compute the effects of nested data, but then one would need much larger samples than one would otherwise need to demonstrate an effect – so, in practice, this can usually not be done with any real rigor.

Controversy 6: the diminishing power of statistical tests on the same data

The next fairly common problem, even with RCTs, is the 'look elsewhere' or 'multiple comparisons' effect: when no interesting effects are found, new hypotheses are introduced and more tests are being run just to dredge up interesting and significant data. However, the more tests are done, the more likely erroneous inferences are to occur, so that spurious, nonreplicable effects might be published. To estimate the sample size you need, you need to have an expected effect size in advance of the study, which can be taken from other similar studies. As a rule of thumb and assuming that we have normal distributions and know that we can expect an effect size of δ around, say, 0.8, for a statistical significance of $p < 0.01$ we already need $N = 58$ subjects in the intervention group and the same number in the control group. For every additional test on the sample we need at least a few extra subjects in the test. However, doing additional tests is often decided afterwards, when the N is already fixed. In those cases, i.e. in the analysis of data for a certain fixed N, a stricter significance threshold for individual comparisons is commonly introduced to compensate for the number of tests being undertaken (or, inferences being made). Often, the 'Bonferroni correction' is followed which says that we have to demand one sigma level higher for every ten additional post-hoc measurements.

Controversy 7: nonattendance of participants in coaching and in research

Another important problem with quantitative research is *attrition* of subjects; or, to a lesser extent, changes in *carelessness* (usually increases in carelessness) of subjects. When participants are asked to answer multiple questionnaires over a sustained period then a drop in completion rates is to be expected. Worse still, this drop is not random but tends to be related to personality (Ward *et al.*, 2017), so the sample becomes *less* representative of the general population of executive-coaching coachees. This attrition problem is much compounded by nonattendance in helping conversations: coachees who do not complete their cycle of coaching. One would suspect that these are the less enthusiastic clients, or they are the clients that are experiencing the smallest effectiveness. The reported effects can become overstated (exaggerated) if those that do not complete final sessions and questionnaires have to be left out of the study. Nonattendance figures are usually above 10% in later sessions and can be further worsened by attrition or carelessness on questionnaire completion.

Controversy 8: nonrepresentative samples

There are quite a few other issues in this budding literature related to the use of amateur or inexperienced coaches, and coaches and coachees from populations which are not representative. I have already mentioned coachees from the research institutes and universities themselves, that are much too young and not in the right roles to be representative of the executive coaching clientele. Then there are the difficulties around variables being tested and the fact that the chosen variables as well as the experimental designs are vastly different between research groups, which means that one should be very cautious pooling those findings together in systematic reviews or meta-analyses.

A wide variety of research into coaching processes and outcomes has now been undertaken. For some influential overviews of empirical papers in the last ten years, see Ely *et al.*, 2010; De Haan & Duckworth, 2013; Blackman *et al.*, 2016; Grover & Furnham, 2016. Athanasopoulou & Dopson, 2018), Theeboom *et al.* (2014), Jones *et al.* (2015), and Burt and Talati (2017) have even attempted some early meta-analyses. However, as Liu and Batt (2010) point out, much of the research into executive coaching has used students or managers on Leadership or MBA courses as subjects, as opposed to experienced managers in an organisational setting (and at least one study, Sonesh *et al.*, 2015, shows that there may be big discrepancies between those two settings). Additionally, most studies so far have investigated links between coaching and performance and other important criteria by utilising cross-sectional designs and subjective self-report measures that may obscure the actual benefits of coaching (Dahling *et al.*, 2016). Furthermore, research has not yet reached the same rigor and status as in other helping professions, as shown by the fact that the application of the 'gold standard in coaching research,' the randomised controlled trial (Passmore & Theeboom, 2015), occurs only in 35, mostly small-scale studies, as will be shown later in section C of this chapter. Indeed, very few corporate coaching programmes have even been formally evaluated (McDermott *et al.*, 2007).

Despite all these issues from a 'truth' or 'evidence' perspective, I have still found it illuminating to read the quantitative research literature in executive coaching, and more widely in the helping professions, because despite all these serious biases and caveats, the large empirical literature does seem to begin to point to certain patterns in the effectiveness of coaching work, which should be generalisable and can therefore inform our practice as workplace and executive coaches, as I will endeavour to show in the next chapters.

Just to summarise, here are some things to keep in mind when you are reading empirical, quantitative research articles in coaching – as you form your own judgement on how serious to take the 'truth' that the authors believe that they have discovered.

1 Scoring bias including recall bias and carelessness
2 Researcher bias, extended to client, commissioner, manager, sponsor, reviewer, and editor bias
3 Publication bias especially against studies where 'only' the null hypothesis was confirmed
4 Same-source response bias, e.g. if coachees provide both independent and dependent variables
5 Absence of control groups: the Hawthorne effect
6 Nonrandomised control and target groups, aggravated by unequal numbers in the two groups
7 Unrealistic samples, e.g. biased towards student coaches and coachees
8 Nested data with many coachees in the sample having the same coach or line manager
9 Number of tests that are run: the multiple-comparisons problem
10 Attrition biases in longitudinal studies compounded by coaching nonattendance
11 Statistical biases: incorrect assumptions such as the assumption of a normal distribution

Remember that all of these are systematic, non-random errors which conspire to give biases in the same direction, namely towards 'errors of the first kind' (or finding a 'false positive,' or a type 1 error), which is the error we make when we believe we have found some evidence for coaching where there was none. They all strengthen each other and bend the 'truth' the same way, towards demonstrating a higher perceived effectiveness of coaching. Fortunately, though, after three decades of quantitative coaching research, we now have so many individual studies that evidence is mounting and a summarising book like this one, which assumes that there are 'truths' about coaching effectiveness worth reporting about, begins to make sense.

Controversy 9: coaching is not very sharply defined

We will begin our overview of coaching research in this chapter with an exploration of the findings in 'health coaching': coaching in support of the provision of clinical care. Although health coaching is also called coaching, the differences with executive coaching are stark: most health coaches are clinical experts, dieticians, or nurses, who use the sessions mostly to instruct, inform, teach, and cajole patients into engaging with more of the treatment or into more healthy habits. In other words, health coaching is largely a form of expert consulting or mentoring, with experts who are in most cases not even qualified as a coach. None of the usual efforts to have a coachee come up with their own themes and goals and then working on these as directed by the client, in an open-ended way, bringing 'creative indifference' with regard to outcomes, trusting the coachee to take their own responsibility.

Health coaching is not executive or workplace coaching. And neither is mentoring or managerial coaching, which we will also be summarising (mentoring outcomes in Chapter 3 and coaching by the direct line manager in Chapter 2). Managerial coaching is defined in some of the articles simply as the time that the manager spends with the employee, the time used to explain and instruct, and to answer questions about current challenges. None of the managers in those investigations have studied coaching, let alone qualified professionally in that field. Nevertheless, their help to the employee is called 'coaching' and there have been some very interesting research papers about what the impact of such a manager's presence is, which I would not want to withhold from a research-interested reader.

The research results themselves seem to invite us to consider *all* clearly adjacent fields: counselling, psychotherapy, life coaching, executive and workplace coaching, health and sports coaching, mentoring, and managerial coaching. The results seem to be saying that there are very basic factors at play around a positive regard, a positive reputation, a 'dominant-friendly' style, the offer of care, space, and attention – and that these are the factors that seem to make the biggest difference in all these professions. If we look again at what all these domains seem to deliver to coachees/mentees/clients/patients, we may notice a dominant pattern, namely that all of these conversations have the common feature of being able to 'wrap around' the needs of the patient, client, coachee, mentee, employee, etcetera – so that they make a difference on virtually every request that might be there. So, they generally deliver on 'goal attainment' *whatever those goals are*. All the domains have in common that they try to help the coachee or employee or client from where s/he is to where s/he wants to be, on a journey that is highly individual but significant for him or her.

The reasons I have left psychotherapy and counselling out of this book are that (1) there is no space since the research in those fields is vast and detailed, and (2) there have already been some very good summaries in the psychotherapy outcome literature, e.g. Wampold (2001), Cooper (2008), Norcross (2011), just to name a few. It is perhaps good to realise right at the beginning that none of the results in this book flatly contradict psychotherapy outcome research and that instead they mostly confirm the findings related to effectiveness, active ingredients, and the broad application of professional treatments. With sports coaching it is similar; there is just too much out there to do justice in this book.

Having made clear that all these helping professions seem to have similar outcomes, it is nevertheless important to note that there is also evidence for the benefits of an added value through more sophisticated in-depth or nondirective coaching – and so the research is not simply saying 'anything goes' in coaching and other helping conversations. We will come back to this in Chapter 2.

Part B: how to establish whether coaching works

Building up 'evidence' about coaching means that we measure results for samples of coaching conversations or coaching assignments in such a way that we can understand something about the sample, with high probability. Such an understanding can then be predictive of other, later samples of coaching conversations. This build-up begins a 'natural science of coaching' where we can say with confidence, albeit only in a general way, what we expect to come out of coaching contracts before we have even started the work.

The only way to build up evidence that coaching does what it sets out to do is to collect quantitative data about its effectiveness whilst at the same time making sure that the effect found can be attributed to coaching, and to coaching only.

It is important to notice that for practical reasons we can only measure quite blunt variables such as 'overall helpfulness' after a certain number of coaching conversations, or a 'reduction of sickness leave days' after a run of coaching sessions, or even a 'significant improvement in 360-degree-leadership ratings' after a full coaching contract. With large enough numbers of clients in the sample, these are examples of statements that one may hope to demonstrate within the sample. These numbers are crude in the sense that they can be measured quantitatively, on a single dimension, and they may only change significantly after a substantial amount of coaching work. Usually, therefore, we are measuring numbers or percentages as a result of a whole series of coaching sessions in a large sample, so even if we can demonstrate significant effects on those numbers, we have still understood very little about the coaching itself. We still do not know what it is within the sessions that has made that number, our 'statistic' or fact about the 'state' of coaching conversations, change. So, even if we can demonstrate a better performance or less absence due to sickness through coaching, we would still struggle to say what it is within the coaching that has made that statistic change. We need much larger samples if we are to relate anything from within the coaching to any of our demonstrated outcomes – nevertheless it is possible to do that as well, through more research, and then we would be able to say what it is about our sessions that made the clients make a certain average change.

The established way of collecting such evidence is the 'randomised controlled trial' or RCT. In such a trial, which is used widely in medicine and psychotherapy, a large group of potential clients is randomly divided into two groups, one of which – the *intervention group*, also called 'experimental' or 'target' group – receives a standard amount of coaching (say six sessions with monthly intervals over a period of six months) whilst the other group – the *control* group – continues the same journey as the intervention group with all circumstances similar *except for* the coaching. They may be on a waiting list or they may be induced by a small payment to complete regular questionnaires (the same questionnaires as the group that is coached is completing at the same intervals, and for the same payment – so still keeping all conditions the same between the two groups, except for the coaching intervention itself).

If one only wants to measure this one thing – *does coaching work?* – then a modest sample size can be sufficient. In the helping professions one can expect a decent effect size of δ at least 0.7 which means that the average person who is treated is better off than 76% of the control group. If one aims for such an effect size, then a sample size of 33 in each of the control group and intervention group can be sufficient to have a statistical power of $p < 0.05$ (so, a one-in-twenty chance that the result is due to type 1 error: Chan, 2003). We will see that many coaching randomised trials have tried to demonstrate something with even smaller sample sizes, which may open up those experiments to criticism. However, if one wants to do other tests as well, such as which characteristics of coachees correlate with a positive outcome, then it is better to go with substantially larger sample sizes.

Let us give the example of one recent study which was done in a realistic environment, in a global pharma corporation (De Haan *et al.*, 2019). This is a rare example of a randomised controlled trial (RCT) in a realistic setting. It could be organised in this corporation because the coaching intervention was already being offered to large groups of female leaders every calendar year. As there so often is, there was a price to pay for having a randomised (waiting-list) controlled trial: all coachees were female, line managers were also expected to hold regular one-to-one mentoring meetings with the coachees, and other than 12 sessions of individual coaching they also received approximately 6 sessions of group coaching throughout the duration of the programme. Maybe in retrospect the rather large strength of the effects that were found were partly due to the fact that the programme also incorporated these managerial support meetings and group-coaching sessions, as part of the overall leadership development intervention.

The study involved two consecutive groups on a leadership-development programme ('Accelerating Difference') designed to increase the ratio of female leaders at all leadership levels. The two starting points of April and September provided ideal conditions for a 'waiting-list control group' study design. Other than basic effectiveness of executive coaching, the study also examined the relative impact of various 'common factors' (i.e. aspects common to all coaching approaches; see the next chapter), with the help of the largest randomised controlled trial to date: 89 female leaders in the target group at T2, and 72 female leaders in the control group, with at least 114 corresponding questionnaires from their 66 different coaches and 115 from their 140 line managers. By asking coachees, coaches, and line managers to rate outcomes on the same scales, we have three independent measures of coaching outcomes. Some of the data structure was multilevel, although average nesting is well under three for the coaches (i.e. a coach does not work with more than three coachees on average) and well under two for the managers – and checks revealed that there seemed to be no biases as a result of nested data.

This was a 'waiting-list' RCT, so before any coaching began, the first email referring to online questionnaires was sent to the coachee, coach, and line manager to set up the experiment and measure baseline data. This questionnaire was closed by the time coaches had been matched to coachees (in Cohort 1, the intervention group). The second questionnaires went out after six months, when Cohort 1 had completed six sessions on average, and Cohort 2 – the control group – was about to be matched to their coaches; similarly, this questionnaire was closed before the control group's first coaching conversations began. The third measurement was again six months later, so it took place after the intervention group's coaching had ended. Completions at T1 were between 18 March and 19 May 2016, at T2 between 3 October and 14 November 2016, and at T3 between 24 April and 30 May 2017.

Baseline data were Name, Gender, Nationality, Country of Residence, MBTI Personality Type,[2] Hogan Personality Type (HPI, HDS, MVPI),[3] Outcome Expectations, Coaching Effectiveness (CE), the Brief Resilience Scale (BRS),[4] the General Self-Efficacy (GSE) Scale,[5] the Psychological Wellbeing Scale (WEMWBS),[6] and the Perceived Social Support (PSS)[7] Scale. Later, at T2 when coach and coachee had met, perceived coaching behaviours were measured with the Coaching Behaviours

Questionnaire (CBQ)[8] and quality of relationship with the Working Alliance Inventory (WAI).[9]

Results of the study will be briefly summarised in Part C of this chapter. Overall, this study contributed to the existing coaching outcome literature in three important ways: firstly, it provided the largest-scale randomised controlled trial to date in the coaching outcome research literature; secondly, it studied the outcome of executive (group) coaching in a naturalistic corporate setting whilst still studying coaching uncontaminated by other leadership development activities such as (cognitive) teaching, instruction, and (personal) training; and thirdly, it is the first to model and demonstrate the impact of coaching on leadership-derailment patterns, by measuring these personality characteristics before and after the intervention (see Chapter 4).

Part C: overview of outcomes of coaching research with randomised control groups

Here is an overview of the most rigorous outcome studies in coaching. Firstly, we will discuss some of the research that was undertaken by clinical research experts in the area of health coaching. Then, I will summarise the best studies that we have into workplace-coaching effectiveness, which is the full body of randomised controlled trials. I know of 35 randomised controlled trials in the wider area of workplace and executive coaching, including some very small-scale ones, and I will summarise them all in the second part of this section.

1 Randomised controlled experiments in health coaching

In the medical field, randomised controlled trials have long shown that coaching can help to support patients. Coaching is always added for the intervention group, whilst the control group stays on 'usual care.' These trials have shown that dedicated health workers who 'coach' patients (usually by means of a series of agreed 30-minute phone calls over a critical period of their treatment or during their recovery process) can make a big difference on a whole raft of measures, from discipline with medicine intake, healthy lifestyles, the cessation of smoking, and all sorts of biomarkers for health. As one of the studies in this section attests, the 'rapidly emerging coaching profession has a natural fit with health care' (Wolever *et al.*, 2010). In other words, the medical field of health coaching seems to be building on the successes of life and executive coaching, with very good research indeed.

We will see that effect sizes of health coaching are very high, much higher than in psychotherapy or executive coaching, partly because of the intensity of interventions, with many coaching sessions and calls over only a few months, and also because of a strong teaching component and the added use of self-coaching: diarising and other homework. The coach tries to be very much in charge of a multitude of ways to improve, get fitter, and get better.

Health coaching in medical settings

From the vast literature on health coaching with more than one hundred randomised controlled trials (and fast growing), I have selected a few influential and typical studies which show that intensive health coaching can boast very high effectiveness in some cases:

Vale et al. (2003) following on from Vale et al. (2002) researched the 'Coaching patients On Achieving Cardiovascular Health' (COACH) programme by randomly assigning half of 792 patients from 6 Melbourne university teaching hospitals after cardiac diagnosis within each hospital: 331 completed the usual care plus COACH Programme and 348 usual care alone over a period of months. Coaches were 2 dietitians and 4 nurses, i.e. one coach per hospital. They found very high effects on total cholesterol levels, the primary target of the coaching ($\delta = 6.5$; $p < 0.0001$).[10] Moreover, significant effects were found on nearly all other parameters as well: a reduction in lipoprotein cholesterol (LDL-C), a significantly lesser rise in blood pressure levels, a greater reduction in body weight (BMI); a lower dietary intake of total fat, saturated fat, and cholesterol; and lower anxiety levels; dietary fibre intake increased in coached patients and decreased in usual care patients; more coached patients reported taking up regular walking than noncoached patients; fewer coached patients reported symptoms of breathlessness and chest pain at 6 months; more coached patients reported better general health and mood at 6 months. There was no impact of the COACH Programme on fasting glucose, smoking behaviour, or depression scores.

DeBar et al. (2006) tested a coaching programme for female adolescents to improve bone mineral density as a prevention of later-life osteoporosis in Oregon, with 101 girls in the intervention group and 108 in the control group. During a 2-year trial both groups received regular check-ups and support, and the intervention group received an additional 4 coaching calls a year, bimonthly group support meetings over and above quarterly adolescent-and-parents group meetings, and weekly self-monitoring postcards. They found high effects on bone mineral density, the primary target of the coaching, after one year (e.g. in the spine, $\delta = 4$; $p < 0.001$), which were maintained after the second year. The intervention also had a substantial effect on the main dietary targets but not on exercise rates.

Edelman et al. (2006) tested an intervention where a coach and a medical expert worked with patients to reduce their 10-year cardiovascular risks in North Carolina, with 56 adults aged 45 and older completing the intervention and 66 assigned randomly to the control group. The coach led 28 two-hour group meetings over the 10 months of the intervention, weekly for the first 4 months, biweekly for months 5 through 9, and then once at the conclusion of the intervention. Participants also had 20- to 30-minute phone sessions with their coach every 2 weeks throughout the intervention. They found a significant change on their main variable: cardiovascular risk ($p = 0.006$ after 5 months), but also positive effects on a broad range of health parameters such as increased days of exercise per week compared with controls (3.7 versus 2.4 days, $p = 0.002$).

Fisher et al. (2009) tested in St. Louis City whether supervised community health workers are able to reach low-income parents of African-American children hospitalised for asthma and to reduce rehospitalisation among them, through a randomised controlled trial with 83 parents in the intervention group and 65 in the control group. The coaches called the parents biweekly for 3 months, after which calls were monthly for the 24 months duration of the intervention. Children with asthma in the coached condition were 61% less likely to be admitted to hospital in the two years following randomisation ($\delta = 3.9$; $p < 0.01$).

Wolever *et al.* (2010) created a randomised controlled design for 27 North Carolina patients with type 2 diabetes in the intervention group who received 14 30-minute telephone-coaching sessions, with 22 in the control group. They assessed whether the 6 months of individual coaching could improve lifestyle behaviours and psychosocial functioning, and reduce haemoglobin. Various adherence-to-medicine measures had a large ($\delta = 0.95$; $p < 0.001$) effect size between intervention and control group, and haemoglobin levels also reduced with $\delta = 0.34$ ($p < 0.05$) in the intervention group only; moreover they found significant improvement in psychosocial measures.

These very large effect sizes show that intensive coaching can have a myriad of effective applications in medicine, leading to remarkable, sustained improvements in physical health and lifestyle changes. They are only some of the main randomised controlled studies in medicine and many hundreds of studies in the area of health coaching. A recent systematic review identified no less than 90 randomised controlled trials in health coaching, including both coaching for rehabilitation and for prevention (Dejonghe *et al.*, 2017). They selected 14 studies that measured longer-term effects, which showed good effectiveness even a minimum of 24 weeks after completion of the coaching. It is worth mentioning again that in this larger group of studies in health coaching it is very rare to find a research design where the intervention consists purely of one-to-one coaching: there are usually many educational and instructional elements built into the intervention as well as coaching. Because we cannot be sure what the part is that was played by teaching and instruction (which is also true, to a lesser degree, for the mentoring effectiveness studies which I will briefly review in Chapter 3), I will not take the many health coaching studies into the main analysis of executive and workplace coaching in the rest of this book.

Health coaching in workplace settings

Prevention studies incorporating telephone health coaching for adults seem to have been considerably less effective than the previously discussed trials for patients. I could only find a few studies in health coaching with workplace applications and they found small effects:

Bennett *et al.* (2005) analysed a randomised controlled experiment where a nurse coached an Oregon older adult monthly over a period of 6 months, starting out face to face and then by phone, using motivational interviewing. Their final sample was 66 in the intervention and 45 in the control group. Results were measured by seven different health status measures, self-scored – only one of these was significantly lowered for the intervention group: illness intrusiveness after 6 months ($\delta = 0.26$; $p < 0.05$).

In a randomised controlled trial design, 367 Dutch hospital workers aged 45 and older received a 6-month intervention, which included two weekly guided group sessions: one yoga and one workout, as well as one weekly session of aerobic exercising, without face-to-face instruction, and three individual coach visits aimed at changing workers' lifestyle behaviour by goal setting, feedback, and problem-solving strategies

(Strijk *et al.*, 2013; N = 363 in control group). Vitality, work engagement, productivity, and number of times of sick leave in the last 3 months were the same in both groups – the only significant difference was amongst those with a high uptake of yoga, who had significantly higher vitality even at 6 months after completing the intervention. And in another, similar study (Van Berkel *et al.*, 2014) 129 Dutch research-institute workers received 8 weeks of weekly mindfulness training sessions followed by 8 sessions of e-coaching, whilst 128 colleagues were in a randomised control group. They did not find any effects on vigorous physical activity, fruit intake, and behavioural vitality determinants after 6 and 12 months.

In a large sample addressing five health risk behaviours (physical activity, fruit and vegetable intake, red meat consumption, multi-vitamin use, and smoking cessation) Emmons *et al.* (2014) researched Boston adults in standard primary care, with a 625-person control group, an 882-person self-coaching intervention group, and a 933-person self-coaching-plus-two-sessions-of-telephone-coaching intervention group. The intervention, with and without coaching, significantly improved the multiple-risk-behaviours score among a large and diverse population of primary care patients, reflecting a between 25% and 50% improvement over usual care (18- and 6-month follow-ups, respectively). However, the differences between the self-coaching and telephone coaching groups were not significant.

Geraedts *et al.* (2014) researched information versus a coaching intervention (consisting of 6 weekly web-based lessons and follow-up by weekly assignments and e-coaching). Participants were employees with high depression scores from 6 large organisations in the Netherlands, randomised into an intervention group of 116 employees and a 115-strong control group. Both groups improved equally ($\delta = 0.26$) and in a sustained way at 12-month follow-up ($\delta = 0.24$); therefore again no additional benefit of the health coaching could be demonstrated. However, it is important to note that attrition rates were very high (as expected with high depression scores).

2 Randomised controlled experiments in workplace coaching

Here starts the overview of outcome studies in workplace and executive coaching, which will take up this chapter and the next. In this chapter I continue to be only referring to randomised controlled studies. Of course, there are many other high-quality pieces of research, such as where conditions are compared in very rigorous ways. However, those studies are not in a good position to answer the key question of this chapter: *does coaching work?* For that purpose one has to compare to a control group of exactly the same composition with the only difference being that those in the control group do not receive coaching during the exact same time of the experiment. All of those studies, exactly 35 in total, that make use of a properly randomised control group, are found in this section. Subsequently, an answer to the all-important question 'What can we conclude about whether workplace and executive coaching works?' can be found in the next section.

Deviney (1994) assigned 45 line managers at a nuclear power plant randomly to three groups: 14 receiving coaching plus 360-degree feedback, 13 receiving coaching with only their own and their manager's 360-degree results, and 18 in a no-treatment control group. Their direct managers were trained in a 3-day workshop to be their coaches. There were three to eight coaching sessions and the 360-degree feedback was retaken after the interventions, approximately nine weeks after the first round of feedback. There were no significant findings overall, although there were some clear trends in the direction of coaching without subordinate feedback being most effective. One reason may have been that the coaching was somewhat confrontational, remedial, and problem-focused in nature.

Taylor (1997) assigned 84 participants undergoing a summer Medical College Admission Test (MCAT) preparation course randomly to one of four groups: 26 to 2-day training only, 16 to maximum 4 coaching sessions only, 26 to training plus coaching, and 16 to a no-treatment control. Stress levels increased significantly during the course, but self-perceived stress was less for those who underwent training or coaching. For high-resilience participants, coaching slightly but significantly lessened post-test perceived stress and training increased post-test perceived stress. For low-resilience participants, training lessened post-test perceived stress and coaching increased post-test perceived stress.

Following on from a PhD project with three small randomised controlled trials (groups of around 20) that demonstrated some significant impact of a coaching workshop and 5 follow-up coaching sessions on objective academic results and anxiety self-ratings (Grant, 2002), a series of further small-scale randomised controlled trials was undertaken in health, educational, and life-coaching settings. In the domain of life coaching, Green *et al.* (2006), Green *et al.* (2007), and Spence and Grant (2007) employed randomised controlled trials with waiting lists for $N = 58$, $N = 56$, and $N = 63$ participants. Note, however, that in the first two studies, 6 and 7 participants withdrew before the second questionnaire, and in the third study there were two treatment groups so in every one of these studies we see numbers per (treatment/control) group lower than 30. Each of these studies used only self-report measures, introducing the risk of same-source biases. They found some significant effects, with the largest effects found for group coaching (Green *et al.*, 2006; later replicated for online group coaching by Poepsel, 2011). Similarly, Grant *et al.* (2009) studied $N = 41$ healthcare managers, with approximately half assigned to a random waiting-list control group and the other half receiving executive coaching. They found that coaching significantly enhanced goal attainment, resilience, and workplace well-being, and reduced depression and stress (all self-scored; all $p < 0.05$). Finally, Grant *et al.* (2010) studied $N = 44$ high-school teachers – of which approximately half were assigned to a random waiting-list control group and the other half received work-related coaching. They found that coaching again significantly enhanced self-scored goal attainment, resilience, and workplace well-being, and reduced depression and stress (δ varying between 0.4 and 1.5). Pre and post *self-ratings* in leadership styles were also significantly different (with δ's around 0.5); however, these rating differences remained insignificant in *peer ratings*. So, in the only article in this series where self- and other-ratings are compared (Grant *et al.*, 2010), the results for other-ratings are insignificant.

Miller *et al.* (2004) found that coaching with feedback was superior to training-only conditions, in a programme designed to help clinicians learn motivational interviewing skills. They randomised into four groups: (a) Workshop only; (b) Workshop plus feedback based on recordings; (c) Workshop plus coaching; (d) Workshop, feedback, and coaching; (e) Waitlist control group. In total 106 clinicians completed at least the 4-month follow-up questionnaire, and there was an 8- and a 12-month follow-up as well. They used objective outcomes defined in terms of independent session ratings based on recordings and client outcome indicators from the same recordings. After workshop effect size difference with the control group was considerable ($\delta = 0.44$; $p < 0.005$) and training and coaching seemed to add to this proficiency but mostly non-significantly. An exception was that only the group with feedback and coaching sustained the improvement in terms of their client responses four months after the workshop (p < 0.01).

Finn *et al.* (2007), following on from Finn (2007), reported on an in-company leadership programme in which a random control group of 12 and intervention group of 11 were created out of those who elected to be coached as part of the programme. The group that was coached showed significantly higher self-reported developmental support, openness to new behaviours and developmental planning, and even came out slightly but not significantly higher on leadership behaviours as rated by their direct reports (whilst not finding significant effects for self-reported positive affect and self-efficacy, and supervisor ratings).

Duijts *et al.* (2008) undertook a randomised controlled investigation into the effectiveness of 7 to 9 sessions of 'preventive' work-related coaching in terms of reducing sickness absence due to psychosocial health complaints. N = 151 employees (all at risk for sickness absence) found themselves randomly assigned to two almost equal-size intervention and no-intervention-control groups, although only 37 of them participated fully in the coaching intervention. The coaching was done by qualified executive coaches which is unusual in health coaching and which is why we need to include the study here with the workplace coaching articles. Again, the intervention group self-reported improved health, whilst the findings on subjective sickness absence were not significant. However, statistically significant reductions in sickness absence could indeed be demonstrated in this group (2.5 days less off work on average in the year following coaching than in the intervention group; p < 0.001). Employees in the coaching group also reported significantly improved health, less distress, less burnout, less need for recovery, and increased satisfaction with their lives.

Dejonghe *et al.* (2017) included the Duijts *et al.* (2008) RCT, because of the longer-term follow-up data collection. Here are two important follow-up studies as well:

- A faithful replication of the Duijts *et al.* (2008) study, with a group of coachees from German private companies who were offered more confidentiality during their coaching, was Telle *et al.* (2016). Their intervention group of 51 received 8 to 12 coaching sessions over 3 months and the control group of 34 received a brochure about how to cope with distress. Similarly to Duijts *et al.*, they found no significant change for self-reported sickness absence days but clear significant differences in self-reported variables such as a lower willingness to work until exhausted ($\delta = 0.8$), more distancing ability ($\delta = 0.7$), and lower emotional exhaustion ($\delta = 0.23$) and lower depression.
- With a much larger and longitudinal sample, Viering *et al.* (2015) were able to show that coaching as support for Swiss adults with a mental disability, with an aim to reintegrate into work, could have a significant impact on return to work. The 88 job seekers in the intervention group received 24 months of job coaching over and above mental health support and other vocational support that the control group of 83 also received, with questionnaires every 6 months. Significant results were obtained for employment rates and number of new jobs obtained (p < 0.01).

Kochanowski *et al.* (2010) compared two randomised groups of 15 store managers in the same supermarket chain, who all received multi-source feedback on their influencing skills and a feedback workshop, with only the intervention group receiving 6 weekly 30-minute coaching sessions from one of the researchers. After 3 months, the feedback instrument was re-run and results indicated that managers who received coaching after the feedback workshop increased their use of collaboration with subordinates more than managers who did not receive coaching ($\delta = 0.45$; $p < 0.05$). One weakness of this study is that the feedback workshops were unmixed so some of the effects found could have come from differences in the separate workshops for intervention and control group.

Taie (2011) created two randomised groups of 60 nurses who were trained in life-support skills after cardiac arrest, and compared their ratings after training plus for the intervention group managerial coaching, at three time points: before and after the programme, and then 4 months later. The intervention group had significantly better results in terms of self-rated skills and knowledge after 4 months ($p < 01$).

There are two randomised controlled trials in driving instruction, where a more 'coaching' approach was compared with a traditional instruction-only approach (Passmore & Velez with 327 drivers and Passmore & Rehman with 208 drivers). These studies show some statistically significant improvements (in terms of number of hours driving that pupils needed to pass the test, the number of tests taken by pupils before passing, and the likelihood of pupils to pass on the first attempt; Passmore & Rehman, 2012), when instructors adopted coaching-type interventions. However, there were no significant findings in the case of one-off coaching sessions (Passmore & Velez, 2012). The Passmore and Rehman (2012) results could be attributed to a more coaching style of instructing, but they may also be attributable to the fact that only the 'coaching' driving instructors had received recent, additional training, which may have changed other elements of their practice.

Goff et al. (2014) conducted a RCT study where 52 US urban elementary and middle-school principals were randomised into 2 groups: 26 received a year of teacher feedback (from on average 34 teachers each) and then a year of feedback (now including 'action items') and external professional coaching (intervention group); and 26 received feedback (also including 'action items') only in the second year when the intervention was happening in parallel. There were 2 to 4 coaching session between terms, i.e. on average 8 coaching sessions in the year of measurement, and 3 feedback-collection terms a year. The outcome measures were constructed from the 'action items' that principals received (two factors: Principal Leadership Development and Teacher Instructional Development). They find changes only on the first factor, with effect sizes of $\delta = 0.15$ per coaching session ($p < 0.05$); the second measure is more about one-to-one teacher interaction and therefore harder to achieve. They find that the principals who agree to more sessions of coaching also had a higher objective need for being coached (which would be in accordance with clients' self-optimising dose-effect curves, see Stiles et al., 2015 – a psychotherapy outcome study where this was shown).

McGonagle et al. (2014) assigned full-time workers with chronic illnesses randomly to either a coaching group of 23 (who received 6 one-hour phone GROW coaching sessions with certified coaches) or a waitlisted control group of 25. Participants completed online surveys at enrolment, at the start of coaching, after coaching ended, and 12 weeks post-coaching. Compared with the control group, the coaching group showed significantly improved work ability perceptions, exhaustion burnout, core self-evaluations, and resilience. Results indicated that the positive effects of coaching were stable 12 weeks after coaching ended.

In a small-scale, longitudinal randomised controlled trial (Singh et al., 2015), a group of 20 London medical students were trained in laparoscopic surgical skills with the help of virtual-reality simulation training. After around 7 hours of training and testing of surgical skills during on average 4 days, the 20 students performed a virtual-reality surgical operation 5 times in a row, with 10 students (controls) receiving a 30-minute online tutorial after each operation whilst the intervention group of 10 received a 30-minute GROW coaching session based on a video recording of that operation. Then all subjects performed 2 medical operations which were assessed by some objective measurements and a trained surgeon assessor using recorded video footage to rate performance on various rating scales. Intervention group students clearly outperformed the control group students on those scales ($\delta \approx 1$; $p < 0.01$). This result was replicated in another randomised controlled trial with 18 much more experienced Canadian surgical residents (Bonrath et al., 2015, with ratings' effect sizes $\delta \approx 1.4$; $p < 0.05$). They also found that after 2 months and on average 4 sessions of structured coaching, the coached registrars were able to more accurately assess their own performance, a prerequisite for future development. Another still-smaller replication was Alameddine et al. (2018).

Losch et al. (2016) assigned 84 students randomly to individual coaching, self-coaching, group training, and a control group. All 3 intervention conditions consisted of 3 sessions of approximately 2 hours each with 10 days in between. Coaches/trainers were students in psychology. Satisfaction and academic procrastination were shown to be significantly higher and lower respectively, for those engaging in individual coaching and group training, and goal attainment was significantly higher only for the individual coaching condition. In Zanchetta et al. (2020) 103 young employees were randomly assigned to receive 3 two-hour sessions of coaching ($N = 36$), similar-length training in groups of 10 ($N = 33$), or to a no-intervention control group ($N = 34$) to help them deal with impostor tendencies. Training turned out to be significantly better to increase cognitive understanding ($\delta = 0.51$ compared to coaching; $p < 0.05$), whilst coaching was superior in terms of helping participants achieve new personalised strategies ($\delta = 0.74$ compared to training; $p < 0.01$), achieving their own coaching goals (but only significant in relation to the control group), and reducing their 'impostor phenomenon' scores (again training and coaching both significant in relation to the control group – but their difference nonsignificant). There was also a significant indirect effect of coaching on 'impostor phenomenon' scores, through the significant reduction of the 'fear of negative evaluation.' From the same research group, a smaller-scale experiment (Junker et al., 2020) showed that coaching for 24 students reduced both their appraisal of stress and their stress responses more than the waiting-list control group of 20 students. However, they were not able to demonstrate a significant difference between control and intervention groups on their main outcome variable, goal attainment.

Tee et al. (2017) was a small 'pilot' RCT study with 39 participants, with the intervention group having 6 weekly sessions consisting of one-hour group training followed by one-hour peer-coaching. They found no significant differences for the trained-and-coached participants.

Williams and Lowman (2018) used a randomised waiting-list control group of 64 mid-to-senior leaders in a large company to assign a group of 32 clients to 2 different coaching conditions (goal-focused and process-oriented coaching): 4 sessions with qualified external coaches during 4 to 6 weeks of intervention. The control group was then also randomly divided in the 2 coaching conditions so that by the end of the experiment there was a comparison group of 32 in each condition. They found a significant increased outcome on leadership competences, but only for self-ratings ($\delta = 0.7$; $p < 0.01$), not for line manager ratings. They found no significant differences for the two coaching conditions, i.e. no significant differences between the more directive goal-focused condition and the more nondirective (tailored) process-oriented condition.

Allan et al. (2018) reviewed a randomised controlled trial where 54 adult participants (average age 42 years) were divided equally over a 10-week coaching intervention by registered and trainee psychologists and a waiting-list control group. The coaching started with feedback on a NEO PI-R ('Big Five') personality tool after which coachees could target facets of their personality which they wanted to change, so Big Five dimensions became outcome variables. Coaches were supervised by weekly supervision groups based on videos of their sessions. Participants took the NEO PI-R 3 more times: midway through the coaching, at the end of the coaching, and during a 12-week follow-up. They showed that regardless of the facets chosen by coachees to work on (which all significantly improved), Neuroticism decreased ($p < 0.001$); Conscientiousness ($p < 0.05$) and Extraversion ($p < 0.01$) increased significantly in the group; whilst Agreeableness remained the same. All changes were maintained from end of the coaching to follow-up, so executive coaching seems to have an impact on these three personality dimensions regardless of the focus of the participants ($p < 0.001$).

In a rigorous randomised controlled trial, Niglio de Figueiredo et al. (2018) gave a group of 72 oncologists a workshop on communication skills and one follow-up session of coaching, plus, for the intervention group only, 3 more sessions of coaching, so they could test the additional effect of 3 more coaching sessions by itself. As outcome measures, they had raters analyse 428 video recordings of the clinicians' consultations with patients: 2 per clinician before-training, 2 after-training (t1), and 2 after-coaching (t2). The training provided theory, role-play with actors, and video feedback regarding the clinicians' own recordings, and the coaching also provided mostly video feedback. The intervention group showed a statistically significant improvement ($\delta = 0.45$, $p = 0.01$) on the rating scales between t1 and t2 and showed a significant advantage compared with the control group ($\delta = 0.41$, $p = 0.04$). Two more interesting outcomes: (1) in the period soon after the workshop there was no significant effect either in intervention or control group, so no demonstrable effects of the workshop alone; (2) some areas of communication were clearly easier to learn (e.g. 'assessing patient's perspective') than others ('dealing with emotions').

McGonagle et al. (2020) randomly assigned 26 US primary-care physicians to 6 coaching sessions (one hour face-to-face and then 30-minute phone sessions over 3 months) with professional coaches, and 24 physicians to a waiting-list control group. They measured at baseline, completion and 3- and 6-month follow-up. They found significant results for the intervention group on self-rated psychological capital, burnout, work engagement, and job satisfaction (the strongest of these being psychological capital: $\delta = 0.93$; $p = 0.002$); and these all remained at increased levels at both follow-up measurements. There were just as many independent variables that were not found to significantly increase in the intervention group: job stress, turnover intentions, compassion, and self-efficacy.

Dyrbye et al. (2019) undertook an RCT involving physicians in the Mayo Clinic's departments of medicine, family medicine, and paediatrics. A group of 41 physicians received an initial 1-hour and five 30-minute follow-up phone coaching sessions every 2 or 3 weeks, by experienced, external executive coaches; whilst 41 others were on a waiting-list control group. Five months after baseline, coachees were doing significantly better than controls on (self-rated) emotional exhaustion ($\delta = 2.0$; $p < 0.001$) and other burnout indicators, and also on resilience ($\delta = 0.9$; $p < 0.05$); however, there was no difference in work engagement and job satisfaction between the two groups.

De Haan et al. (2019) was the largest RCT undertaken to date in coaching, in a realistic environment for executive coaching: a global healthcare company, comprising approximately 100,000 employees based in over 120 countries (see section B of this chapter for a longer description). It involved two consecutive groups on a leadership-development programme which was exclusively based on coaching and designed to increase the ratio of female leaders at all leadership levels. The two starting points of April and September provided ideal conditions for a 'waiting list control group' design. The study examines the relative impact of various 'common factors,' involving 180 coachees, 66 coaches, and 140 line managers of the coachees to rate outcomes on three independent measures of coaching outcomes. This RCT found strong indications that executive coaching can be an effective intervention; not only in the eyes of the coachees but also in the eyes of their line managers, with effect sizes δ larger than 1. Although the study was undertaken within the healthcare industry (just like Grant et al., 2009), it seems likely that these findings are globally generalisable over many industries, because the coachees were globally mobile senior and mostly general managers, not technical healthcare experts. This study also found a first indication that that executive coaching can have an effect on the leader's personality ($\delta = 0.58$; $p < 0.05$), particularly since the effect was not observed in the control group.

A further RCT study reported on by De Haan et al. (2020) had an even larger group of 105 business-school students at a London university who were coached by an equal number of qualified coaches, whilst another 105 students formed the control group. Data was collected over eight data points for all participants, enabling the researchers to model the dose-effect curve type change expected over the course of, and following the coaching sessions (see Figure 3.4 in Chapter 3). Responses were collected from both students and coaches, in order to again overcome issues of purely self-reported measures. Again, effect sizes δ over the 6-month journey were between 0.9 and 1, indicating similarly large effects. Furthermore, in this study significant change was established on a range of parameters: coaching effectiveness, resilience, stress reduction, and goal attainment scores.

Fontes and Dello Russo (2020) organised a waiting-list RCT within a marketing company with 32 marketing professionals in the intervention and 24 in the control group. The intervention consisted of 4 one-hour GROW coaching sessions in 4 months. They measured self-scored 'psychological capital' (a combined measure of hope, optimism, self-efficacy, and resilience), self-scored job satisfaction and organisational commitment, and multi-source performance ratings from peers and line managers. They found strong effects on psychological capital ($\delta = 1.1$; $p < 0.01$), job satisfaction and organisational commitment, and no effect on three of the performance criteria; however they do find a significant effect on the fourth, Collaboration ($\delta = 0.67$; $p < 0.05$). This particular dimension, Collaboration, comprised only one item in 19 on the 360-degree instrument, so it is wise to exert some caution as to their non-self-scored findings.

It is reassuring to see how the last five RCTs mentioned earlier in workplace coaching find very similar effect sizes of around 0.9–1.1 in very different contexts (senior manager coachees vs. professional coachees vs. student coachees; global business setting vs. medical practice vs. marketing professionals vs. local business-school setting; leadership development programme vs. stand-alone coaching vs. paid subjects in student context; three very different groups of qualified coaches with a different 'technique' base, etcetera). The five RCTs find effectiveness both on 'coaching effectiveness,' and on other variables such as goal achievement, resilience and well-being improvement, and burnout and stress reduction, as well as psychological capital and multi-source ratings. We will come back to this rich variety of effects later in the book.

There are two more near-randomised controlled trials worth mentioning. In each case the experiment was set up in a realistic setting with proper randomisation, but organisational pressures and attrition meant that intervention and control groups were no longer fully randomised. One of these studies found significant effects and the other had to confirm the null hypothesis. Egan & Song (2005) found that 54 new managers in a multinational retail organisation that were coached by external executive coaches received higher line-manager ratings than 49 managers in the control group ($\delta = 0.6$; $p < 0.05$) and differences on self-scored performance goal orientation, job satisfaction and organisational commitment were also significant. Ungerer et al. (2019) found that 36 new German entrepreneurs in innovative technology-based firms who had received state-sponsored external coaching did not acquire significantly more survival capability than the 57-strong control group, as no significant results were found on any of the indicators of survival capability.

3 Limitations of past research

Most of the current research base in coaching, including these randomised controlled trials which are the best standard of overall effectiveness in the coaching field, does show major weaknesses including:

1 the use of nonrandomised samples (e.g. most of the studies summarised in Chapter 2);
2 the scarcity of reliable data because of small sample sizes (e.g. Grant et al., 2002–2010; Losch et al., 2016; Tee et al., 2017);
3 the predominance of self-score measures, inviting the possibility of same-source bias (e.g. whilst the Duijts et al., 2008; Grant et al., 2010; Fontes & Dello Russo, 2020; De Haan et al., 2020 studies used randomised allocation, we have noted that only the self-reported improvements were statistically significant, the results on more objective measures being largely nonsignificant). De Haan et al. (2019) use self-scores and scores by other interested parties (coaches, coachees, line managers); however the fact that all three parties themselves contributed to the coaching may still have led to an over-estimation of the coaching outcome;
4 Only 7 of the 35 randomised controlled trials in coaching were undertaken with an *executive*-coaching sample, i.e. with organisational line managers as clients of coaching, in other words, as part of leadership development proper.

We clearly still need further large-scale studies where membership of target and control groups are randomly assigned, and which make use of a variety of outcome measures and not just self-scoring. Nevertheless, the combined evidence from these 35 articles does help to convince most commissioners and coaches that coaching is usually an effective intervention. Moreover, in the next chapter we will find many different studies concluding the same thing, including some of the most rigorous and well-designed experiments, which even if they did not work with a no-intervention control group are nevertheless very worth taking into account.

Part D: what it means for coaching practice

On the basis of the 35 RCT studies in Part C of this chapter which are probably the most rigorous RCTs in executive coaching to date, we can now be relatively sure that coaching is indeed an effective intervention. Nearly, all of these 35 studies show a convincing, significant advantage of the 'coached' (experimental) groups over the control groups (except for Deviney, 1994; Passmore & Velez, 2012; Tee *et al.*, 2017, where there are no differences between control and intervention groups). The studies that do show significant results use a wide range of outcome indicators ('dependent variables'), which again is hopeful. However, they also show a huge range in effect sizes, although studies that have a similar design do seem to yield similar effect sizes.

I believe these results that have been created over the years through the hard work of many researchers should help us feel confident that professional helping conversations work, and not only in mentoring or therapy but also in workplace coaching. Clearly, the research has been done with a variety of coaches in a variety of countries, which should also give us confidence. There is no evidence yet that different coaches – e.g. coaches with different approaches or backgrounds – have distinct results, i.e. no evidence that certain coaches are more effective than others. See also the coming chapters which look more into the ingredients of effectiveness in coaching.

Effect sizes vary wildly between the studies, from small effects to very large effects, $0.2 < \delta < 1.5$. In order to determine overall effect sizes, we need an agreed definition of the effect we are measuring, e.g. on which ratings, by whom, after how many sessions of coaching. Generally, it is to be expected that self-scores produce much higher effect sizes, as well as small-scale studies. It is encouraging though to see substantial effect sizes on manager scores (e.g. in De Haan *et al.*, 2019). Where personality changes were measured, e.g. in Allan *et al.* (2018), De Haan *et al.* (2019) and Zanchetta *et al.* (2020), the effect sizes were considerable ($\delta = 0.5$ to 0.9 with $p < 0.05$), especially when considering that it has to be much more work to change your personality than to achieve your goals.

Our own meta-analysis[11] shows that the pooled effect size is somewhere in the middle, slightly lower than the impact of 6 sessions of psychotherapy, namely around $\delta = 0.6$. One of the most rigorous studies, Niglio de Figueiredo *et al.* (2018), shows a relatively low effect size of 0.41 but that is on an objective outcome criterion and can be attributed to just 3 additional coaching sessions (which was the only difference between intervention and control group in their case), so may compare well with the higher effect sizes after 6 sessions in the more rigorous studies.

We need to remember that effect size δ in clinical research is normally a function of the clinical 'dose,' in this case the number of sessions – although there is some interesting evidence that in the grand scheme of things this is perhaps not the case (see Stiles *et al.*, 2015) and we have indications that clients and coaches may somehow negotiate the 'right' amount of coaching. In other words, effect size – at least on self-scores – has been found to be constant over a large range of total sessions in psychotherapy (Stiles *et al.*, 2015). This may mean that on average patients and therapists have a powerful mutual understanding to determine the dose that they require or ensure that the required change happens within the agreed 'dose' by e.g. adapting their focus or takeaways per session.

Summary of Chapter 1: 'Does executive coaching work?'

If we look at the only research that can possibly establish the effectiveness of coaching beyond any doubt, **large-scale randomised controlled trials**, then we do not have many, in fact less than a handful, but they all agree that coaching works and they give a broad **effect size estimate** of $\delta \approx 0.6$. This would mean that those that are being coached are better off than 72% of those that are not receiving coaching.

In this chapter we reviewed a total of 35 large and small randomised controlled trials in workplace coaching and they are probably the best we have in response to the general question, 'Does executive coaching work or not?'

Other than showing a good **effect size** these research articles show effectiveness in different countries; in workplace, health, and executive coaching; and on a variety of **outcome variables**:

- (objectively scored) On-the-job behaviour, such as better patient treatment for GPs and improved skills of pupils of driving instructors;
- (peer-scored) Improvement of 360-degree ratings and coach- and manager-rated effectiveness;
- (self-scored) Job-related skills, confidence and knowledge;
- (self-scored) Improved self-efficacy beliefs, goal-attainment, satisfaction, and outcome expectancies;
- (self-scored) Improved resilience, workplace well-being, and career satisfaction;
- (self-scored) Improved health and life satisfaction, less depression, stress, burnout, and need for recovery.

Nevertheless, our quantitative research literature into coaching effectiveness still suffers from some major weaknesses:

- the exclusive reliance on *self-score measures* in more than half of the studies;
- the scarcity of reliable data because of *small sample sizes* well under $N = 100$ in four out of five studies;
- the focus on *executive* coaching in only a fifth of the studies in this chapter.
- the use of *randomised* controlled trials: RCTs were at the core of all 35 of the studies selected to be in this chapter; however, RCTs constitute only about one out of five of the outcome studies in this book.

The remainder of this book discusses well over 125 further studies that shed more light on coaching effectiveness, and still other studies in adjacent fields like mentoring. These studies do not work with a randomised, no-treatment control group, so they have to 'assume' general coaching effectiveness. Nevertheless, many of the studies are able to demonstrate much more detail about which aspects of coaching make coaching more effective (the so-called active ingredients; see Chapter 2) and which outcomes can be expected from coaching (the so-called dependent outcomes; see Chapter 4).

Notes

1 In physics however the five sigma threshold is generally agreed upon as the hallmark of a 'scientific discovery,' because it has only a one-in-3.5 million chance of a false positive; e.g. when the Higgs boson was confirmed to be first detected in 2012. Within the same year the particle was confirmed even with seven sigma accuracy, which seems important enough given that it was an entirely new and highly foundational building block of matter.
2 See Myers *et al.* (1998) for background on the Myers-Briggs Type Indicator MBTI.
3 See Hogan and Hogan (1997) for background on the Hogan suite of personality instruments.
4 See Smith *et al.* (2008) for background on the Brief Resilience Scale.
5 Self-efficacy measures were introduced by Bandura (1997).
6 See Tennant *et al.* (2007) for the Warwick-Edinburgh mental well-being scale WEMWBS.
7 For Zimet's multidimensional scale of Perceived Social Support see Zimet *et al.*, 1988.
8 For Ashridge's Coaching Behaviours Questionnaire see De Haan and Nilsson (2017) and Chapter 5 of this book.
9 Working alliance, as originally defined by Greenson (1965), is a measure for the strength of the coaching relationship. Bordin (1979) suggested that the working alliance can be thought of as a combination of agreement on tasks, agreement on goals and strength of bonds. Based on Bordin's (1979) model, Horvath and Greenberg (1986) designed the Working Alliance Inventory with three sub-variables: tasks, goals, and bonds. This is now the most widely used of many well-validated tools to measure working alliance
10 In the earlier Vale *et al.* (2002) randomised controlled trial with 245 coronary heart disease patients, the effect size had been very similar ($\delta = 6.0$; $p < 0.0001$), and an equivalence was found between the four phone coaching sessions in the trial and lipid-lowering pharmacotherapy. Just as in psychiatry we find here that helping conversations and drugs are about equally effective (compare Wampold, 2001).
11 Viktor Nilsson and I will publish our meta-analysis of those 34 coaching randomised controlled trials where we could retrieve all relevant data, in 2021.

An interlude before Chapter 2

This chapter is about what it is in coaching that works. Which styles and techniques, which coaches and clients achieve the most or the ambitious objectives? A part of this question is, which coaching interventions yield the best results? Often research distinguishes between optimistic and future-focused techniques versus nondirective and insight-focused techniques. Another part of the question is, which clients will benefit the most from coaching? Research has suggested that clients who are already resilient and good self-motivators might benefit the most; but perhaps it is those who are more open, vulnerable, and willing to doubt? These are subtle issues that every coach will recognize. Here is a recent example of how these general research questions look in practice, at least for me.

Alexandra is a senior banker with a successful career in general management spanning various decades and continents. She was increasingly experiencing the bank for which she worked as a 'golden cage' and contemplated a progression of her career in a different industry. Her coaching contract therefore focused on the need to gain clarity regarding developing her career longer term. Alexandra mused that every time she started looking around for a job outside her organisation, she tended to get promoted. Through coaching she wanted to regain the initiative when it came to her career.

I collected some views from her colleagues who were generally quite impressed with her, but they added that she spread herself quite thinly at times, and that she was known to become extremely passionate and almost 'manic' at senior meetings where she tended to ask most questions of senior management, but then also answered half of those questions on behalf of the same senior management group that she was part of. When taking up multiple roles at management conferences did not work out so well, she was known to sulk or leave early.

Alexandra told me how when she was very young, she suffered a major loss, the loss of her first caregiver. To add insult to injury, in her early years she also experienced a detached style from her other parent who preferred to focus more on work than on raising her, so she spent many hours alone and became precocious and responsible at a very early age. Through reflection she had done earlier with a therapist, she could relate this to some of her patterns now, such as her regular bursts of manic activity or her stretching of her own responsibilities. I was moved and listened deeply and attentively when she spoke about these things, and I thought I heard something else underneath the panic, a certain sadness, a loneliness which was not so apparent but that I felt – or imagined – was nevertheless there. When I first mentioned this, in our second session, she did not recognize it very much. I thought to myself, was I projecting it?

Was I projecting these consequences of a huge loss onto her story of her childhood, or was there something there, something the panic – from which she could bounce back amazingly quickly – did not allow much sight of?

Many of our sessions started with an intense and upbeat download, a kind of a mini version of panicking. All the terrible things that had happened in the past few weeks, all the great successes of the last weeks, they were all presented in rapid succession and seemingly with a lot of confidence and fluidity. Normally this would fill almost half the session. And once it even filled the entire session which made me feel quite uncomfortable. It felt as if we had achieved 'nothing' and I had not been able to come into my role as a coach. Usually though, after listening the best I could, not being able to add very much and not hearing many questions or doubts in the material, I would in due course be rewarded or 'let in' as a coach in the second hour. Then, gradually, Alexandra made contact with how the negative experiences at work really made her feel, and how the manifold successes still left her with a rather empty feeling. At that point there was a change in facial expression and a kind of a grey hue over her face, a heavy brow, thoughtfulness, and silence. In those moments, not only could we do some productive coaching work, but we could also make contact with that sadness and loss that had permeated so much of her life from the beginning.

With this client I felt solution-focused techniques worked very well with the career orientation objectives. We talked through many scenarios and we imagined miracle futures. We worked step by step as opportunities presented themselves. I think we could have just used these directive techniques, and nothing else. Even though there was a longing underneath and the feeling of having to tread a solitary path across the slight but acute sadness underneath her passion and liveliness, we could also have left these alone. Maybe those deeper feelings did not really contribute to effectiveness or 'results,' and yet they did present themselves, so they were summarised by both of us in the sessions. I believe those moments contributed to her feeling of being understood at a deeper level. In any case we will never know because we had only one chance to have every conversation, and we could not have the alternative conversations that we might have had. Another occasion for a slight longing and sadness, which again, we shared and spoke about.

Alexandra was obviously a very resilient client. And in my view her resilience allowed her to be very vulnerable without feeling resentful, without any loss of face. It was as if she had both a high self-efficacy and resilience and a high vulnerability and distress – and I wondered how these opposing tendencies could ever be measured well on simple psychometric scales.

Chapter 2

What works in executive coaching? What makes coaching really worthwhile?

In this chapter we will look at active ingredients which have been proposed and verified by researchers. Active ingredients are aspects of coaching that demonstratively lead to better coaching results. As part of looking for active ingredients in coaching contracts I will introduce a larger literature with a variety of studies so that we have a fuller overview of what studies have been undertaken and what ingredients of coaching effectiveness have been proposed and quantitatively verified. Even though some of the studies added in this chapter are retrospective (non-experimental) or do not have a control group, they are sometimes very cleverly designed and statistically convincing. This means that even though they cannot comment on *general* effectiveness of coaching, they can still provide very strong clues as to the *aspects* of coaching that might work.

Part A: some controversies

This chapter looks at quantitative research that is going more deeply 'into' the coaching work, looking at general parameters or 'variables' that may be present inside that work and may make a difference when it comes to outcome, such as context and circumstance, style of working and structure of sessions, or background, role, and personality of coachees, or even background and personality of coaches.

Controversy 1: what to do with studies of a different standard than RCTs

Interestingly, in order to establish what works in coaching, we do *not* need to establish that coaching works. The latter issue, about general effectiveness of coaching, needs very elaborate testing: the kind of research we have seen in Chapter 1, to make sure that anything that works in coaching, any of the outcomes or changes through coaching, can be attributed to coaching and to coaching only. The general outcome issue needed the detail of the first chapter of this book to be somewhat convincingly dealt with. Now when it comes to the question about what it is in coaching that works, we can lower the standards of research and thereby widen our net.

To find significant patterns in terms of what works in the coaching intervention, we only need to make comparisons *within* a sufficiently representative sample. We can use the RCTs that have been summarised earlier to see whether coaching outcomes correlate with any of the differences within the sample, such as age, gender, personality, or other attributes of the group of coachees. But we can also use pure coachee samples, which may be a lot easier to come across, and still find meaningful outcomes as long as those samples are representative of all coachees. In other words, trials without control groups can be very informative, as long as they are not skewed towards only biased coachees, such as coachees who do not want to bring up anything negative about the coaching, which one would likely get if a coach surveys his or her own client base (as is the case in some of the weaker articles summarised in this chapter).

So, to sum up the argument here, we do not need rigorous studies with randomised control groups to understand what makes coaching conversations and coaching contracts work and for whom. However, it is important not to read any understanding about the effectiveness of coaching into such analyses without control groups, as some of the summarised articles in this chapter nevertheless have done. Many coaches have concluded that coaching is effective from clients ascertaining that it has been helpful to them, or they have even estimated the benefits of coaching from their clients' estimates about how much money they had made through decisions that could 'only' have come about through coaching ('only,' in their own minds). If one reads simple client reports as evidence for the effectiveness of coaching, one will get gross overestimates of the coach's impact, as we will see later.

Let us take an example from psychotherapy. In the United Kingdom the outcome review forms that therapists and patients use have been standardised for a long time and are now being used by many tens of thousands of therapist-patient partnerships every year, across primary, secondary, and tertiary care; university and voluntary care; and even large parts of the private sector. This standardised instrument was launched in 1998 and called CORE-OM (Clinical Outcomes in Routine Evaluation-Outcome Measure).

The wide use of this survey with 34 questions about a patient's current well-being, problems, functioning, and vulnerability to risks, taken at least at the beginning and end of treatment, led to studies with many tens of thousands of patients, i.e very high levels of statistical power (see, e.g., Stiles et al., 2015, 2008). In Stiles et al. (2015) the experience of over 26,000 patients is studied with a dataset that included start and end CORE-OM measures from both patient and therapist.

It is clear from the effect sizes reported, which tend to be δ between 1.4 and 2.1, i.e. much higher than we see in randomised controlled studies, that outcomes and effects are easily overestimated when only patient and therapist review forms are being used. In part this is because of post-hoc rationalisation: patient and therapist have invested time so they are bound to look back positively; and in part also due to the Hawthorne effect mentioned in the first chapter: the sheer discipline of reflection on mental health, and of answering CORE-OM and of being part of a study leads to improvement, quite apart from the sessions themselves.

Nevertheless, there are clear advantages of studying the self-reported outcomes in some detail, as Stiles et al. (2008, 2015) also argue. Effectiveness research which compares conditions within real-life assignments (as opposed to experimental studies) balances the risks of standard randomised controlled trials (such as university student populations or control-groups selection biases associated with lack of randomisation or the lack of assurance that coaching assignments were delivered in a standard way), by a greater realism and external validity of the research sample.

One of the things these and other studies were able to confirm was that there was no measurable difference between different therapy approaches across very large datasets: integrative (41.2%), person-centred (36.4%), psychodynamic (22.8%), cognitive-behavioral (14.9%), structured/brief (14.6%), and supportive (14.0%) therapy turned out to be all equally effective (Stiles et al., 2015). Even more surprisingly, they found that recovery and improvement rates are equal for widely diverging numbers of sessions (up to 40 sessions in total), which suggests amazing self-regulation and client agency.

Controversy 2: the technique versus common-factors debate

When looking at possible active ingredients, historically some important distinctions have been made, which can be briefly summarised as follows:

1 *Technique*: technique-related contributing factors are the nature and timing of specific interventions, overall technical approach and methodology, and underpinning philosophy of change and improvement. Underpinning philosophical or ideological differences are usually grouped around different conceptions of human change – and they inform different coaching methodologies, such as GROW, Solution-Focused, Systems Psychodynamic, Gestalt, Person-Centred, and others (see De Haan & Burger, 2005 for an overview).

2   *Common factors*: all contributing factors which are common to all techniques and approaches, such as structure and planning of sessions, the helping relationship, the strength of commitment to an ideology, coachee-related factors, coach-related factors, and client circumstances unrelated to coaching such as receiving a promotion or finding new important friendships, partnerships, or income.

There has been and still is quite a bit of controversy around which of these two sets of factors is more important for outcomes. In the more extensive research in the helping professions generally there is relatively scant evidence on 'technique'; i.e. all different, professional techniques and approaches lead to the same outcomes (see, e.g., De Haan, 2008). Within coaching there is still a lot more to do to measure the full range of techniques, and of all the possible 'common factors' mainly those related to the coachee's personality (and motivation) and the coach-coachee relationship have been researched thus far, and much less so the personal circumstances of the coachee nor the coach-related factors.

Active ingredients, and in particular the so-called common factors, seem a promising avenue to a better understanding of coaching, so that we know how to structure and design our coaching contracts for the best result. As we will see later there are some clear findings that indicate that common factors are important, but there are also some clear controversies to be resolved (e.g. in some studies the coach technique does not matter at all whereas in other studies it does clearly; in some studies the client's core self-evaluations such as self-efficacy, self-esteem, and emotional stability are clearly related to objective outcomes, in others they are not), and there are clear indications of mediation by the strongest common factors, i.e. by certain factors such as resilience having the most direct influence on results.

Controversy 3: difficult to compare different studies when they use different constructs

When reading about the research into active ingredients, it is important to note that there are often different constructs (surveys) to measure the same properties, e.g. for resilience, optimism, and the working alliance each, there are many different validated questionnaires. In this book I will assume that the constructs are essentially picking up the same underlying variable, so occasionally I will compare different measures of, say, resilience or the coaching relationship, without drawing attention to that difference between the measures. It is not necessarily a bad thing for outcome research if different validated instruments are being used, particularly if the same significant relationships can be demonstrated with different instruments. Such corroboration would give us as readers more confidence that there is a significant underlying psychological or conversational mechanism that we are beginning to uncover.

Sample size is not always defined in the same way either. For reasons of fair comparison, I have chosen throughout this book to give the sample size that enters the main analysis so the number of participants that has participated in the final data collection – unless otherwise stated.

As to self-scores and ratings by others, we also have to assume sometimes in this chapter that the coachee's perceptions of outcome are indeed a meaningful measure of effectiveness, even though we know that they may be biased in favour of coaching.

One might argue that effectiveness only happens when the coachee takes action and does something with the coaching, or when colleagues and clients notice a positive difference in the client's work, or even when the performance of the wider organisation is positively affected by the coaching. In this chapter we will not have such high demands on what effectiveness might mean so that we can present a wider range of coaching research. That client effectiveness scores can be relevant as well as more rigorous outcome variables is also supported in psychotherapy research – see, for example, the aforementioned Stiles *et al.*, 2008, 2015.

If the articles in the first chapter were already quite diverse in their choices of sample, variables, and experimental design, in this chapter the sheer diversity of studies is mind-boggling. Many studies can be criticised for not defining variables well enough, for having subjective outcome variables (or, when performance outcomes were objectively rated by trained raters, it is not always clear if the raters were blind to whether the subjects had had coaching or not), and for having very small N, but I have decided to keep them in the selection, since they may still give us an idea for replication or an argument for some 'working' aspect of coaching conversations. As will be shown in Part D of this chapter, if all the articles are taken together, some clear and coherent patterns about active ingredients do emerge.

Controversy 4: where does 'technique' end and do 'common factors' begin?

In this chapter I will not only review the studies into common factors in coaching but I will also present the research base regarding coaching technique, and show that it is indeed possible to demonstrate that certain techniques make a difference or that certain forms of coaching are more suited to certain forms of challenges than others. After surveying all the articles that I could find, I am convinced that there is a research base in coaching studies which shows that technique is non-trivial and that we cannot assume that 'all techniques and approaches are the same when it comes to effectiveness,' as is often concluded in psychotherapy. There will always be a controversy even within the study of technique: some will argue that what the studies measuring specific techniques are picking up are general features of *any* technique; i.e. much more holistic 'common factors' in coaching, the overall 'halo' of the coach, the general sense of welcoming and well-being experienced by the client. This debate will probably rage on for some time to come because it is not always possible to say if a technique, say a single intervention, is just that, a technique; or if it is instead predominantly an expression of the whole personality of the coach, or perhaps even a confirmation of the whole picture of coaching that the client already has. In some sense techniques are *also* common factors: every approach has some form of technique, some preferred interventions or phasing of interventions. Therefore, all approaches have many 'techniques' in common even if they sound very different. Techniques pertaining to all approaches are by definition a 'common factor.'

To complicate matters further, in the study of 'techniques' coaches are often asked to display different techniques with different clients. However, in that experimental design the coaches always know which 'technique' they are adopting in a session, which may influence them in other ways. If the condition is such that they have to use techniques that they are less fond of, they may become poorer coaches overall, irrespective of their faithful rendition of the 'technique' or not. So coaches can be expected to feel different in the various conditions being tested, not just in terms of their 'technique' but also more generally in their motivation to coach in that way. Every coach's overarching philosophy or ideology will prefer one condition over the other. That deeper preference might make them different coaches in the two (or more) conditions of the experiment – quite apart from different techniques that they are supposed to display in either.

It looks as though this debate between 'technique' and 'common factors' can survive any evidence and can never be decided on the basis of empirical evidence alone. As soon as a 'common factor' such as the working alliance is found to be an effective ingredient in coaching (in other words, as soon as a significant relationship can be demonstrated between higher working alliances and higher performance or effectiveness as a result of coaching contracts), a 'person-centred' coach will claim the finding as evidence for the value of unconditional positive regard, whilst a 'cognitive-behavioural' coach will say that it is evidence for the agreement on goals, which is another aspect of the working alliance.

Conversely, when a technical approach, such as future- and vision-oriented coaching is shown to be superior to other coaching techniques, a solution-focused coach will claim the finding as evidence for a positive psychology orientation, whilst a person-centred coach will still argue that it is evidence for warmth and a positive orientation towards the client. These debates between schools will never stop even when research can answer all questions that we might bring, simply because they are driven by other factors such as the importance of aligning oneself with a brand in the marketplace, or the deep attachment to one's *alma mater*, the original school where we trained as coaches, or even the personality differences that attract us all to different explanations and psychological schools.

Part B: how to establish the 'active ingredients'

As noted, in some ways the standard of statistical significance for establishing 'active ingredients' of coaching is lower, because we do not need to also demonstrate effectiveness. When we measure active ingredients, we can just assume that coaching is effective and then look at conditions which significantly make it more or less so. We do not even need a control group for finding active ingredients because we can make simple, within-sample comparisons. On the other hand, within-sample comparisons are themselves weaker instruments and they may pick up an effect when it was not there in the general population.

Let us look at De Haan et al. (2016) as an example of a large-scale study without control groups, i.e. a study containing only within-sample comparisons.

In that study, the participating coach-coachee pairs were selected through our own networks of experienced and qualified executive coaches. We made clear that we were primarily interested in executive coaches but we did not exclude other coaches from our sample. The coaches were employed by or associated with different institutions, such as Ashridge Business School, the Society for Coaching Psychology in Italy, the Dutch Association for Coaching and Supervision, Intercoach, and the Oxford School for Coaching and Mentoring, among others. A snowball sampling technique was used, as follows. Each coach completed an online 'coach survey' and then invited clients to complete an online 'client survey.' Clients nominated an organisational sponsor, who was invited by us to complete the equivalent 'sponsor survey' where possible and appropriate.

From an initial dataset of 4,070 coach and coachee questionnaires, 3,790 matching coach and coachee questionnaires could be identified, so it was possible to study a total of 1,895 coaching relationships (366 different coaches from 34 countries, augmented by 92 matching sponsors questionnaires). The exact number of coaching relationships included in each analysis varied according to coach and coachee completion rates. It was not possible to ensure the full completion of all scales or prevent the possibility of errors and missing data and thus the sample size reported differs slightly according to the scale being analysed. Data collection took place over an 18-month period from November 2011 to May 2013.

All coach and coachee surveys could be completed in ten minutes. The coach surveys collected relevant background information on gender, MBTI type, coaching credentials, and self-efficacy. For every assignment, the coaches answered questions about the type of coaching and the context of coaching (e.g. stand-alone or part of leadership development). The coachee survey asked for name, gender, MBTI type, nationality, professional role, and for permission to contact a 'manager,' 'HR director,' or 'business partner' who had sponsored the coaching work. For the remainder of the questionnaires, the coach and coachee questionnaires were identical and included the number of sessions to date, months of coaching to date, own initial expectations, and the coach/coachee's initial expectations of outcomes.

Coaching Effectiveness (CE) was assessed using 4 items on a 7-point response scale: (a) 'successful in creating reflective space'; (b) 'successful in creating new insights'; (c) 'successfully engaged in new action or behaviour'; and (d) 'overall coaching outcome.' Responses were calculated as the averaged score across these four items.

The *Working Alliance Inventory* (WAI) was used as a measure of the strength of the coach-coachee relationship (Horvath & Greenberg, 1986). Prior permission was obtained to adapt this 36-item instrument, which is used widely in therapy for measuring the strength and quality of the relationship between therapist and client, in order to measure the coach-coachee relationship. The WAI consists of three subscales: Task, Goal, and Bond. The term Task refers to what coach and coachee agree need to be done in order for the coachee to reach his or her goals for coaching. A typical item is, 'I am clear as to what my coach wants me to do in these sessions.' The term Goal refers to the outcomes that the coach/coachee hopes to gain from coaching. A typical item is, 'The goals of these sessions are important to me.' The term Bond refers to what extent the coach/coachee trusts, respects, and feels confidence in the other person. A typical item is, 'I believe my coach is genuinely concerned for my welfare.'

The General Self-Efficacy scale was used to assess the coach/coachee self-efficacy (Schwarzer & Jerusalem, 1995). This scale consists of 10 items on a 4-point Likert scale. Sample items include: 'I can always manage to solve difficult problems if I try hard enough,' 'If someone opposes me, I can find the means and ways to get what I want,' and 'It is easy for me to stick to my aims and accomplish my goals.'

Sponsor questionnaire. The sponsor questionnaire contained only the questions about initial expectations (for themselves and their colleagues) and the questions about effectiveness. Reliability estimates were calculated for all of the scales and ranged from adequate to (mostly) high.

48   Chapter 2: What makes coaching really worthwhile?

The main dependent variable was 'coaching effectiveness' (CE), and the independent variables were the working alliance (as assessed by coach and coachee independently), the 16 different Myers-Briggs 'types' of coach and coachee, and the self-efficacy of the coachee.

Results of the study will be summarised in Part C of this chapter. Overall, this study contributed to the existing coaching outcome literature in three important ways: firstly, it provided the largest-scale international coaching research study to date involving a total of 3,882 completed questionnaires; secondly, it studied the contribution of common factors such as the roles of the coach-coachee working alliance, personality, and self-efficacy in relation to coaching effectiveness in some detail; and thirdly, is our strongest evidence for the working alliance being an active ingredient, as seen from both the coachee's and the coach's perspective – with some indications that the contribution of tasks and goals within the working alliance is more important than that of bonds.

In line with the model specified in Figure 2.1, we checked and found that the strength of the coaching relationship mediates significant influences of (a) coach personality,

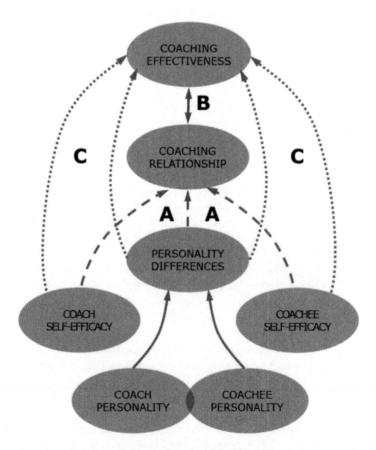

Figure 2.1 Graphical depiction of the various common factors studied as independent variables. The research investigates both direct influences of the independent variables on CE (dependencies B and C) and the probability of mediation of this influence through the strongest dependency, the coaching relationship (dependency A plus B as compared to C).

(b) coachee personality, (c) coachee self-efficacy, and (d) coach self-efficacy on CE as reported by coach and coachee. As coach-coachee personality differences did not predict CE, and separately coach and coachee personality scores were weak predictors of CE with only small effects, and because there was no clear pattern of effect of coach-coachee personality match/mismatch on CE, we reduced the model and used mediation analysis (Baron & Kenny, 1986) to regress self-efficacy and aspects of the working alliance (Task, Bond, Goal) on CE separately for coachee and coach within the sample (De Haan et al., 2016).

Part C: overview of more evidence with an eye for possible active ingredients of coaching

There is a growing quantitative research literature into the active ingredients of coaching. In this section, I have grouped many of the existing, original research studies in coaching together, in seven separate blocks of studies: evaluation or field studies, studies with more objective outcome variables, manager-as-coach research, studies with objective outcome variables and a control group, studies that are designed to compare conditions, studies that are designed to compare coach techniques, and studies that compare face-to-face with virtual coaching.

In the fourth category: studies with objective outcome variables and a control group, we have already seen 35 of the RCT-studies in Chapter 1. In this chapter, we now also allow nonrandomised control groups. Moreover, there are a great many studies with control groups to report on, certainly if we widen the net a little to 'mentoring outcome studies,' 'managerial coaching' (coaching by managers after a short coaching course, or not), and 'health coaching' (essentially to support clients of care or employees close to burnout, with supportive coaching), and to retrospective studies. This section will show that amongst these there are certainly many that are very rigorous, on a par with many of the randomised controlled studies in Chapter 1.

Many of these studies are also trying to demonstrate the effectiveness of coaching, even though their experimental design may not be the best suited one to do that. What is striking is that the field studies which did not make use of a contemporary control group, e.g. Peterson, 1993; Olivero et al., 1997; Thach, 2002; Orenstein, 2006; Bowles et al., 2007; Perkins, 2009), found large effects ($\delta > 0.75$), generally larger than those found in psychotherapy. On the other hand, the more rigorous studies involving control groups (such as Nieminen et al., 2013; Dahling et al., 2016; Evers et al., 2006, and the work done in mentoring outcome studies – see Chapter 4) only found small effects, generally smaller than those found in psychotherapy ($\delta < 0.5$; compare with average $\delta \approx 0.8$ in psychotherapy – see Wampold, 2001). However, these are studies with internal coaches or mentors, whilst many of the studies without control groups involve more significant coaching programmes with qualified professional coaches, which may also be a factor in the higher effects.

The same is true generally for effect sizes rated by others compared with those rated by self (see, e.g., Ellinger et al., 2003) – the latter tend to be much larger than those more objectively obtained. So, it is important to remain somewhat sceptical and keep an open mind about the exact significance of results when appreciating this vast and impressive research output.

1 Overview of coaching outcome research I: evaluation or field studies

Most empirical research into executive coaching is concerned with the value of coaching from the perspective of the client, with the research taking the form of an extensive evaluation of 'customer satisfaction.' On some occasions, clients are asked to estimate how much their coaching has contributed financially to the bottom line of their organisation (e.g. McGovern *et al.*, 2001; Parker-Wilkins, 2006). As could have been guessed, clients are usually very positive about the coaching they have experienced, if only because they have invested in it as well, and in these studies clients give coaching a highly unrealistic return-on-investment of many hundreds of percentage points. Dello Russo *et al.* (2017) show that a large group of 576 employees find their organisation less political if they experience their manager as a better coach ($p < 0.01$). However, these and many other field studies consist essentially of satisfaction scores. They can easily spread to other values such as in this case money and ethics, but as argued in Chapter 1 they cannot be statistically converted into objective outcomes traceable to the coaching conversations per se.

Luthans and Peterson (2003) with 20 managers in a manufacturing organisation show that after 3 months others' ratings (and self-ratings) increased significantly when they had only one feedback cum coaching session plus a few informal follow-ups.

One field study describes a consulting intervention incorporating leadership coaching in 7 units of a large Danish hospital (containing $N = 128$ employees; compared with 7 nonrandomised control units, $N = 103$), where the consulting intervention went so badly that on most self-scored outcomes the intervention group fared worse than the control group (Aust *et al.*, 2010). From the descriptions one can see that most consulting interventions were thwarted or discontinued, and that the uptake of leadership coaching was also very mixed.

Smith and Brummel (2013) explored the relationship between executive involvement, perceptions of developability, and individual development plans with a specific measure of executive coaching success (change in the leadership competencies that were the focus of the coaching engagement), for 30 senior-management clients in different organisations, who said they had spent on average 82 hours being coached by external coaches or in doing their 'coaching homework.' The results indicated that the three self-scored ingredients were significantly related to self-experienced coaching success.

Grant (2014a) did a pre- and post-coaching measurement for 31 clients and showed how they reported increases in goal attainment, enhanced solution-focused thinking, a greater ability to deal with change, increased leadership self-efficacy and resilience, and decrease in depression.

Hui and Sue-Chan (2018) researched a group of 51 managers (Chinese MBA alumni) and their 373 direct reports (average age of all subjects below 30). The direct reports rated the coaching style of the managers in terms of 'guidance' and 'facilitation'; and the managers rated both the adaptive performance and the task performance of the direct reports. Direct reports also rated their own job-related feelings of anxiety. Guidance was negatively related to adaptive performance and positively related to task performance, whilst facilitation the reverse: negatively related to task performance and positively related to adaptive performance. Adaptive performance also partially mediated the relationships between the two styles of coaching and task performance. Guidance coaching was positively related to anxiety and facilitation coaching was negatively related to anxiety, whilst anxiety partially mediated the impact of the two styles of coaching on adaptive performance. So, in sum, guidance coaching helps with the task performance but makes employees more anxious or negative, whilst facilitation coaching helps with both anxiety and adaptive performance which then also helps with task performance (all findings $p < 0.01$).

Schermuly *et al.* (2020) studied the coaching experience (on average a little over 4 sessions and 120 days of coaching) of 19 owner-managers of on-average 14-year-old companies with on-average 10 employees, who had recently filed for bankruptcy. They measured well-being, coping resources, stress levels, exhaustion before and after the coaching, cognitive performance, and also objective stress hormones through hair samples. They found significant positive changes through coaching, on well-being (no less than $\delta = 0.88$; $p < 0.001$), exhaustion, and cognitive performance, but not on the most objective measure: stress hormones, nor on the only coach-rated measure, working alliance.

Wasylyshyn *et al.* (2006) and Kombarakaran *et al.* (2008) both show high outcome ratings for in-company coaching programmes. Wasylyshyn *et al.* (2006) provides ratings from $N = 28$ clients and $N = 17$ 'others' (direct colleagues of clients) in a pharmaceutical company. Kombarakaran *et al.* (2008) provides ratings from $N = 104$ clients and $N = 29$ coaches. In these studies the majority of those surveyed report high value or 'sustainability of learning' from coaching.

Schlosser *et al.* (2007) measured the outcome of executive coaching across a range of variables and industries and from the perspectives of manager/sponsor ($N = 14$), client ($N = 56$), and coach ($N = 70$). Whilst a significant positive outcome was reported for all subjects, a significantly lower rating for the managers, in terms of return on investment, was reported. Hooijberg and Lane (2009) show that 232 participants in one-off multi-source feedback coaching sessions wanted their coach to take an active role in interpreting their results and in making action recommendations.

Mukherjee (2012) looked particularly at the effect of coaching on the coaches rather than the coachees. He collected coachee responses to 19 recently qualified internal coaches in a large production company in India, looking at their 'transaction styles' using a transactional-analysis lens. He found a statistically significant ($p < 0.05$) increase in effective styles on 3 of 6 ego states, namely for Nurturing Parent, Adult, and Adaptive Child.

In another field study, Sonesh *et al.* (2015) compared student coaching (55 MBA-student-coaches and 44 student-coachees) with executive coaching (89 licensed coaches and their coachees in industry) and found out that many dependencies were different. Results showed that, only in the student sample but not in the industry sample, coachee motivation was significantly related to coachee goal attainment and coachee insight; so coachee motivation mattered more in the student sample. Moreover, working alliance and information sharing partially mediated the relationship between a coach's psychological mindedness and coachee goal attainment, also only in the student sample.

In a different approach, taken by Grant and Cavanagh (2007), the results of a self-report measure of coaching skill (scored by $N = 38$ coaches after a 45-minute coaching session was correlated with their 38 clients' assessment regarding the same skill.

This correlation was significantly positive ($\delta = 1.4$; $p < 0.001$) thus providing a good indication that coaching skill can be inter-subjectively established. The suggestion of this study is also that higher coaching skills lead to better outcome, so this would indicate that 'technique' of coaches does matter for outcome. However, it is a general 'skill' that they measured so the research can equally be seen as supportive of common factors.

Toegel and Nicholson (2005) measured changes in multi-source feedback for 89 investment bank managers over 10 months after a group feedback workshop and a single executive coaching session. There was a significant improvement in ratings for the coachees from their direct reports ($p < 0.001$). They also showed that improvement was significantly related to coaching effectiveness ratings from the coachees and to same-gender coaching dyads.

Burke and Linley (2007) measured aspects of a diverse group of 26 senior managers' goal-setting before and after a single GROW session of coaching. They found that self-reported 'self-concordance' of their goals, i.e. alignment with their personal values of their goals, and their commitment to their goals had significantly increased after the single session. Rank and Gray (2017) studied factors contributing to 59 coachees' self-reports of reflection or satisfaction with the coaching, finding that high 'self-presenters,' i.e. more charming coachees, give higher scores to coaching, whilst conversely coachees low in self-presentation ability may benefit more strongly from coaching. Gan and Chong (2015) organised a field study amongst 172 clients in Malaysia to find that rapport and commitment were significantly correlated with effectiveness, in the clients' minds.

O'Connor and Cavanagh (2013) describe an experiment in a university where 20 leaders received 8 coaching sessions whilst 102 colleagues in their 'network' also completed questionnaires, as a no-intervention control group. Individual self-report measures of well-being and goal attainment as well as 360-degree feedback on transformational leadership were assessed at baseline and then again in pre- and post-intervention periods. Well-being and goal attainment, and 360-degree leadership qualities were shown to increase in the coachees, with well-being slightly more than in the network control group. A social network analysis was done at all three time points, measuring frequency and quality of interaction with other individuals in the network. During the intervention period, only those that received coaching saw the quality of their communications with others as more positive. However, whilst the coaching intervention did appear to improve the quality of communication from the coachees' perspectives, it was perceived by those around the coachees to have become less positive. Maybe changes in communication can be initially confusing and anxiety provoking, accounting for the lower perceived positivity of the interaction – or there was a lag in competency after coaching. Those observed to have increased their psychological well-being the most over the intervention period tend to be most closely connected to those that received coaching, as measured through closeness and centrality in the coachee neighbourhood network.

2 Overview of coaching outcome research II: incorporating objective outcome variables

The following studies explore the effectiveness of coaching by looking at independent variables over and above client, coach, or manager satisfaction, but with no control group.

Hazucha et al. (1993) showed that for 48 managers in a utility company, various developmental activities including coaching could increase 360-degree feedback scores after 24 months. Interestingly, ratings by others went up to come in line with the higher self-ratings. Peterson (1993) studied $N = 72$ leaders from various organisations at three points in time (pre-coaching, post-coaching, and follow-up) with outcome defined by their own coaching objectives and five standard 'control' items, rated by at least themselves, their manager and their coach (multi-source ratings). The coaching programme was intensive and long-term, with typically 50+ hours of individual coaching with a professional coach over at least a year. Peterson found that clients, on average, achieved significant improvement on all measures of outcome related to coaching objectives (effect sizes $\delta > 1.5$). Olivero et al. (1997) studied managers who had taken part in a 3-day educational training course followed by 8 weeks of coaching. They found that both the training and the coaching increased productivity considerably, with most of the increase attributable to the coaching (increase of 22.4% with training alone and of 88.0% with training and coaching; i.e. almost fourfold; a difference which was significant at the $p < 0.05$ level). In another study by Thach (2002), $N = 281$ managers participated in 4 one-hour sessions of coaching over 5 months with a 360-degree (multi-source) feedback process before and after the coaching. They found an increase in 'leadership effectiveness' both as rated by the coaches and their co-workers (average increase 60% but no significance reported). Seifert et al. (2003) show that a feedback workshop can add significantly to the impact of a 360-degree instrument. Orenstein (2006) shows the same positive effect of coaching on 360-degree ratings with only a single client.

Carson et al. (2007) studied 59 teams of around 6 MBA students who were engaged in a consultancy project for a client organisation and received coaching from a faculty member. They found that this form of external team coaching was positively related to the level of shared leadership in the teams, and shared leadership in turn predicted externally measured team performance. Teams with an unsupportive internal team environment were still able to develop high levels of shared leadership, so long as they received a high level of coaching. Coaching was therefore mostly related to shared leadership when the internal team environment was unsupportive (this is similar to Buljac-Samardzic & Van Woerkom, 2015, which we look at in the next section). Shared leadership within the team predicted team performance.

Bowles et al. (2007) looked at effectiveness in terms of increased productivity in army recruitment managers ($N = 30$) and executives ($N = 29$) who received coaching as compared to productivity changes in a nonrandomised group of experienced recruitment managers over a similar, but not contemporaneous, time interval. The individuals who were coached showed greater productivity gains ($\delta = 0.43$ with $p < 0.05$ for the middle managers and $\delta = 0.75$ with $p < 0.01$ for the executives). An earlier pilot with the same population (Bowles & Picano, 2006) could not find significant effects of a 6-month coaching experience for 19 managers (first sergeants) on productivity. However, more involvement with coaching as rated by the coach, who was a senior leader in their organisation, was correlated with greater work satisfaction in the coachee ($p < 0.01$).

Perkins (2009) studied the effectiveness of executive coaching on improving leadership behaviours in meetings, as rated by the coach. Using quantitative and qualitative methods with a small sample ($N = 21$), pre- and post-coaching measurement of meeting behaviours were scored by the coach and author, with a clear improvement of behaviours reported (effect sizes δ > 0.95 for 9 out of 11 behaviours measured, and p < 0.01). There may of course have been researcher bias in these scores as the author – the coach who rates his own clients – might understandably want their clients to do well.

George *et al.* (2020) undertook a retrospective study to determine which external coaches of nurses for safe childbirths in India had been the most effective. Demographics were collected for 10 coaches and (observation-based) practice-adherence criteria for their coachees, by observing 1,052 child deliveries. A significant (p < 0.0001) inverse relationship was detected between the coach's age (or else years of experience) and the nurses' adherence to the practice checklist.

3 Manager-as-coach research with objective outcome variables

Wageman (2001) undertook a rigorous, large-scale study into the management of 34 self-managing teams in Rank Xerox, through both in-depth interviews with full teams and with the help of quantitative surveys. As outcome variable she used objective data averaged over a full year, to measure team performance. She found that coaching did not affect performance directly, but only leaders' design (structuring) activities affected team task performance. However, design and coaching interacted, so that well-designed teams are helped more by effective coaching and they are also undermined less by ineffective coaching than are poorly designed teams. Design features seem to be necessary conditions for good teamwork, but if they are in place coaching does make a significant difference. In short, the impact of leaders' coaching on their teams appears conditioned by the way in which they set the team up in the first place.

Ellinger *et al.* (2003) showed how in an industrial setting, on the shop floor of warehouses, 458 employees' perceptions of coaching skills of their 67 line managers were correlated with their performance, as rated independently by those same line managers (δ = 0.3; p < 0.05). Moreover, line-management coaching behaviour as perceived by employees was a highly significant predictor variable for employee job satisfaction (δ = 1.4; p < 0.01). Shanock and Eisenberger (2006) find the same relationships between perceived line manager's support and line-manager-rated in-role performance (δ = 0.26; p < 0.01) and beyond-role performance (δ = 0.7; p < 0.01) for 135 employees of a chain of discount electronics stores. Agarwal *et al.* (2009) confirms these results in a US sales force, over several managerial levels, but suffers from only reporting same-source effects. Similarly, Gregory and Levy (2011) looked into employee coaching of 1,290 employees by 221 line managers at front-line management level in a manufacturing organisation, and found that line managers' self-scored 'individual consideration for their employees' actually correlates strongly with employees' ratings of the coaching relationship (δ = 3; p < 0.001). Again, Huang and Hsieh (2015) and Hsu *et al.* (2019) show that for 324 and 689 Taiwanese employees, their perceptions of coaching skills of their 324 and 689 line managers were correlated with their line-manager-rated performance (δ = 0.35 and 0.56, respectively; p < 0.01) which again was predictive of employee empowerment, career proactiveness, and team commitment. Finally, Kim and Kuo (2015) have researched 280 manager-employee pairs in the Taiwanese insurance industry. Contrary to the other studies they did not find that employee-rated managerial coaching was related to manager-rated employee performance; however the coaching was significantly related to manager-rated organisational citizenship behaviour of the employee ($\delta = 0.3$, $p < 0.01$).

Heslin et al. (2006) have shown in two experiments that $N = 45$ ($\delta = 0.8$; $p < 0.05$) and $N = 92$ ($\delta = 1$; $p < 0.01$) managers are rated by their direct reports to be better coaches if their 'implicit person theories' are more towards thinking about people as changeable and malleable towards positive change (i.e. more 'incremental implicit person theories' as opposed to the more fixed 'entity implicit person theories'). They also showed, through a small-scale randomised controlled trial with 32 in the intervention group and 29 in the control group, that more 'incremental interpersonal theories' can be induced into managers with the help of a short training programme, after which these managers demonstrate a significantly higher willingness to coach, and they also demonstrate higher numbers of more quality suggestions for a 'poor performing employee' on a video recording.

Liu and Batt (2010) investigated a group of 2,327 telephone operators and their line managers during a 5-month longitudinal study and showed that the amount of 'coaching' (mostly individualized feedback and guidance based on monitoring of calls, behaviours, and keystrokes) received from direct line managers predicted objective performance improvements; i.e. a 0.09 second-per-call improvement of call-handling time ($p < 0.01$). Uniquely, both coaching time and call-handling time could be measured objectively because of the nature of the operators' work where every single one of the circa-1,000 calls a day was measured, but also the personal time with their line managers was measured. The performance effect of coaching was stronger when line managers made greater use of group rewards, when work automation was lower, and when process changes were less frequent.

Latham et al. (2012) looked into three restaurant managers' coaching of a group of around 90 restaurant servers in three restaurants whose performance was being monitored through mystery guests' feedback, based on around 1,200 mystery shopper visits in 17 months leading to 1,200 thirty-minute feedback/coaching conversations. The three restaurants obtained clearly higher server performance and a higher customer count in the period when specific coaching conversations based on mystery shopper feedback were provided daily ($p < 0.05$). Server performance and customer count were lower in pre- and post-coaching time periods when no feedback from a mystery shopper was made available to the servers ($p < 0.05$). There was some evidence for a long-term effect of the coaching as well, because post-coaching customer count remained higher for around 6 months, although that could have been the mystery guests returning on their own account. By the end of the experiment it was easy to calculate a substantial growth of revenue through the mystery shoppers and the resulting feedback and coaching sessions, over and above the payment for the agency and the mystery shoppers themselves.

Dahling et al. (2016) also investigated managerial coaching on the basis of objective measures, in a group of 1,246 pharmaceutical sales representatives and their 136 district managers: managers' accompaniment on field visits could be measured (in terms of number of field visit days per year, ranging between 1 and 20), and the coaching skills of the managers were rated by their own supervisors during a sales training programme for the representatives, but also by the average team role clarity that their direct reports experienced. Outcomes were measured as the percentage of goal attainment (which varied between 31% and 150% of the assigned sales goal). Ratings of managerial coaching skill had a significant effect on representatives' sales goal attainment ($\delta = 0.3$; $p < 0.01$) and team role clarity as well, to a lesser extent ($\delta = 0.1$; $p < 0.05$).

In another study of relatively hands-off managers, Buljac-Samardzic and Van Woerkom (2015) researched line managers' team coaching in the Dutch long-term care sector where teams are in different locations and highly autonomous with regard to their managers, who were line managing at least 2 teams on average. They measured 423 team members (rating managerial coaching and team reflection) of 122 teams which had 49 managers (rating team performance); 2 measurements with a year in between. Team coaching did not predict team reflection a year later but it did predict team effectiveness as rated by the managers ($p < 0.01$). However, there was a stronger relationship between team coaching and team effectiveness a year later, when team reflection had been low and only then ($p < 0.01$). There was even a detrimental effect on efficiency when team reflection was high ('excessive managerial coaching'; $p < 0.05$). This research shows that the success of managerial coaching depends on the match between the intensity of coaching interventions with the highly self-directed and autonomous teams' ability to organise their collective reflection process without interference.

Weer *et al*. (2016) looked at the contrasting effects of facilitative versus pressure-based coaching on changes in team effectiveness, on a sample of 714 managers in a technology multinational firm and their teams, over a 54-month period of time. Sample items for facilitative coaching: 'Coaches group members to help them improve performance on the job,' 'Is a helpful coach and trainer,' and 'Discusses how group members' work and goals relate to the organization's goals and projects.' Sample items for pressure-based coaching: 'Punishes or yells at people when they make mistakes,' 'Seems to feel it is necessary to apply pressure to get results,' and 'Complains vigorously if goals are not met.' With 'team effectiveness' rated only by the managers and the two forms of coaching and also 'team tension' and 'team commitment' only by the teams, the effects found on team effectiveness (namely a direct effect from pressure-based coaching on the slope of team effectiveness: $\delta = -0.47$; $p < 0.05$ and an indirect effect through both forms of coaching and then team commitment on the same slope: $\delta = 0.87$; $p < 0.001$) seem very robust.

Woo (2017) polled 275 employees from 17 different South Korean companies who were also mentored and showed that the coaching by their manager only became significantly related to their organisational commitment when they rated the mentoring highly – but only if they experience their manager and the mentor as similarly helpful ('homogeneous').

There are many smaller-scale studies that also seek to demonstrate the effectiveness of managerial coaching, e.g. Pousa and Mathieu (2014).

4 Overview of coaching outcome research III: employing control groups

Miller (1990) compared two groups of corporate employees attending a communication-skills development programme; one group of 17 received more formal coaching on the trained skills than the other group of 16. The line managers of those 17 in the intervention group received extra training in coaching skills. On returning to the workplace, the experimental subjects received coaching by their managers for a period of 4 weeks, whilst control subjects received no such formal interaction. Post-test comparisons of self-scored and observer-rated communication scores in control and experimental groups showed no significant differences between groups.

Smither et al. (2003) is still one of the most thorough studies on the impact of executive coaching. Their design involved a (nonrandomised) control group and conclusions were based on more objective criteria than evaluations by the coachees, namely evaluations by independent researchers together with coachees' superiors, colleagues, and staff (multi-source feedback). This research involved 1,202 senior managers in one multinational organisation who all received 2 consecutive years of 360-degree feedback. The researchers found that the 286 managers of this sample who worked with an executive coach were significantly more likely than other managers to (1) set specific goals ($\delta = 0.16$; $p < 0.01$); (2) solicit ideas for improvements from their superiors ($\delta = 0.36$; $p < 0.01$); and (3) obtain higher ratings from direct reports and superiors in the second year ($\delta = 0.17$; $p < 0.05$). This was a significant result particularly given there were no more than 'two or three' coaching sessions per coachee (Smither et al., 2003, p. 29).

In a nonrandomised sample with 76 German students, Willms[1] (2004) compared a self-coaching programme with three 90-minute sessions over a period of 16 days with a nonrandomised control group which had only one self-coaching session. After approximately 16 weeks the degree of goal attainment ($\delta = 0.51$; $p = 0.01$) and the positive affect ($\delta = 0.41$; $p < 05$) of the self-coaching group was significantly higher than that of the control group. The degree of goal attainment was significantly predicted by persistence measured at baseline ($p < 0.05$).

Gyllensten and Palmer (2005) looked into the effects of coaching on depression, anxiety, and stress with 16 coachees from a UK finance organisation and 15 similar managers in a control group. They collected a pre- and post-coaching questionnaire which included job satisfaction, stress indications through HIT, and strain through DASS-21. Although they found more lowering of stress and anxiety in the intervention group, these results were not significant.

Jones et al. (2006) offered 11 leaders 7 sessions of coaching following a 360-degree feedback workshop, after which the leader's flexibility (including resilience) was measured at three time points. At the same time there was a waiting-list nonrandomised control group of 12 taking the same measurements. They found some evidence for increasing flexibility (which included resilience) through coaching, although strictly speaking all their results are only near-significant.

Evers et al. (2006) measured self-efficacy beliefs and outcome expectancies, on each of three dimensions. Their study compared a pre-intervention and post-intervention measurement and also involved a (nonrandomised) control group. Although the sample was quite small (30 managers in both the experimental and the control group) they did find some empirical evidence for a positive outcome of the coaching intervention. There was a significant increment for the coached group over the control group for one of the three dimensions in both self-efficacy beliefs ('setting one's own goals') and outcome expectancies ('acting in a balanced way') ($\delta \approx 0.5$ with p

< 0.05). However, the intervention was short with an average of only 4 coaching sessions.

Moen and Skaalvik (2009) trained 11 senior leaders through a coaching programme – group coaching and external executive coaching – who then formed the intervention group, to coach their 52 middle managers, whilst in a nonrandomised control group 8 executives worked with 56 middle managers without further training. They show significant findings in terms of managers' self-efficacy, goal setting behaviours, (self) attributions of success, and need satisfaction.

Despite using a very small pre-post nonrandomised control group design, with only 8 secondary school principals coached (by the first author) for 10 weekly 1-hour highly structured coaching sessions, whilst 6 other principals were assigned to a control group, Cerni et al. (2010) were able to show that hundreds of staff rated the principals in the intervention group significantly higher on transformational leadership skills – just like Goff et al. (2014) who also looked at principals' coaching.

In a large public-sector organisation all 61 staff that had received coaching in the last two years formed the intervention group and the control group ($N = 57$) was a nonrandomised sample taken from the rest of the staff (Leonard-Cross, 2010). She found that self-efficacy was significantly higher ($\delta = 1.4$; $p < 0.001$) in the intervention group and satisfaction levels were higher too.

Kines et al. (2010) looked into the help that coaching can provide in the construction industry with biweekly feedback/coaching for 4 foremen by the researchers, whilst 3 other foremen and their workers served as controls. Workers were interviewed over the full 16-week intervention period (1,693 interviews also taking place in a 10-week pre-measurement and a 16-week post-measurement so 42 weeks in total) about the frequency of safety-related communication. Moreover, 22,077 safety-performance observations were done over the same period, which had been shown in other studies to relate with job-related safety. Feedback-based coaching to construction site foremen regarding the content of their daily verbal exchanges resulted in significant increases (in intervention sites only) in those verbal exchanges ($p < 0.001$), workers' safety performance and the physical safety level of the work site ($p < 0.001$) and the general safety climate ($p < 0.03$).

Bright and Crockett (2012) studied a combination of a 4-hour training with a single short telephone external coaching session 3 weeks later with help of a 73-person intervention group and 42-person nonrandomised control group. They found a number of self-scored improvements in performance and time management in the intervention group, with high significance ($p < 0.01$).

Vidal-Salazar et al. (2012) performed an experiment where 40 small businesses in a Spanish town received a diagnosis to help them through a crisis period and 20 of the business owners, nonrandomly selected, also received coaching by the business experts who made the diagnosis and who then visited them at their home or organisation once a week (3 sessions of 2 hours and 3 shorter catch-up telephone calls). The results showed that the coached group significantly ($p < 0.05$) increased their understanding and their application of the proposed management and HR measures and were also more satisfied.

Nieminen et al.'s (2013) quasi-experimental study followed 469 managers, 227 of whom received 4 or 5 sessions of executive coaching and a multi-source feedback

(MSF) session, whilst 242 received only the MSF. Results indicated that managers in both groups improved similarly as rated by direct reports, peers, and line managers, whilst only those managers who received the executive coaching intervention improved according to self-ratings ($\delta = 0.21$; $p < 0.01$), i.e. clear evidence for MSF feedback instruments yet no objective evidence that coaching contributes to enhanced performance. However, managers had been allocated to the two groups based on non-random selection methods, the coached group comprising managers who had recently been promoted and had fewer years of leadership than the non-coached group.

Bozer *et al.* (2013, 2014, 2015) studied coachee characteristics in a quasi-experimental field study with 12 coaching sessions for 72 coachees and 29 of their peers in a nonrandomised control group, with data from their 28 direct managers. They found clear effectiveness in terms of career satisfaction ($\delta = 0.87$; $p < 0.001$) but surprisingly the control group performed better in terms of line-manager-rated task performance (although the peers really only 'caught up' with the intervention group's before-coaching scores; $\delta = 0.54$; $p < 0.05$). Bozer *et al.* (2013) also found a positive relationship of learning goal orientation, self-efficacy, and pre-coaching motivation to career satisfaction.

Ladegard and Gjerde (2014) studied leaders who had received coaching for 8 sessions by experienced external coaches, although the numbers were limited with only 18 coachees and 6 nonrandomised controls (80 of their direct reports were studied for subordinate feedback). There was a statistically significant relationship between managers' trust in subordinates and reduced turnover intentions of the subordinates. Ladegard and Gjerde (2014) showed that coachee-scored 'facilitative behaviour' of the coaches correlated to higher outcomes in terms of self-scored leadership efficacy and trust.

Gardiner *et al.* (2013) describe an experiment where 69 Australian rural general practitioners volunteered for a 9-hour cognitive-behavioral coaching retreat with pre- and post- self-coaching homework. On their before-and-after ratings the GPs were found to be significantly less stressed and more inclined to stay in their job than the nonrandomised control group of 205. Moreover, three years later, and in comparison with the whole remaining population of 312 GPs in South Australia, their retention rates were 94% compared with 80 % in the others ($p < 0.03$).

The next three are retrospective studies so for that reason no randomisation:

- Hoven *et al.* (2014) analysed the short- and long-term employment outcomes of 2,480 homeless clients participating over 4 years in a labour market programme which includes elective coaching (638 of the clients chose to take the full 16 sessions over 6 months). Clients being supported by a job coach have significantly higher (more than three times higher) chances of gaining employment than those not being supported. This holds particularly true for the youngest age group, who tend to perform worst on the programme. Furthermore, results also indicate that job coaching improves clients' chances of successfully sustaining employment. These results are impressive but probably overestimates, because the more

motivated and higher-education-background clients chose the coaching more often (non-random and retrospective design).
- Poluka and Kaifi (2015) compared two groups of 77 each from a database within the telecoms industry which had taken a training programme – with the non-randomised intervention group also taking five days of 'ride-along' coaching by experts, straight after their training. It was shown that the coached telecoms engineers had a consistently higher performance after 30, 60, and 90 days ($p < 0.001$). Their increase in productivity was 61.8%: a figure comparable with what Olivero *et al.* (1997) found earlier. The results may have been affected by the retrospective design since the average educational level of the intervention group was also higher than that of the control group.
- Oberschachtsiek and Scioch (2015), in a very large-scale ($N > 418.000$) investigation of German support structures for new business owners, show that coaching and training did not make a meaningfully significant difference in the viability of their businesses.

In a small-scale quasi-experimental study, MacKie (2014, 2015) assigned executives and senior managers in a not-for-profit organisation non-randomly to a coaching and a waiting-list cohort, with cohort sizes of 14 and 17, respectively. Both groups received 6 sessions of strengths-based coaching with experienced external coaches, at different times. The results revealed that participants displayed strong and statistically significant increases in their transformational leadership behaviour after coaching ($\delta = 0.9$; $p < 0.01$), and this difference was reported by peers, direct reports, and superiors within the organisation but not by the participants themselves.

In another small-scale study (Teemant, 2014), 16 urban elementary school teachers received an instruction workshop to enhance their proficiency and 7 coaching sessions by an external 'instructional' coach, with 5 teachers in a nonrandomised control group. The coached teachers did much better on a classroom observer-rated instrument which was related to their earlier workshop, and they still easily outperformed the control group in another measurement a year later (30-minute observations by independent raters).

Reyes Liske and Holladay (2016) investigated a group-plus-individual-coaching intervention for leaders in a large US healthcare organisation (nonrandomised controls from same organisation; 62 in intervention and 32 in control group, so a lot of attrition in the control group), and found significant increases of 360-degree leadership ratings, also by peers and superiors, and significant differences in terms of promotion and retention rates a year later, as well.

Andreanoff (2016) studied the impact of peer coaching on academic attainment with a nonrandomised 65-strong intervention group and 93 in the control group of university students. The control group had been matched in terms of academic attainment. The objective module grades on two measures of those who received coaching were higher than those who did not ($\delta = 0.35$; $p < 0.01$), an effect which was still mostly there in the next semester and led to a better retention in the coached group of students.

Jordan *et al.* (2016, 2017) studied the effects of group coaching by their student-coaches on the career orientation of secondary-school pupils. Note that there were some overlapping data in these articles. In the first article they have 46 volunteering coachees in nonrandomised coaching groups with 10 weekly sessions of 90 minutes (with 2 or 3 coaches for a group of 4 to 7 pupils) and 56 in the control group. They show how the career group coaching is effective for the groups of adolescents who report a higher gain of the coaching participants in career planning, career decision-making self-efficacy and career decision status compared to the control group, despite starting out at lower levels than the control group. In the second article (Jordan et al., 2017), 104 pupils were coached by 57 student-coaches. They showed that these coaches increased their occupational self-efficacy, goal orientation, and career adaptability during the train-the-coach course ($p < 0.05$) and they could show that higher levels of coaches' goal orientation and career adaptability led to stronger increases of clients' career decision-making self-efficacy during the coaching process.

In a large-scale study Ebner et al. (2017) undertook an experiment with 4 sessions of group coaching in a military university (sessions every 2–3 weeks; 2 coaches per group of 6 to 12 students). They found a significant effect on both self-efficacy and self-management in 92 coaching clients compared with 417 nonrandomised controls ($p < 0.05$). They also found that coaching does increase stress-reducing coping strategies like situation control (but not social support) and also reduces stress-enhancing coping strategies (namely rumination, but not avoidance; $p < 0.05$).

Peláez et al. (2019) and Peláez et al. (2020) presented two nonrandomised controlled trial studies with external coaches working with senior managers in the Spanish automotive sector. In the first trial, there were 56 managers in total and those in the intervention group (2-hour group coaching and 3 individual coaching sessions) significantly performed better not only in their own eyes but also in the eyes of their supervisors. They also self-reported better work engagement, though most of the gains were dropped to nonsignificant at 4-month follow-up. In the second trial at a later date in the same plant (Peláez et al., 2020), 23 somewhat more senior managers in the experimental group than the 14 in the waiting-list control group received pre-assessment feedback, 5 coaching-based leadership group workshops, and 3 individual (external, GROW) executive coaching sessions over a period of 3 months. Ratings on leadership skills were collected from participants but also from most of their line managers and their direct reports. Clear differences were found for intervention and control groups, and the pre-, post-, and even 4-month follow-up measurements for the intervention groups showed significant progress on all variables (self-rating, line-manager-rating, direct-report-rating on leadership skills and performance; a combination of self-efficacy, hope, resilience, and optimism; work engagement; $p < 0.05$). The choice of a leadership-training-plus-coaching intervention and a skewed control group is of course a little problematic in this study, including the fact that many of the feedback-givers were themselves participants in the programme so may have been positively disposed towards it anyway. Nevertheless, it does seem to offer further evidence that coaching (combined with training) improves leadership performance, resilience, optimism, and self-efficacy.

5 Overview of coaching research which compares conditions

This newer body of research in coaching outcome assumes general effectiveness of coaching and then compares conditions to determine the degree to which various aspects of the coaching, of the coach, or of the client impact the outcome. If one accepts the assumption of general effectiveness (e.g. as demonstrated by the studies quoted in Chapter 1) the experimental conditions of this type of research can be a lot less stringent. In particular, client, coach, or sponsor satisfaction can be used as the outcome variable, and one does not need to employ randomised control groups, because the various conditions create proper comparison samples within the study (De Haan & Duckworth, 2013). One should however still be wary of small sample sizes, since effects are bound to be exaggerated without the control groups.

I have found the following 29 studies which explore the question of *what sort* of coaching is effective; in other words, *which* coaching models, personality matches, or coaching behaviours make a significant difference to clients?

Sue-Chan and Latham (2004) compared the impact of internal and external coaches with a wide difference in reputation in terms of (perceived) expertise and credibility. This outcome study involved MBA students in two countries (total $N = 53$) and compared the performance in terms of team playing and exam grades and found small but statistically significant differences at $p < 0.05$, between faculty, peer, and self-coaching with the first the most impactful. As in Perkins (2009) earlier, this study may suffer from researcher-bias as the external coaches/tutors did the scoring of performance.

Similar to Sue-Chan and Latham (2004), Franklin and Doran (2009) put 52 student-volunteers into two peer-coaching conditions, both with some coaching training; with one condition (containing 27 subjects) receiving more information about preparation for change and adaptive learning. They were then independently assessed together with 2,103 of their peers, the assessment forming an objective outcome criterion, and it was only the condition which had the extra preparation that led to a large effect ($\delta = 0.6$) on academic performance. There were also significant increases in both conditions in self-scored self-efficacy and resilience.

In a longitudinal study, Behrendt (2006) shows that 8 manager-coachees view their own 52 performance conversations with employees as being more successful when in the observer analysis of their 35 video recordings (up to 5 sessions per manager) the observer notices that the coach works more on resourcefulness and relationship during the session (large effects; $p < 0.01$). He also notices a surprising small significant negative correlation between the manager's estimate of the coaching relationship and the manager's rating of his own following performance conversation. He further finds some indications that psychodrama coaching is more effective than systemic-Rogerian coaching. This latter result has to be taken with some caution since the author is clearly more committed to the psychodrama coaching, and the coaches in the two conditions were different professionals, so other differences may have played a role.

Scoular and Linley (2006) looked at how both (1) a 'goal-setting' intervention at the beginning of the conversation and (2) personality (dis-)similarities between coach and client as measured by MBTI impact perceived effectiveness. The sample size was $N = 117$ clients and $N = 14$ coaches. No statistically significant difference resulted for outcome measurements at 2 and 8 weeks after the session between 'goal-setting' and 'no goal-setting'; but when the coach and client differed on particular aspects of the personality instrument (the MBTI 'temperaments') the outcome scores were significantly higher.

Stewart et al. (2008) looked at how both client personality and client self-efficacy correlate with coaching outcome. They measured so-called 'BigFive' personality factors (Digman, 1990) and general self-efficacy for 110 clients and correlated these with coaching outcome. They found moderate positive effects for conscientiousness, openness, emotional stability, and general self-efficacy (all around $\delta = 0.4$; $p < 0.05$) but warned that other factors are likely to play a role as well.

Spence et al. (2008) have undertaken an experimental study that compares three randomised conditions: 4 weeks of mindfulness training followed by 4 weekly sessions of coaching; coaching followed by mindfulness training; and health education seminars, for 14, 15, and 13 adults concerning their health goals. Results showed that goal attainment was significantly greater in the coaching format than the educational format. No significant differences were found for goal attainment between the two mindfulness-and-coaching conditions, suggesting that the delivery sequence had little bearing on outcomes.

Vandekerckhove (2010) compares choices of 1,752 applicants to Belgian medical school entrance to be coached and/or make use of online coaching, finding that coaching does lead to significantly higher marks ($\delta = 0.56$ and 0.32 for the two forms of coaching, respectively; $p < 0.01$). He also summarises older outcome literature for the effects of coaching/tutoring on university entrance exams.

Boyce et al. (2010) studied 74 coach-client relationships in a US military academy where clients were cadets and coaches were senior military leaders who had had some training in executive coaching. The study analysed the impact of relational aspects (rapport, trust, and commitment) and matching criteria (demographic commonality, behavioural compatibility, and coach credibility), on coaching outcome. Their main findings were that matching had no significant impact on outcome, whilst rapport and trust, as assessed by both client ($\delta = 2$) and coach ($\delta = 1.2$), affected client-scored outcomes significantly.

With a sample of internal coaches working alongside a leadership development programme within a manufacturing company involving 31 coach-client pairs, Baron and Morin (2009) were able to show that coaching clients' rating of the working alliance as a measure of the coaching relationship correlated with coaching outcomes (measured in terms of changes in coachee self-efficacy, $\delta = 0.5$) whilst coaches' ratings of the working alliance did not correlate with outcomes significantly. Coachees' ratings of the working alliance mediated the impact of coachee-rated self-efficacy on self-rated outcomes.

De Haan et al. (2011) examine how various executive coaching interventions make a difference to clients. A total of 71 coaching clients, from as many organisations, reported on the various interventions of their coaches and these ratings were compared with their evaluations. In that work, De Haan et al. found no distinction among specific coach interventions, leading to the conclusion that effectiveness is much less correlated with technique or intervention than by factors common to all coaching, such as the relationship, empathic understanding, positive expectations, etcetera.

De Haan et al. (2013) built on the previous study to research the relative impact and importance of various common factors for 156 new executive coaching clients and 34 experienced coaches. The purpose of this research was to look at various elements common to *all* coaching approaches (the 'common factors') and to measure which of these are likely to have the highest positive impact on clients. The study showed that client perceptions of the outcome of coaching were significantly related to their perceptions of the working alliance, client self-efficacy, and perceptions of coaching interventions ('generalised techniques') of the coach. The client-coach relationship strongly mediated the impact of self-efficacy and the majority of techniques on coaching outcomes (except for perceived explicit focus on goals and helping the client to make discoveries), suggesting that the relationship is the key factor in coaching outcome.

Working with two nonrandomised groups of teachers in training (pre- and post-measurement), of which 48 teachers were required to take synchronous (group) e-coaching and 49 teachers were not, Anthony et al. (2013) are able to show that the e-coaching has increased the self-efficacy only for the coached group ($\delta = 0.4$; $p < 0.02$). They also showed that those teachers with the lowest self-efficacy at the beginning of the year took more e-coaching sessions and ended up with similar self-efficacy levels, another example of a self-adjusted take-up of coaching (see also Goff et al., 2014). A smaller but similar experiment by Hunt et al. (2019), investigating a group of 40 female entrepreneurs, 24 of which received 6 months of online coaching, again demonstrated that self-efficacy grew only in the coached group.

Hui et al. (2013) set out to measure differences between different styles of coaching: guidance coaching and facilitative coaching. In this study, 127 adults from diverse backgrounds but mostly students were randomly assigned to 3 sessions of 25 minutes of computer training in Excel or PowerPoint, with 2 coaching conditions (i.e. 4 groups of around 32 in each condition): (1) guidance including explaining, giving answers, teaching, instructing and (2) facilitation including developing and facilitating your own solution and your own approach by supporting and encouraging. After the coaching all participants do the same challenging task on both Excel and PowerPoint; i.e. a 'coached' task (same software they have been coached on) and a 'transfer' task (different software). For coached task performance, participants who received guidance coaching performed better than those who received facilitation coaching ($p < 0.01$). For transfer task performance, participants who received facilitation coaching performed better than those who received guidance coaching ($p < 0.05$). Hui et al. (2019) reported on the influence of implicit person theories in this experiment, showing that holding an 'entity theory' that human attributes are innate and unalterable moderates the relationship between 'guidance' coaching and task performance on the 'coached' task. Similarly, holding the 'incremental theory' that personal attributes can be developed moderates the relationship between 'facilitation' coaching and task performance on the 'transfer' task.

Hui and Sue-Chan (2018; reviewed earlier in this chapter) extended this research to management coaching, and Hui et al. (2017) did the same for student-tutors as coaches of 297 younger (circa-18-year-old) university students. They found that facilitation coaching was indirectly related to academic performance ($p < 0.05$) through its significant impact on 1 out of 4 emotions (cheerfulness, dejection, quiescence, and agitation) and this effect was more pronounced ('moderated') if guidance coaching was also present – although one can interpret their results also as both styles of coaching having a small, indirect, and positive impact on exam results.

Grant (2014b) compared four aspects of the coach-coachee relationship to investigate which was more related to specific measures of coaching success. The four aspects were (a) autonomy support (bonding); (b) the extent to which a coachee feels satisfied with the actual coach-coachee relationship; (c) the extent to which the coaching relationship was similar to an 'ideal' coach-coachee relationship; and (d) a goal-focused coach-coachee relationship. In a within-subject study, 49 coach-coachee dyads conducted 4 coaching sessions over a 10- to 12-week period (as part of a 5-day coach training programme). Results indicate that satisfaction with a coach-coachee relationship does not predict coaching effectiveness; however satisfaction does predict autonomy support ($\delta = 0.6$; $p < 0.05$) and proximity to an 'ideal' relationship ($\delta = 0.6$; $p = 0.05$) moderately predicted coaching success; whilst a goal-focused coach-coachee relationship was a more powerful predictor of coaching success ($\delta = 0.9$; $p < 0.01$). The findings affirm the importance of goals in the coaching process.

Real-time coaching with visual feedback of radiation levels nearly halved the exposure to their hospital procedure's radiation for experienced pain consultant doctors as compared to real-time visual feedback only (Slegers et al., 2015). But note that the coaching is more like instruction, pointing out risks of radiation to the doctors.

A different kind of between-subject design by Chinn et al. (2015) explored the experiences of a group of 215 coachees from different industries and showed that the degree of the external coach's relevant professional and relevant industry experience as a choice criterion in matching did not correlate with outcome. Also, there was no relationship between shared coach-client professional or industry experience and goal achievement. The authors convincingly show that the coach's experience in the profession or industry of the client does not matter a great deal.

Gessnitzer and Kauffeld (2015) had observers rate the working relationship of 31 videotaped coaching dyads by means of interaction analysis and also working-alliance questionnaires for coachees and coaches. They found that coachee-initiated goals and tasks as rated by the observers were positively related to coaching success later, as rated by the coachee after the final session. However, coach-initiated goals and tasks had the opposite effect. They also found that observer-rated bonding behaviours did not influence coaching success.

De Haan et al. (2016) was a large-scale study of executive coaching exploring the perceived effectiveness of coaching from the perspectives of coach, coachee, and sponsor, and measuring potential active ingredients including the coach-coachee working alliance, coachee self-efficacy, personality, and 'personality match' between coach and coachee. Using a retrospective design, data was collected from 1,895 coachee-coach pairs (366 different coaches) from 34 countries, and 92 sponsors, for a total of 3,882 matching surveys. Results indicate that coach and coachee perceptions of coaching effectiveness (CE) were significantly related to both coach- and coachee-rated strength of the working alliance (δ around 1.4 for coachee-rated CE and δ around 0.4 for coach-rated CE) and to coachee self-efficacy (δ around 0.5 for coachee-rated CE and δ around 0.2 for coach-rated CE) but unrelated to coachee or coach personality nor to personality matching. The coachee-coach working alliance mediated the impact of self-efficacy on CE, suggesting that the strength of this working alliance – particularly as seen through the eyes of the coachee – is a key ingredient in CE. In addition, a strong emphasis on goals in the working alliance can partially compensate for low coachee self-efficacy. The task and goal aspects of the working alliance were stronger predictors of positive CE than the bond aspects, highlighting the importance of a task and goal focus in the coach-coachee relationship.

In a pair of studies Tee et al. (2017, 2019) gave an interesting example of how hard it can be to demonstrate objective outcomes of coaching conversations. In the first study, 39 participants were randomly assigned to control and experimental conditions, with the intervention group having 6 weekly sessions consisting of one-hour group training followed by one-hour peer-coaching. They found no significant predictions for 4 'core self-evaluations' comprising Self-esteem, Self-efficacy, Emotional stability, and Internal locus of control. In the second study, there were no control groups; however a much larger 135-strong target group of students engaged in 6 monthly co-coaching conversations. This time an objective outcome criterion was used: the percentage scores of their academic achievement which were also explicitly part of their coaching through goal-attainment tracking. They found no significant impact of any of the 4 core self-evaluations dimensions on (objectively measured) goal attainment.

Zimmermann and Antoni (2018, 2020) published two longitudinal studies of coaching with overlapping datasets: students on a coaching programme recruited one client each for 4 to 11 sessions of coaching. Zimmermann and Antoni (2018) followed one coaching assignment for every one of 33 dyads formed by these new coaches (256 sessions in total). They found the usual increase of goal-attainment over time for the coachees and could also demonstrate that two out of three coach-reported groups of interventions (1) around clarification or meaning-making and (2) improving mastery and coping, significantly predicted coachee goal-attainment ($p < 0.05$). In the second study with 52 student-coach dyads and 317 sessions in total (Zimmermann & Antoni, 2020), client satisfaction was predicted from coach ratings of the relationship and the degree of the coach's 'resource building.' Clients whose coaches reported an enhancement in the coach-client relationship relative to their mean level perceived higher coaching satisfaction in the following session ($p < 0.05$). Also, self-scored occupational self-efficacy, as well as satisfaction of needs, mediated the impact of the clients' perceived resource activation on coaching satisfaction in the following session ($p < 0.001$). Clients who perceive higher occupational self-efficacy rate the coach-client relationship higher and consequently are more satisfied with coaching, as found in earlier models ($p < 0.001$; Baron & Morin, 2009; De Haan et al., 2013, 2016, 2019).

De Haan et al. (2019), in their large-scale RCT within a global healthcare corporation, tested several aspects that are common to coaching contracts and found more evidence for the central importance of the strength of the working alliance as seen from both the coachee and (to a lesser extent) the coach perspectives, which mediated the effects for coachee well-being and perceived social support. In addition, they found some significant impact for coachee self-efficacy, resilience, and 'bright side' personality aspects. Finally, they found some first significant indications that personality and career derailment aspects may show demonstrable improvement through coaching.

Jones et al. (2019) conducted a field study in a UK nonprofit organisation where 53 participants were in an intervention group that engaged in 4 one-hour long 'GROW' coaching conversations over approximately 4 months (coached by the first author) and 31 in a waiting-list control group. Three of the Big Five personality aspects were measured, as well as core self-evaluations, goal orientation, and self- and line-manager ratings of performance. Coaching had a significant effect only on self-rated performance. They could demonstrate that coachees with greater Openness within the Big Five benefited more than those with less Openness.

In Ebner et al. (2020) high-school pupils received feedback on a psychometric and then attended either a single one-on-one coaching session ($N = 50$), or participated in a single, structured group coaching session ($N = 18$), or only received feedback without coaching (N = 64); with pre- and post-coaching measurements spanning 10 weeks. Contrary to the expectation that one-to-one coaching and group coaching could help with self-efficacy and life satisfaction, and could moderate the impact of the tough feedback on incongruities, none of these effects were found – and there was even one significant contrary effect for one-to-one coaching on life satisfaction. These findings could be due to testing only a single coaching session or the fact that the participants chose which experimental group they wanted to belong to.

6 Overview of coaching research which compares techniques of coaching

When researchers have compared different approaches, styles, or techniques of coaching they have usually created experiments where they could make use of randomisation in the design, so all studies in this section have been done with well distributed groups undergoing different techniques or approaches.

It is important to bear in mind that much of the work in the area of coaching 'technique' was done by researchers who wanted to validate a particular method of coaching (such as solution-focused coaching, or PEA-coaching) from the outset, i.e. by researchers who already strongly believed in these techniques before embarking on the investigation. This can create automatic and subconscious biases in us as we are doing our quantitative research (see, e.g., Wampold, 2001) and consequent over-estimation of effects, as mentioned in Chapter 1. Now we have not just coaches studying coaching with quantitative methods (and therefore as professionals in the field being biased about it), but also coaches with a particular belief about a technique or model studying that technique or model to see it being 'validated' with quantitative methods. In each of the next empirical articles the authors cannot help but advertise and list advantages of their chosen method of coaching before the experiment even begins, and afterwards they may look at the results in the best possible light, building on their pre-existing allegiances. As far as I can see no one historically increased their own doubts about their chosen technique by doing an investigation to validate it. In my summary I will therefore have to be slightly more critical and detached, but without in any way wanting to diminish the very helpful results that they have indeed obtained.

In a randomised controlled set-up for 118 students with four conditions made up of coachees that have been primed with either fixed implicit person theories (IPTs) or incremental implicit person theories, and witness a peer being coached in a generally critical or supportive coaching condition, Sue-Chan *et al.* (2012) show that supportive, 'promotion' coaching has slightly better results than challenging or critical 'prevention' coaching – and that coachees with a fixed IPT do slightly better with the similar condition of negative, 'prevention' coaching. Note that in this experiment none of the participants were directly coached; they all viewed a live, rehearsed role modelling of one of the coaching conditions. In a second study in Sue-Chan *et al.* (2012) this result was replicated for a sample of 249 factory workers who scored their own IPTs and their line managers' coaching styles.

Similar findings were produced by Jarzebowski *et al.* (2012) with an entirely different, much smaller experiment. Coachees were primed into a 'promotion' mindset just before doing a leadership-skills written task, after which, in the fifth and final coaching session, they received positive 'promotion' feedback ('congratulations, you have achieved . . .' etc.) in the fit condition (17 participants, randomised) or positive 'prevention' feedback ('congratulations, you have met the standard . . ." etc.) in the non-fit condition (12 participants). It could be shown that those in the promotion feedback or matching feedback condition had demonstrably higher motivation ($p < 0.05$), indicating that it is helpful if the feedback from the coach matches the implicit mindset of the coachee. Hui *et al.* (2013) were able to show that more directive 'guidance' coaching had better effects on a similar challenge whilst more nondirective 'facilitation' coaching led to better results on a transfer condition where coachees had to work on a less similar challenge, and that this effect was moderated by IPTs in precisely the same manner as in the research of Sue-Chan *et al.* (2012): a fixed IPT creates better results for 'guidance' coaching on similar challenges whilst an incremental IPT creates better results for 'facilitation' coaching on adaptive challenges (Hui *et al.*, 2019). This work was extended by Hui and Sue-Chan in 2018, who found similar differences for coaching by line managers.

Williams and Lowman (2018) compared two different coaching interventions, the more directive goal-focused ('I help my coachee to identify and set realistic and challenging goals') and the more nondirective process-oriented coaching ('I tailor my own approach to fit the preferences and needs of the coachee'). Although process-oriented coaching seemed to effect slightly bigger changes in self- and line-manager rated leadership competences, no significant differences between the two conditions were found.

Similarly, Sun *et al.* (2013) studied a group of mental health workers who received once-a-month sessions of either (randomly assigned) more in-depth 'transformational' coaching (21 coachees) or more directive 'skills coaching' (19 coachees) from internal more senior coaches. They found that the transformational coaching encouraged the development of stronger coaching relationships, both in terms of the working alliance and the 'real' relationship. In the same Australian recovery-oriented care service, Deane *et al.* (2014) compared 'transformational' again to 'skills' coaching in a larger randomised assignment for 188 mental-health practitioners (with a lot of incomplete data). They found a significant improvement in their quality of goal planning in the 'transformational' coaching condition and not in the 'skills' coaching condition, as rated by independent experts between time 1 and time 3 ($p < 0.05$).

Seven studies (not counting pilots) compared the effects of specific 'problem-focused' and 'solution-focused' coaching questions on positive and negative affect, self-efficacy, goal approach, and action planning. These were not studies of coaching assignments or coaching conversations – only of students answering different types of questions about their 'issues' online, as part of a one-off self-coaching session following the online questionnaire.

Grant (2012) assigned a total of 225 psychology students randomly to either a problem-focused (PF) or solution-focused (SF) 'coaching' condition. All participants described a real-life problem that they wanted to solve and set a goal to solve that problem. They then completed a set of measures that assessed levels of positive and negative affect, self-efficacy, and goal attainment. In the problem-focused coaching condition 108 participants then responded to a number of online problem-focused coaching questions and finally completed a second set of the same measures. The 117 participants in the solution-focused coaching session completed a mirror image of the problem-focused condition, responding to solution-focused questions including the 'Miracle Question.' Both the problem-focused and the solution-focused coaching conditions were effective at enhancing goal approach. However, only the solution-focused approach significantly increased positive affect, decreased negative affect, and increased self-efficacy (p < 0.01). This study was replicated in Spain with a total of 204 nursing and psychology students giving the same significant results (Neipp et al., 2016).

McDowall et al. (2014) randomly assigned British adult employees from a range of British organisations to either a solution-focused 'feedforward' (N = 32) or a review, 'feedback' coaching (N = 22) session. After the single session, self-efficacy, strengths confidence, and goal attainment were significantly better for the feedforward than for the feedback condition (p < 0.01), and mood was near-significantly more positive too. There is always the problem that two coaches being more in favour of feedforward than feedback, contributed to obtaining better results in the former condition.

Theeboom et al. (2016) in two separate studies assigned 61 and then 54 students randomly to PF and SF coaching conditions, asked them to come up with a real-life problem related to study stress or time management, and completed a first set of measures to assess levels of positive and negative affect, and emotional exhaustion. After answering the same questions as in Grant (2012) the students received a second measure of positive and negative affect and were asked to do an attentional control task (first cohort of 61) or cognitive flexibility test (second cohort of 54). Theeboom et al. (2016) found the same broad relationship between SF questions and both positive affect (p < 0.001) and the cognitive flexibility test (p < 0.05), yet no significant relationship to attentional control.

Braunstein and Grant (2016) randomly assigned 140 students to four conditions made up of PF and SF questions in combination with Approach and Avoid Goals, and so participants were asked to write their issue down but also their (approach or avoid) goal with this issue. This study replicated the earlier results with regard to affect, self-efficacy, and perceived goal attainment, but did not show any statistically significant effects of choosing an approach goal versus an avoid goal.

Grant and O'Connor (2018) randomly allocated 512 students to four conditions: comparing (1) PF coaching questions and (2) SF coaching questions and (3) positive affect (PA) induction and (4) a SF plus PA condition (SF + PA). The findings of this study were that PA induction and SF coaching questions were equally effective at enhancing positive affect, increasing self-efficacy, enhancing goal approach, and developing action steps. Whilst positive affect makes a valuable contribution to coaching outcomes, combining PA induction with SF questions produces superior outcomes to PA or SF questions alone in terms of self-efficacy, goal approach, and action steps.

Grant and Gerrard (2020) randomly assigned 80 students to PF, SF, or PF + SF questions conditions through the same process as the other studies and measured one new variable: pre-existing dysfunctional attitudes. Again, earlier significant relationships between SF and affect, self-efficacy, and goal approach were replicated; but the PF + SF condition behaved like the PF condition, not equal to or better than SF alone, as was expected. Dysfunctional attitudes were found to have a detrimental impact on negative affect following both PF and PF + SF questions but not following SF. They concluded therefore that SF questions may be particularly helpful with dysfunctional attitudes.

These studies are impressive in the sense that we have fairly large randomised group comparisons and the same basic significant findings are confirmed every time, so this seems to be one of the most rigorous designs and among the best-replicated research in all of the coaching literature, even though it is not really studying coaching but only one small part of coaching, namely the response to questions. We can learn from these studies that solution-focused or 'feedforward' questions do put the 'issue holders' in a different frame of mind, namely a more positive one similar to the induction of positive affect, which in some cases leads to them seeing more options for their issue (Grant & O'Connor, 2018) and may make them more flexible in a cognitive test as well (Theeboom *et al.*, 2016).

There has been another group studying the differences between what these different researchers from Case Western University call problem-focused or NEA-coaching and vision-focused or PEA-coaching. They have tried to establish links between the effectiveness of coaching interventions and well-known neuronal pathways. They model the coaching relationship as a Positive Emotional Attractor or PEA that can help coachees balance out the Negative Emotional Attractors or NEAs in their life and work. They also warn that bad coaching, which creates a stressful environment for the coachee (such as in some forms of remedial coaching and mentoring, where 'management' stipulates the objectives and the coach is experienced as a representative or extension of management) runs the risk of strengthening the NEA so that negative effects can be expected. This leads them to speak about 'PEA coaching' versus 'NEA coaching' in some of the articles – two conditions that can be linked with the work by Grant, Theeboom, and the others previously mentioned on positive questioning and positive affect – and extending that work into proper live conversations between a 'coach' and a 'coachee.' They compare in their research the 'visioning'/PEA condition wherein the coach uses the participant's own hopes, strengths, and desired future ('Ideal Self') as the primary framework for the coaching session. In the 'improvement needs'/NEA condition the coach uses the participant's perceived improvement needs, weaknesses, and current reality ('Real Self') as the primary framework.

Jack *et al.* (2013) randomly divided 20 participants into 4 conditions, each with a 30-minute interview session: PEA-coaching followed by a PEA-question on a screen whilst they were inside nuclear magnetic resonance imaging 3 to 5 days later; NEA-coaching followed by a NEA-question whilst in magnetic resonance imaging 3 to 5 days later; and PEA- or NEA-coaching followed by a neutral question whilst in magnetic resonance imaging 3 to 5 days later. They found statistically significant enhancements for brain areas that they argued related to visioning (after PEA-coaching and -question) and for other areas related to the parasympathetic nervous system (after PEA-coaching and -question) and also for areas related to the sympathetic 'arousal' system (after NEA-coaching and -question). The association with different interviewers, i.e. more 'positive' versus more 'negative' relationships with the interviewers, and the activity in different brain areas, seems to argue for a positive, supportive coaching relationship furthering more 'visioning' 'creative thinking' and 'restorative' activities. We have to be careful of course because it is only a single study and there were only 5 participants in each condition, but it did deliver coherent and significant results. One could argue whether these positive effects found are only true for 'positive psychology' PEA-coaching or much more generally for any kind of helpful working alliance. Given what we know about the small contribution of technique and specific interventions, one would err towards the working alliance and a general positive coaching relationship rather than the specific optimistic questioning.

Howard (2015) also tested the PEA versus NEA model with a small-scale experiment involving a single 360-degree feedback 'coaching' session of one hour. The 18 participants were randomly assigned to a 'PEA'-style coach or an 'NEA'-style coach. As with the previous experiment one could argue they were both rather 'directive' ways of coaching, where the coach-style was rather central to the conversation: the coach in the first case focused on the perceived positives for the coachee, and in the second case on the perceived challenges for the coachee. This had nothing to do with free association, letting the client set the agenda, or other nondirective approaches as other professionals would understand coaching to be (see for a wider range of core models of coaching De Haan & Burger, 2005). The study measured outcomes in terms of the use of different emotive words during the sessions, the presence of cortisol in saliva after the session (indicative of arousal), and satisfaction with the session. The only significant differences found, with low significance, were in quantities of emotion words used by the client, namely words indicating sadness and anger (which occurred more in the NEA condition) and leisure (occurring more in the PEA condition) and some differences as well in the distribution of sadness- and future-oriented words during the three phases of the session. No significant changes were found in cortisol-levels.

Another group working from Braunschweig University used videos of coaching sessions to study specific techniques as they occurred. These were impressive experiments studying coaching interventions at the micro level, and quite similar to the previous two groups of papers, they also found that dominant-friendly (or, in other jargon: solution-focused, PEA) coaching leads to significantly better results than the opposite: hostile-submissive interventions. Here is a brief overview of the work done at Braunschweig, with the caveat that many of the datasets overlapped so that independence between the studies was not complete:

> Ianiro *et al.* (2013) analysed thousands of moments of interaction during 33 first coaching sessions with trainee psychologists as coaches and young professionals as clients, in terms of both the client's and the coach's interpersonal behaviour, over two basic dimensions: affiliation and dominance. Findings suggest that both (1) the coach's dominance behaviour and (2) similarity of dominance and affiliation behaviour between coach and client predict positive client ratings of goal-attainment after 5 sessions; whilst (2) also predicts positive client ratings of the relationship quality after 5 sessions. Building on this, Ianiro and Kauffeld (2014) found that the coach's dominance behaviour also predicted the working alliance as scored by the coachee. Moreover, these authors further found that coach mood (and also coachee mood) correlated significantly with the coach's own dominant-friendly behaviour and with the working alliance as ultimately scored by the coachee, but only on the 'good mood' and 'calm' sub-scales, not on that of 'awakeness,' because the latter was negatively correlated with dominant-friendly coachee behaviour. Gessnitzer and Kauffeld (2015) showed with a similar group that only observer-rated working-alliance behaviours with respect to 'agreement on goals and tasks *initiated by the coachee* turned out to correlate with coaching outcomes, not working-alliance ratings by coach or coachee. Ianiro *et al.* (2015) showed how dominant-friendly coaching behaviour significantly evoked dominant coachee behaviour and vice versa (whereas other dominant coach behaviour, namely both neutral and hostile, in fact evoked dependent coachee behaviour).

Dominant coachee behaviour related in turn to positive outcomes in terms of self-scored effectiveness on goals. Moreover, the complementary hypothesis also appears to be true: dependent coachee behaviour was significantly negatively correlated to the same outcomes. Furthermore, as Will *et al.* (2016) showed, two (observer-rated) aspects of empathy (paraphrasing and naming coachee feelings) in the behavioural analysis of the video images induced a positive response in coachees with a frequency that could be classed as significant. Gessnitzer *et al.* (2016) managed to show that open questions and offering support by coaches led to more 'self-efficient' coachee statements (as did offering solutions, a very directive intervention, but only in the very first session), and that the support of coaches after a 'self-efficient' statement can significantly lead to more 'self-efficient' coachee statements immediately after. Will *et al.* (2019) examined the role of a coach's expressed empathy and appreciation within different phases of a first coaching session. Results yielded that coaches' positive-supportive behaviour differs significantly across all phases, and that expressed positive-supportive coach behaviour was significantly linked to the client's interest in change. Jordan and Kauffeld (2020) followed on Gessnitzer *et al.* (2016) by exploring the effect of the coaches' solution-focused questions on clients' solution statements and 'self-efficient' behaviour in the middle (third) session of 23 coach-client pairs. Clients' solution statements followed significantly after solution-focused questions (lag 1 and lag 2; $p < 0.01$) and those solution statements predicted their goal attainment two sessions later ($p < 0.05$); however those statements did not predict client-efficient statements with a short lag, whilst those client-efficient statements did predict goal and career orientation two sessions later ($p < 0.05$). Klonek *et al.* (2020) used the first of 5 coaching sessions for 53 coach-coachee pairs to validate different ways of measuring the micro behaviours and correlating them with overall perceived empathy and working alliance, using independent pairs of observers (and no self-reported data whatsoever). They could demonstrate the validity of their tools and pinpoint behaviours in the moment that observers consistently rate as empathetic, such as using summaries, bonding with the client, appreciation, and even positive humorous expressions; and similar with the working alliance: e.g. closed questions and directive behaviours were negatively related to working alliance in the minds of observers.

7 Overview of coaching research which compares virtual and face-to-face coaching

Now that the whole world has very rapidly gone virtual due to the corona-crisis in 2020, we should expect much more research into the particular quality (advantages and disadvantages) and the effectiveness of (various forms of) virtual coaching as compared to face-to-face coaching. There have already been a few studies that have compared different modalities and they are summarised here. By and large they seem to conclude that differences in effectiveness cannot be found, which confirms older research in the helping professions that shows that different forms of facilitation are equivalent and that therefore virtual coaching may have an advantage as it comes with wider access and lower thresholds to attendance (see, e.g., Caulat & De Haan, 2006).

Poepsel (2011) studied the effectiveness of web-based virtual group coaching by creating a waiting-list randomised controlled trial looking into the outcomes of an

8-week structured e-coaching journey making use of regular tasks and homework and online discussion forums with a qualified coach. Adults from the general population were randomly assigned to an 8-week coaching condition of 12 or waiting-list control group of 16. He found small, significant differences for goal-attainment and well-being, but not for hope – similar outcomes to Green et al. (2006) who had the same study design except their group coaching was face-to-face.

In a health coaching study by Fischer et al. (2019) Swiss adults (age: 42 ± 11 years) were assigned randomly to a 62-strong control and two intervention groups which received 12 bi-weekly short telephone calls with ($N = 73$) or without ($N = 82$) additional twice-a-week SMS prompts. The control group received only one written physical-activity instruction and recommendations at the beginning of the trial, which the other two groups received as well. At post-test, self-reported physical activity increased by 173 min/week in the coaching group and by 165 min/week in the coaching and SMS group compared to control (significant at $p < 0.05$ level). These group differences remained similar in the 12-month follow-up test. According to the objectively assessed fitness monitoring, the coaching group increased by 32 min/week and the coaching and SMS group by 34 min/week, compared to the control group (significant at $p < 0.05$ level). In the follow-up test, the objective fitness levels of the intervention groups no longer differed from baseline, but group differences persisted as the control group decreased below baseline. Dropout rates in the control group were also about double the other conditions which shows that the positive effect on fitness is possibly underestimated. Additional SMS prompts did not result in a further increase in physical activity, so additional 'asynchronous virtual coaching' did not boost the results of telephone coaching. It is worth noting that many of the health coaching studies covered in Chapter 1 also exclusively made use of short telephone coaching sessions with which they could generally demonstrate a large, significant impact.

In a retrospective within-sample comparison of pure face-to-face and pure telephone coaching (5 hourly sessions over around 4 months) Van Dun (2020) studied 209 nonrandomised face-to-face and 120 telephone coachees. He found no differences on the outcome variables vitality and goal attainment, so telephone coaching was shown to be equally effective on those two dimensions. A similar result was found in another retrospective, within-sample comparison by Vandekerckhove (2010): personal tutoring was only slightly more effective than non-interactive online tutoring in preparation for medical entrance exams.

In sum, it seems virtual telephone coaching is as good as face-to-face coaching and even has some practical advantages for clients. There is some evidence in favour of online synchronous discussion forums and e-coaching as well, whilst there is little support for the efficacy of SMS prompts and asynchronous coaching. However, these conclusions are as yet based on very little research.

Part D: what it means for coaching practice

From all that has been researched in the 160 robust empirical studies presented in this chapter and the previous chapter, we can now infer something about what it is that makes coaching effective, or what makes coaching work. In other words, which aspects of coaching might be making a positive difference in terms of overall effectiveness? In still other words, which are the 'active ingredients' in coaching?

In this section I will look into all the independent variables that have been tested in coaching research – and in particular those independent variables that have been researched and appear to make a difference. Interestingly, as is very normal in social research, all variables that have been tested do appear to make a difference as well, although there are some clear differences of degree.

The labels and groupings in this section are slightly arbitrary – e.g. the preparedness and motivation dimensions could just as well be part of the coachee's personality rather than his or her attitude towards coaching or towards work and challenges more generally. Moreover, the reason for a high motivation, say, could be very different from one coachee to another in the intervention group.

More generally, as with all research into personality, we do not really know to what extent we are beginning to identify stable *traits* or are picking up dynamic *states* or moods at the time the research was done. Many of the same factors that may cause change in coaching are themselves changed as a result of coaching, as we shall see in Chapter 4. Just as it is not always easy to distinguish between weather and climate, particularly if you have only a small-scale experiment. Say you go to a new place for one week: was the humidity, temperature, air pressure that you had in that week indicative of the climate, or was it just what the weather was like that week? Very hard to answer with a small sample of days. Similarly, it is hard to distinguish between more and less stable parts of the personality if you only have relatively small sample research, and nearly no longitudinal research.

It is interesting that there are several instances (described later) where we find a contradiction in the data, i.e. certain studies are saying that a certain ingredient makes a big difference, whilst there are other studies saying that they cannot demonstrate a correlation with the same ingredient. However, for those willing to inquire, in each of these cases it will be easy to see which of the contrasting voices to take more seriously, from the different standards of research as covered in previous sections.

First factor: the coach

Do we know if the coach makes a difference to coaching? It would seem obvious and important to know, yet very few measurements have been done. One would need quite large samples with many different coaches well represented, to draw clear conclusions.

Firstly, Sue-Chan and Latham (2004) did show that the coach's *reputation* matters a lot: their results with peer-coaches were much poorer than with business-school faculty-coaches. Even though the faculty members were not professional coaches, their sheer reputation seemed to have made all the difference. Similarly, Grant (2014b) showed that the coach's proximity to an 'ideal' coach ($\delta = 0.6$; $p = 0.05$) or ideal coaching relationship moderately predicted coaching success. Boyce *et al.* (2010) add a small degree of predictive significance for the coach's credibility. Finally, Bozer *et al.* (2014) show that a coach's academic background in psychology was positively related to executive coaching effectiveness as reflected in greater improvement in coachee self-rated self-awareness but also in line-manager rated job performance. Moreover, the coach's credibility in the eye of the coachee predicted coach-rated (in Sue-Chan & Latham, 2004) and coachee-rated (in Bozer *et al.*, 2014) job performance.

Heslin *et al.* (2006) show that the coach's *ideology* is important too, and that 'implicit person theories' matter and that these mindsets affect managers' willingness and even their ability to coach others. Specifically, individuals holding an 'entity theory' that human attributes are innate and unalterable are disinclined to invest in helping others to develop and improve, relative to individuals who hold the 'incremental theory' that personal attributes can be developed. Sonesh *et al.* (2015) adds to this idea that the coach's *frame of mind* matters: in some cases, the coach's *psychological mindedness* was significantly related to outcome.

It does seem that a *generally positive outlook* and appreciative questioning may help to move clients into a calmer and more positive frame of mind (e.g. Ianiro *et al.*, 2013; Jack *et al.*, 2013; Howard, 2015; Grant & O'Connor, 2018). I would suggest this is not a specific technique but more a 'common factor' of coaching: the friendly and optimistic and confident approach that a coach may naturally offer to every client. Having said that, I can also find indications from these studies that specific techniques based on friendliness and positive assertiveness are more effective than the converse. When we checked in our large dataset, the coach's own *self-efficacy* was not related to outcome (De Haan *et al.*, 2016), so there is not that much evidence that optimism or self-motivation makes a better coach.

Jordan *et al.* (2017) finally show that higher levels of coaches' *goal orientation and career adaptability* led to stronger increases of clients' career decision-making self-efficacy during the coaching process.

Younger coaches seem to be more effective: effectiveness of the coach is inversely related to the coach's age and years of experience (George *et al.*, 2020), presumably because young and relatively inexperienced coaches were less directive.[2]

Second factor: the technique of the coach

In a series of articles, De Haan *et al.* (2011, 2013, 2019) found little or no distinction amongst a wide spectrum of specific coach interventions although they all correlated significantly with outcome. This seems to say that if a coachee experiences a high benefit or achieves a good outcome, all the various behaviours and techniques of her or his coach are appreciated (and similarly for less successful work: if it did not work for the coachee, *all* coach behaviours are seen as less helpful). In any case, not much of a distinction was made by most coachees in terms of the particular approaches of their coaches. So, these researchers arrived at the conclusion that effectiveness is much less correlated with technique or intervention than by factors common to all coaching, such as the quality of the relationship, empathic understanding, positive expectations, etcetera. It has to be said though that in these research programmes all of these techniques were measured in a general way, i.e. referring to all of the coaching as a whole, and not in terms of particular moments or the timing of interventions. Facilitative coaching behaviours were also measured from the coachee's perspective and shown to correlate to outcome by Ladegard and Gjerde (2014), but those behaviours do fall within the wider spectrum of behaviours shown to be correlated with coachee-scored outcome (De Haan *et al.*, 2011).

Williams and Lowman (2018) compared two different approaches (goal- and process-oriented coaching) and found no significant differences between the two, supporting the idea that coachees look more holistically at coach techniques. If coachees look mainly for 'general technique,' then Grant and Cavanagh (2007) seem to confirm this: they found that coaches who rate themselves as more skilful in general have higher outcomes in the eyes of their coachee. Dahling *et al.* (2016) also showed that manager-coaches' general skill and offer of 'team role clarity' both had a significant effect on delivery (sales goal attainment of sales reps).

Behrendt (2006) shows that managers rate their own performance as higher if their coach works more on resourcefulness and relationship during the session (as rated by an observer on the basis of a video recording). Zimmermann and Antoni (2018) found that the coach's self-reported clarifications or strengthening of mastery in their sessions were significantly correlated with coachee-rated goal attainment. McDowall *et al.* (2014) also showed that solution-focused feedforward techniques raise self-efficacy, strengths confidence and goal attainment significantly more than 'feedback coaching'.

Some research has found a limited contribution of 'technique': Scoular and Linley (2006), studying single sessions of coaching, found no difference for a 'goal-setting' intervention at the beginning of the conversation. Sue-Chan *et al.* (2012), Jarzebowski *et al.* (2012), Hui *et al.* (2013), Sun *et al.* (2013), Deane *et al.* (2014) and Hui and Sue-Chan (2018) each used randomised group sampling to find significant differences between two measurably different coaching styles and each found a slight superiority for the more facilitative and supportive styles:

- 'prevention' based (challenging) coaching achieves better results with coachees with fixed implicit person theories, and 'promotion' based (supportive) coaching does the same overall and in particular for those with incremental implicit person theories (Sue-Chan *et al.*, 2012; Jarzebowski *et al.*, 2012).
- more directive 'guidance' or 'skills coaching' helped with task performance (Hui & Sue-Chan, 2018) or more similar tasks; whilst less directive 'facilitation' helped with adaptive performance (Hui & Sue-Chan, 2018) or new, less similar tasks on a software challenge (Excel versus PowerPoint; Hui *et al.*, 2013).
- more in-depth 'transformational' coaching encouraged the development of stronger coaching relationships compared to more directive 'skills coaching' (Sun *et al.*, 2013) as well as better objective professional service-delivery outcomes (Deane *et al.*, 2014).

Hui and Sue-Chan (2018) also indicate indirect impacts of different coaching styles: 'guidance' coaching being related to more anxiety and 'facilitation' coaching related to less anxiety; whilst 'facilitation' through 'adaptive' performance also helps with the 'task' performance over time.

Behrendt (2006) finds significantly higher client ratings favouring psychodrama coaching over systemic-Rogerian coaching, although this does not materialize in subsequent higher objective outcomes for psychodrama. Moreover, Grant (2014b) found that a goal-focused coach-coachee relationship was a good predictor of coaching success ($\delta = 0.9$; $p < 0.01$).

Ianiro *et al.* (2013, 2015), Ianiro and Kauffeld (2014), Gessnitzer *et al.* (2016), Gessnitzer and Kauffeld (2015), Will *et al.* (2016), Will *et al.* (2019) and Jordan and Kauffeld (2020) show that certain coach feelings (rated by the coaches themselves) and coach behaviours (rated by neutral observers) lead to greater effectiveness: dominant-friendly and positive-supportive behaviour (as defined by Leary, 1957), similarity of behaviours of dominance and affiliation (which also leads to a better coaching relationship as rated by the clients), a coach's calm and positive mood, empathy in terms of paraphrasing and naming feelings, support for self-efficacious statements, and solution-focused questions. Note that in their research client ratings of the relationship and of effectiveness were often only made after 5 sessions whilst coach behaviours were measured in the first session, which indicates causality in their findings. Vande Walle *et al.* (2020) also found coach 'constructive' styles on the same Leary circle to be more effective, but only for first coaching sessions. Hooijberg and Lane (2009) confirm that their clients wanted their coach to be actively involved in interpretation and action plans, i.e. to be 'dominant-friendly' as well.

Weer *et al.* (2016) in a very large and longitudinal experiment found both a direct negative effect from pressure-based managerial coaching as rated by the team on the slope of (manager-rated) team effectiveness over time: $\delta = -0.47$; $p < 0.05$ and an indirect opposite effect of pressure-based versus facilitative managerial coaching as rated by the team, through team commitment, on the slope of (manager-rated) team effectiveness over time: $\delta = 0.87$; $p < 0.001$). Several studies build on this and show that both solution-focused questions and creating feel-good, positive environments do indeed make clients feel better and more positive (Grant, 2012; Ianiro *et al.*, 2013; Jack *et al.* 2013; Howard, 2015; Braunstein & Grant, 2016; Theeboom *et al.*, 2016; Grant & O'Connor, 2018), show more interest in change (Will *et al.*, 2019), come to more solutions themselves (Jordan & Kauffeld, 2020), and in some cases become more resourceful at coming up with cognitive solutions (Theeboom *et al.*, 2016), but there is not much evidence from research that they will actually solve their problems better and more quickly through so-called solution-focused interventions. Technical solution-focused questions seem to have the same effect as the induction of a positive climate through imagining a positive recent event (Grant & O'Connor, 2018) and quite possibly of being warm, positive, and visioning- or strengths-oriented (Jack *et al.* 2013; Howard, 2015).

So, in conclusion, clients want the techniques of the coach to come across as positive and helpful, they benefit when the coach is generally confident and friendly, and they will respond differently to 'instruction' type interventions than to 'facilitation' type interventions; i.e. to generally directive versus nondirective coaching.

It is worth looking separately at differences between 'coach techniques' and 'trainer techniques':

> Several experiments have shown that individual coaching has clear demonstrable benefits over and above group training: Olivero *et al.* (1997), Taie (2011), Poluka and Kaifi (2015), Losch *et al.* (2016) and Zanchetta *et al.* (2020). This would show that a more client-tailored approach to learning and a one-to-one relationship which involves typical coaching behaviours (i.e. more listening, summarising, exploring, hypothesising behaviours as compared with training and teaching) can lead to a very substantial uptick in transfer, effectiveness, or productivity. Hui *et al.* (2013) and Zanchetta *et al.* (2020) in particular show that training (or in Hui *et al.*'s 2013 case, 'guidance coaching') is more helpful with cognitive acquisition whilst coaching helps more with dissimilar or new cognitive tasks (Hui *et al.*, 2013), and with individual strategies, goal attainment and impostor tendencies in young employees (Zanchetta *et al.*, 2020).

Conversely to coaching helping with training and instruction, there is also some evidence that training and instruction can help with coaching: Franklin and Doran (2009) show that active help (teaching) of future coachees including some preparation for change and adaptive learning leads to better results in terms of objective performance of the coachees (on their student marks).

Finally, self-coaching – i.e. coaching as prescribed 'home work' without a coach – has been found to be significantly effective when compared with a no-coaching control group (Willms, 2004) but also as less effective than coaching by a coach, when directly compared (Sue-Chan & Latham, 2004; Losch *et al.*, 2016)

Third factor: personality of the coachee

Scoular and Linley (2006) found some effects for personality dissimilarities between coach and client as measured by their MBTI preferences. However, this result was not replicated by other, larger studies looking into MBTI (De Haan *et al.*, 2013, 2016, 2019; Vande Walle *et al.*, 2020); in fact, even contradicted by Vande Walle *et al.* (2020), who found that personality dissimilarities between coach and client on the MBTI were actually less effective, but only for one dimension (judging versus perceiving) and only for first coaching sessions. Neither the MBTI preference of the coachee, nor the MBTI type preference of the coach, nor the MBTI matching differences between coaches and coachees, could be shown to make anything but tiny differences to coaching outcome: in the larger-scale research (De Haan *et al.*, 2019) the only small but significant results ($p < 0.02$) that were found seem to indicate that extraverted coaches and coachees achieve more agreement on tasks within the working alliance, which is perhaps a consequence of interacting more. Furthermore, coaches with an intuition preference may achieve slightly higher outcomes, and the feeling-feeling match seems to result in the highest bond, yet at the same time also in the lowest effectiveness. More generally, MBTI preferences have been critiqued as lacking the required validity to be amenable to quantitative research (Pittenger, 2005).

Stewart *et al.* (2008) found positive effects for conscientiousness, openness, emotional stability within the Big Five personality model. Jones *et al.* (2014) also asked coachees to complete a Big Five personality model questionnaire and found a significant link only between extraversion and perceived effectiveness ($p < 0.05$; $N = 30$). Jones *et al.* (2019) replicated this with a control group, but could only demonstrate significance for openness (despite also measuring conscientiousness and emotional stability), and in terms of only self-rated performance (and not line-manager rated performance).

De Haan *et al.* (2019) also found weak yet significant relationships between coachee personality and outcome for some bright-side personality factors, namely adjustment, ambition, and interpersonal sensitivity, broadly confirming the results by Stewart *et al.* (2008). However, these findings were relatively small and not consistent over all times and sources, so it is too early to interpret them.

Rank and Gray (2017) found that clients low in self-presentation ability (charm) may benefit more from coaching even though they give lower satisfaction scores. Similarly, Buljac-Samardzic and Van Woerkom (2015) and Carson *et al.* (2007) showed that if levels of reflection and support (respectively) are low in teams then team coaching has a much higher impact towards the team's effectiveness. The coachee's implicit person theory (IPT) has also been shown to make a difference as an IPT in accordance with coaching style strengthens the effects of that style, i.e. a 'fixed' IPT strengthens the link between 'guidance' coaching and 'fixed' tasks, whilst an 'incremental' IPT strengthens the link between 'facilitation' coaching and 'adaptive' tasks (Hui *et al.*, 2019).

In summary, for client personality there are several first indications that personality as rated on Big Five personality dimensions does impact significantly on the expected outcomes, with openness, emotional stability, extraversion, conscientiousness, adjustment, ambition, and interpersonal sensitivity all found to correlate significantly but weakly with coaching outcomes. Nearly no significance has been found though for the much less validated MBTI model of 'personality type.'

Other than these basic building blocks of client personality, there are some indications that low 'charm' and low levels of reflection may lead to a fertile ground for coaching, with higher impact of coaching interventions.

Finally, there are also some first indications, e.g. Hoven *et al.* (2014) and Poluka and Kaifi (2015) that people from a higher educational background benefit more from coaching.

Fourth factor: general preparedness and motivation on the side of coachees

There is a wide-ranging research literature around the topic of client 'preparedness' or 'psychological capital', including measures of self-esteem, self-efficacy, emotional stability, internal locus of control, resilience, perceived support around the client, motivation, hope, general well-being, health, happiness, etcetera. The first four of these are sometimes called 'core self-evaluations' (see, e.g., McGonagle *et al.*, 2014; MacKie, 2015; Tee *et al.*, 2017). The active ingredient for this effect is not very well known; we may be dealing with personality aspects like resilience, robustness, even bloody-mindedness, or with attachment styles, or with optimism or even narcissism, we do not know. The measurements are usually done at a time well before the beginning of coaching, so we can exclude momentary shifts in motivation, mood, and optimism as the source of these effects.

Smith and Brummel (2013) found that expectancy and hope were related to outcome. MacKie (2015) reported a statistically significant relationship between client 'readiness' and client core self-evaluations (Self-esteem, Self-efficacy, Emotional stability, Internal locus of control) and coaching effectiveness, but this could not be replicated by Tee *et al.* in two studies with similar sample sizes (2017, 2019). A major difference may have been the fact that in the Tee *et al.* studies students were used as (peer) coaches, whilst Mackie made use of professional, experienced coaches from a business school. Jones *et al.* (2019) found the opposite, namely that coachees with lower core self-evaluations (and an avoid goal orientation) benefited more from the coaching. Braunstein and Grant (2016) also looked at expectancies, namely the difference between approach and avoid goals, but found no difference. It seems the picture for core self-evaluations and (avoid) goal orientations is very mixed at this point.

Some more consistent findings are around self-scored learning goal orientation and pre-coaching motivation, which were correlated to better outcomes in terms of self-reported job performance, according to Bozer *et al.* (2013). Scriffignano (2011) confirmed the former: the coachee's learning goal orientation (focus on development and mastery) correlated with outcome, whilst performance goal orientation (focus on achieving goals and comparison with others) did not. Sonesh *et al.* (2015) confirmed the latter, i.e. also found coachee motivation to be correlated with outcomes (but only for the student sample not for the industry sample).

Stewart *et al.* (2008), Leonard-Cross (2010), Baron and Morin (2009), Bozer *et al.* (2013), De Haan *et al.* (2013, 2016, 2019), Mackie (2015) and Zimmermann and Antoni (2020) all found moderate to large significant effects for general self-efficacy as an independent variable. All those who compared the strength of the self-efficacy contribution with relationship factors, such as Baron and Morin (2009), De Haan *et al.* (2013, 2016, 2019) and Zimmermann and Antoni (2020), found that self-efficacy was significantly related to outcome, but weaker than the working alliance (see the following for relationship ingredients such as the working alliance), which tended to mediate the self-efficacy direct effects.

Taylor (1997) found indications that a coachee's *resilience* and Willms (2004) that a coachee's *persistence* correlates with better outcomes. De Haan *et al*. (2019) found significant effects for coachee well-being, resilience and perceived social support, which were again mediated in full by the coaching relationship (working alliance).

Smith and Brummel (2013) show a better coaching experience significantly correlating with coachee-scored executive involvement, perceptions of developability and individual development plans.

Conversely, dysfunctional attitudes in the coachee have been showed to lower the effectiveness of problem-focused coaching questions whilst solution-focused questions are relatively immune to those attitudes (Grant & Gerrard, 2020).

In summary, one could argue that every single preparedness variable that has been proposed (hope, expectancy, motivation, self-esteem, emotional stability, internal locus of control, perceptions of developability, self-efficacy, learning goal orientation, functional attitudes, coachee well-being, resilience, and perceived social support) correlated significantly with coaching outcome in the overwhelming majority of studies. Incidentally all these self-scored variables also tend to correlate (and strongly!) with one another, so there may be only one or very few underpinning 'preparedness' variables if one could look at the whole gamut of measurements and do a factor analysis.

All in all there is something worryingly elitist about these results because they do seem to show that a coachee who is already robust and resilient, a coachee who is relatively optimistic and can self-motivate, will do better in executive coaching. Logically, this means that a pre-existing 'preparedness gap' is only going to grow through coaching. Given that the provision of coaching in many organisations is already skewed towards the top layers, we do need to think about an equity gap in coaching and its consequences for the organisations we work in.

Fifth factor: coach-client matching and diversity

Boyce *et al*. (2010) analysed the impact of matching criteria (demographic commonality, behavioural compatibility, and coach credibility), on coaching outcome. Their main findings were that matching had no significant impact on outcome. Chinn *et al*. (2015) support this by showing the external coach's relevant professional and industry experience as a choice criterion in matching does not correlate with outcome and even that shared coach-client professional or industry experiences do not predict the client's goal achievement.

There is more evidence against external matching coming out of the MBTI studies where coach-coachee matches on the MBTI preferences are being compared – and no correlations with outcome are found (De Haan *et al*., 2013, 2016, 2019). The only indication that personality matching might work comes out of one finding that a 'motivational match' between the coachee's implicit person theories and the coach's guidance versus facilitation style moderates the coaching effectiveness (Hui *et al*., 2019).

Gender match: Toegel and Nicholson (2005) found a small positive effect on outcomes for same-gender coaching pairs, and De Haan *et al*. (2016) a tiny positive effect for female coaches who achieved higher outcomes as compared to male coaches; $\delta = 0.12$; $p < 0.05$). Other studies that analyse gender match are Gray and Goregaokar (2010), Bozer *et al*. (2015; based on the same dataset as Bozer *et al*., 2013), and De Haan *et al*. (2019). However, these studies all conclude that the coach-coachee match has little effect on coaching outcomes.

So, in conclusion, neither demographical matching, nor personality matching, nor gender matching, seems to have a profound impact on the coaching relationship. This is an important finding because it suggests that all 'outside' matching by third parties, such as coaching firms or HR professionals, is unnecessary and possibly unhelpful. The best way of matching a coachee to a coach seems to be by making use of the next factor: the emerging relationship. This means offering the coachee a few coaches (suitably qualified coaches) to meet and choose between.

Sixth factor: coach-client relationship during coaching

Boyce *et al.* (2010) found that relationship trust and rapport, as assessed by both client ($\delta = 2$ and $p < 0.01$) and coach ($\delta = 1.2$ and $p < 0.01$), affected outcomes significantly. Baron and Morin (2009) and De Haan *et al.* (2013, 2016, 2019) confirmed a significant relationship between client-rated working alliance and coaching outcomes. These findings are confirmed by Sonesh *et al.* (2015) who found that client-rated working alliance was related to client-rated outcome and Zimmermann and Antoni (2020) who found that the coach's relationship scores were related to client-rated outcome. In Baron and Morin's 2009 (relatively small) sample, coaches' ratings of the working alliance did not correlate with outcomes significantly. Trust is also confirmed as a variable related to outcome by Kim and Kuo (2015), for managerial coaching.

De Haan *et al.* (2013, 2016, 2019) showed with three different samples that client and coach perceptions of the working alliance were significantly related to client perceptions of client-assessed coaching effectiveness ($\delta = 1.4$ and $p < 0.01$ for client estimates of working alliance WAI; $\delta = 0.4$ and $p < 0.01$ for coach-estimates of WAI; see De Haan *et al.*, 2016, 2019). Moreover, De Haan *et al.*, 2019, even found a correlation between line-manager estimated coaching effectiveness and coach-estimates of WAI ($\delta = 0.6$ and $p < 0.05$). Baron and Morin (2009) and De Haan *et al.* (2013, 2019) show that the client-coach relationship strongly mediated the impact of self-efficacy, well-being, perceived social support, demographic matching (on compatibility and credibility; Boyce *et al.*, 2010), the coach's psychological mindedness (Sonesh *et al.*, 2015), and the majority of the coach's techniques on coaching outcomes (except for perceived explicit focus on goals and helping the client to make discoveries; De Haan *et al.*, 2013), suggesting that the relationship is a key factor in coaching outcome. Working alliance – particularly as seen through the eyes of the coachee – appears to be a key ingredient in effectiveness. In one study, De Haan *et al.* (2016), the task and goal aspects of the working alliance were stronger predictors of positive CE than the bond aspects.

On the other hand, Grant (2014b) found that satisfaction with a coach-coachee relationship did not predict successful coaching effectiveness, although bonding aspects of the relationship ('autonomy support') did predict effectiveness. Also, in De Haan *et al.* (2016) the bonding aspects of the working alliance were slightly but significantly more weakly related to outcome.

Similarly, Gessnitzer and Kauffeld (2015) found that coachee-initiated goals and tasks as scored by objective observers were positively related to coaching success. However, coach-initiated goals and tasks had the opposite effect. They also found that bonding behaviours did not influence coaching success. However, Gan and Chong (2015) found that rapport and coachee commitment were correlated significantly with effectiveness in the clients' minds. Conversely, Graßmann and Schermuly (2016) show that relationship quality as rated by clients was inversely proportional to the number of negative side effects they reported at two times during their coaching.

Clearly, there is convincing evidence that relationship factors such as in the three subscales of the Working Alliance Inventory (agreement on tasks, agreement on goals, bond) and other relationship aspects such as rapport and trust, have a significant relationship to outcome which is so strong that it tends to mediate other client-related ingredients such as coachee motivation, self-efficacy, well-being and perceived social support, and client-coach matching. Moreover, in different studies the working alliance measures from the coachee, the coach, and an observer looking at video recordings of coaching sessions (Gessnitzer & Kauffeld, 2015) were found in a diversity of settings to correlate with effectiveness scores as measured by clients, coaches, and even line managers (De Haan et al., 2019). So, the working-alliance coaching outcome relationship seems to be robust to different sources and ways of measuring, even though we also know that there is little – yet consistently and significantly positive – correlation between working-alliance scores from coaches, coachees, and observers.

All of these findings together have led to various authors pronouncing the coach-coachee relationship as the 'best predictor' of coaching outcome (McKenna & Davis, 2009; De Haan & Duckworth, 2013), particularly if it is the coaching relationship as rated by the client (De Haan, 2008). The coaching relationship certainly seems the 'active ingredient' that shows the greatest effect sizes. Moreover, it is one of the few ingredients that coach and coachee can influence together – and will influence, all the time! – during the coaching work, so it seems an ingredient of great import for coaches to know about. Hence, I will devote the next chapter to this single active ingredient in coaching. I will show that more recent research has also thrown some doubt and controversy on the importance of the 'coaching relationship as seen by the client.' It now seems working alliance may be just another one of those coachee-related factors, such as 'preparedness' or 'psychological capital' (see the fourth factor, earlier) and therefore may not measure the actual relationship between coachee and coach nearly as well as we think.

Seventh factor: systemic or organisational influences

The rapid growth of executive coaching over the past three decades seems to indicate that coaching is mostly helpful in the modern, volatile, uncertain, knowledge-intensive service economy, and that certain jobs where perhaps more complex and strategic decisions need to be made lend themselves most for coaching support. However, there has not been a lot of research into the organisational context most conducive to executive coaching. Liu and Batt (2010) also showed that the performance effect of coaching was stronger when line managers made greater use of group rewards, when work automation was lower (i.e. independent decision making was higher), and when process changes were less frequent (perhaps to do with the fact that this was managerial coaching or mentoring and the knowledge transfer would become quickly obsolete with more frequent process changes). These are some first indications of an area that really merits a lot more research.

Conversely, there are some indications of 'ripple effects' back from coaching towards peers and colleagues and further into the organisation (O'Connor & Cavanagh, 2013), which we will look at more in Chapter 4.

Finally, Wageman (2001) was able to show that, provided a good team design (structure) is in place, the leader's coaching of the team can help a great deal, but if such structures are not there then coaching matters little.

Summary of Chapter 2: 'What works in executive coaching?'

In this chapter another 125 original and empirical coaching-research reports have been reviewed, and with the collection grown to 160 coaching outcome research studies, we have a much better idea of the many factors that have been shown to be significant within the coach-coachee contract:

1. The **coach** and his or her personality, psychological mindset, changeability views, and credibility/reputation/background/age
2. The **technique** of the coach, specifically the added value of
   a. coaching versus instruction (the latter including teaching and training)
   b. positive, solution-focused techniques versus more critical, problem-focused techniques
   c. dominant-friendly techniques versus hostile-submissive techniques
3. The **coachee** and his or her personality or background
4. The general **preparedness** and motivation of the coachee
5. The coach-client **matching** and diversity
6. The coach-client **relationship** during coaching
7. The **organisation**: systemic or organisational influences

In this chapter we also reviewed the full set of 160 rigorous research articles to identify the **active ingredients** within those factors.

The active ingredients that have now been most rigorously demonstrated are, in order of declining importance:

- **Generally positive relationship quality** between coach and client: trust, rapport, bonding, agreement on tasks, agreement on goals ($\delta > 0.6$);
- The coach's **reputation** ($\delta = 0.6$ in one case) and change mindset ($\delta = 0.8$);
- Generally positive, friendly, visioning techniques of the coach – or being **warm and welcoming and confident**;
- A small contribution from the **coachee's personality, e.g. openness**, emotional stability, extraversion, conscientiousness, adjustment, ambition, and interpersonal sensitivity ($\delta = 0.4$);
- **Preparedness** by the coachee: hope, motivation, self-esteem, self-efficacy, learning goal orientation, well-being, resilience, and perceived social support ($\delta = 0.2$);
- Another even smaller contribution from the coachee's **diversity**: female coachees and coachees with higher education do slightly better ($\delta = 0.12$).
- **Conducive organisations,** where e.g. line managers made greater use of group rewards, when work automation was lower, and when process changes were less frequent.

The next chapter of this book will go into a lot more detail regarding the most intriguing, perhaps strongest one of these, the only one that coach and client can influence at any moment during their coaching work, namely the **relationship between coach and coachee.**

Notes

1 This is the only reference in this book that I was not able to read in full. I base myself on long summaries kindly communicated to me by the project's supervisor, Siegfried Greif.
2 This phenomenon has also been found in psychotherapy, e.g. Goldberg *et al.* (2016), where other explanations are given than the one in George *et al.* (2020).

An interlude before Chapter 3

The quality of the coaching relationship is often regarded as a prime ingredient for good coaching results. I have noticed in my work as an executive coach how much difference a good working relationship makes. And how it seems important for coach and coachee to be able to reflect on the here-and-now relationship in the room; and to explore this relationship as a lens through which we can view the coachee's work patterns and relationships. I have been researching the working alliance as one manifestation of the coaching relationship for more than a decade. Once, in 2014, collecting data for the De Haan *et al*. (2016) large-scale study on the impact of the working alliance on coaching effectiveness, I found an interesting counterexample to our pervasive view at the time that the working alliance is related to effectiveness.

As part of our research we offered participating coaches a confidential and anonymous insight into their own effectiveness as coaches. Once we had obtained ten matched questionnaires from ten different clients of a coach, about aspects like working alliance, self-efficacy, and effectiveness, we offered the coach an overview of their average scores from those ten coachees. The coaches could request a phone call if they were not clear about the findings, which was helpful to some since not every practicing coach was used to reading the response patterns to validated questionnaires and the correlation coefficients that we could share with them.

In one of those phone conversations, I spoke with a coach who had slightly below-average effectiveness scores, but his relationship scores were much lower, nearly 50% below the average and generally quite concerning, particularly for the 'bond' dimension of the working-alliance measure. This was the reason why he had requested a conversation, and I could see that the pattern was applicable across all of his ten or more clients. On further questioning, it emerged that this was a coach who did mainly *remedial* coaching work. To be precise, he worked with senior managers who were being given a final chance to keep their jobs by taking sessions with him and demonstrating that they can improve as a result. The way of working and the tone in which this coach described his customary direct feedback to his clients about their performance sounded tough and frightful to me. It appeared almost astounding that this coach's effectiveness scores were nevertheless hovering just under the average. That could probably be best explained by the fact that many of his clients did indeed manage to keep their jobs, by working productively with this coach, as he confirmed.

The remainder of our conversation was devoted to whether it is possible to coach clients who are backed up against the wall in such a way, whilst maintaining or even strengthening the relationship. He explained that it worked very well for him and that he obtained many referrals from his client organisations. He added that even though he focused very much on the negative, certainly initially, he thought his clients did experience him as frank, honest, and entirely on their sides. We wondered together if it would be possible to obtain the same results as so far, whilst building higher relationship scores. In other words, would it be possible for the coach to give the same feedback in such a way that it actually strengthened the relationship? The coach concluded that he might try this by showing more explicit warmth and empathy whilst at the same time still addressing the shortcomings of his coachees (in the eyes of himself, their clients, direct reports, or bosses). He seemed to find a new initiative for his work: by assuring the coachees more explicitly that, as a coach, he commits himself entirely to his coachee, and therefore is only trying to help him or her learn and grow and keep their jobs, even under very difficult circumstances.

Chapter 3

The coaching relationship as 'best predictor'? How does the working alliance help to achieve outcomes?

The coaching relationship in the form of the 'working alliance' between coach and coachee has been proposed as the best predictor of coaching outcomes and the foremost active ingredient that coach and coachee can influence and optimise during their work together. This chapter investigates that claim. Even though working alliance is indeed a very good predictor of overall outcome from coaching, we find little evidence that sessional changes are predicted by the working alliance from session to session. From two recent studies, which are the only ones to have measured the working alliance over time, from both a coach and a client perspective, we have to conclude that there is no correlation between 'working alliance' and 'outcome increase per session.' The same has been observed in several psychotherapy studies. If this is generally true then the working alliance is only related to overall outcome and may have much more to do with a response bias (through general trust or optimism) than with a proper driver or active ingredient of coaching outcomes.

Part A: some controversies

As we have seen, there is now a lot of evidence for the coaching relationship as the 'container' or a 'vehicle' for the coachee to achieve his or her goals and other results with coaching. This goes back to the original definition of coaching as offering a 'vehicle' (literally, a 'coach' – a word originating from the Hungarian village Kocs where very good coaches/carriages were once made) for learning and development. The coaching environment or relationship is then the direct surrounding of the coachee, where space is offered, conditions are peaceful and reflective and safe, so that the coachee can do his or her own work to forge ahead with the goals. The relational field is increasingly seen as the core active ingredient for coaching, particularly in the way that it is experienced by the client. To measure this ingredient we need to ask, is the relationship clear and helpful and conducive, is it pleasant, is it agreeable, wholesome, secure?

As mentioned before, the most widely used tool to measure the coaching relationship in coaching is the Working Alliance Inventory (WAI; Horvath & Greenberg, 1986) which consists of three subscales: Task, Goal, and Bond. The term *Task* refers to what coach and coachee agree needs to be done for the coachee to reach his or her goals for coaching. A typical item is, 'I am clear as to what my coach wants me to do in these sessions.' The term *Goal* refers to the outcomes that the coachee hopes to gain from coaching. A typical item is, 'The goals of these sessions are important to me.' The term *Bond* refers to what extent the coachee trusts, respects, and feels confidence in the other person. A typical item is, 'I believe my coach is genuinely concerned for my welfare.'

A lot of the discussion around the coaching relationship has been driven by earlier and much more extensive work in psychotherapy outcome (McKenna & Davis, 2009). There is now a very strong evidence base in psychotherapy showing that working alliance as perceived by the patient is a very good predictor for outcome ($\delta \approx 0.6$; $p < 0.001$; Flückiger et al., 2020).

All of this started with a broad summary of the psychotherapy outcome literature that Michael Lambert made in 1992. In his summary which took the form of what became an influential pie chart (see Figure 3.1), he suggested that 40% of change through therapy would be 'extra-therapeutic' (i.e. due to support and life's circumstances outside the therapy), 30% would be due to 'common factors' to all therapies, including the therapeutic relationship, 15% would be due to techniques, and 15% would be due to expectancy (the 'placebo' effect). An updated version of this pie chart, based on much more research since 1992, is displayed in Figure 3.2. It shows that the extra-therapeutic factors have now rightly been left out of the pie chart (although they are still considered to be the strongest influences on therapy even if they come from the outside) and the expectancy effect is not made explicit anymore, since it cannot be distinguished from other (personality) factors in the client, something we also saw in Chapter 2 (we cannot determine if expectancy, motivation, hope, and preparedness factors are part of the personality of the client but we can attribute them clearly to the client). In the new figure we can see that there is now broad consensus in psychotherapy research that the patient contribution is the largest, around 30%, that the relationship is the next largest single factor (12%), and that the therapist contribution (7%) is around the same size on average as the technique contribution (8%).

What works in executive coaching? 89

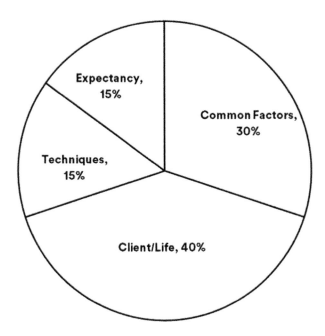

Figure 3.1 The Lambert pie chart from 1992 estimating the different active ingredients in therapy, with relationship 'common factors' on 30%.

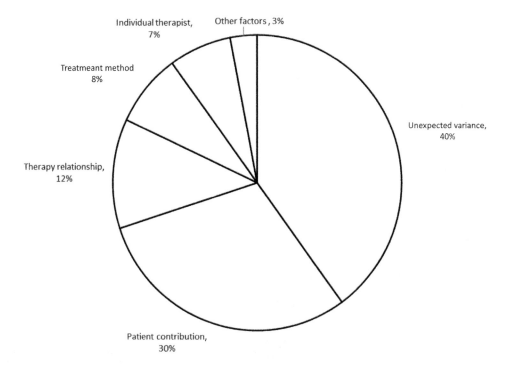

Figure 3.2 The updated Lambert pie chart (Norcross, 2011) with the therapy relationship on 12%, which is the largest contribution to do with the therapy itself.

In this chapter we will take a closer look at the coaching relationship and what we now know about its importance for coaching outcome. But first let us look at some broader controversies amongst scientists which pertain to the coaching relationship measurement.

Controversy 1: does the 'medical model' apply?

One important controversy surrounds, rather fundamentally, the 'medical model' upon which outcome measurements are based. Randomised controlled trials in medicine usually try to measure if a specific chemical compound, or a few compounds, can make a measurable and significant difference to our health. This type of research is based on *specific* ingredients and traceable, identifiable, *linear* reactions which can be measured and isolated as the 'cause' behind a working ingredient's effectiveness. When it comes to the helping professions, we have very few specifics that we can measure. Only with highly manualised treatment methods (or maybe in the future in robotic applications where every specific intervention can be measured and kept constant in terms of e.g. timing and duration from session to session) can we research specifics. However, manualised treatments are unpopular and even demonstrated to be inferior in psychotherapy, partly because of their rigidity and limitations in terms of moving with what the patient brings to the session. Nevertheless, current research findings are interpreted by some as only intermediary steps towards measuring something specific about coaching assignments. For more information about the medical versus contextual model controversy, see Wampold (2001).

To restate the controversy in different words, contextual common factors such as 'client preparedness,' 'coach personality,' or 'coaching relationship' are seen by some as too soft, too general, too vague, to ever be of use in the measurement of active ingredients. For instance, if we find (as we do) that the quality of the coaching relationship makes a measurable difference to outcomes, could that not be due to *specific* aspects of that relationship, such as the specific yes-or-no agreement on specific goals for the sessions? Or do we really have to assume that something as vague, loose, and multifaceted as 'the coaching relationship' is the smallest 'unit' of measurement, which cannot be broken down further? Many operationalisations of a positive coaching relationship have nevertheless been put forward, of which the most common is the Working Alliance Inventory, short or long version, which has been used in most of the coaching research described in this book (an exception being Boyce *et al.*, 2010, which simply used a six-item measurement of rapport, trust and commitment altogether).

Controversy 2: does the 'therapy model' apply?

Another controversy surrounds how relevant it is to look at psychotherapy outcome research to understand outcomes of executive coaching. Some will say they both belong to the wider helping professions, and nothing contradictory has been found in both fields. Others are much more sceptical and quote the many differences in training and practice. In any case, with a growing research base of our own in executive coaching, as summarised in earlier chapters, we have less and less of a need to look over to psychotherapy to understand best predictors such as the coaching relationship. On the other hand, psychotherapy research has shown that researchers sometimes need data from many thousands of patients to report truly significant predictions. And when it comes to the relationship or working alliance, there is a sense in psychotherapy that there are still major controversies to be resolved, because there are so few longitudinal studies that can really explore the relevance of that therapeutic relationship from session to session. We will come back to this later in this chapter.

In an attempt to address this controversy, I have decided in this book not to base conclusions on psychotherapy research and instead to include only relevant research from more adjacent, workplace-related fields than psychotherapy, in particular managerial coaching (in Chapter 2) and mentoring (in this chapter), to give the widest possible interpretation of coaching results and not to rely on psychotherapy studies.

Controversy 3: causality is still open to debate

Talking about the 'coaching relationship' as the 'best' predictor of outcome and the 'only' predictor that can be influenced during the sessions, seems to be somewhat premature when we have not even established causality. Nearly all significant findings in coaching and most findings in psychotherapy have been based on a single measurement of the Working Alliance, usually at the beginning of the work, e.g. after session one (or, as in Boyce et al., 2010, at the very end of coaching). That is not enough to establish prediction of later outcomes, certainly not enough to predict improvement from session to session. Authors such as Gessnitzer and Kauffeld (2015) and De Haan et al. (2019) have argued that because working alliance was measured independently (by coaches or observers of video recordings) and at an early stage, and was then found to correlate with effectiveness assessed by the coachee at a much later stage, there was evidence for prediction and causality. But this need not be the case: it is impossible to exclude the possibility that clients who are more motivated also rate the coaching relationship more highly, irrespective of coaching results. As long as they then maintain this more positive view of the sessions, they will also register higher outcomes at the end. This could be independent of their observing any difference through coaching or achieving any of their own outcomes of the sessions.

As Flückiger et al. (2020) also confirm, most of the relationship measurements in psychotherapy have also been done only once in every therapeutic or coaching contract, usually at the beginning. Whenever we have only one measurement we cannot rule out that this aspect is only relevant in a general sense – and also we cannot rule out 'reverse causality,' i.e. in this case, better coaching outcomes causing a better coaching relationship.

Controversy 4: the puzzle of 'the' relationship

It is easy to talk about 'the' coaching relationship and that is what researchers, coaches, and coachees tend to do. The psychometric questionnaires confirm this idea as they ask participants in research to give 'the' relationship aspects a number, in the case of the Working Alliance Inventory on a scale from one to seven. On the other hand, we know from all the findings that coach, coachee, and observer ratings of the relationship do not strongly correlate: Gessnitzer and Kauffeld (2015) find correlations which are positive but below 0.11 for measurements by these three parties, and De Haan et al. (2016, 2019) find positive correlations between coach and client ratings of WAI well below 0.24 for all measurements at different times. All correlations between relationship measures seem to be significantly positive (see De Haan et al., 2016, which has the largest sample), but small.

So, truthfully, there is no 'coaching relationship': we are all sitting in this 'vehicle' for development, and seeing it from a different angle, feeling and seeing different aspects of the encounter. Whenever we talk about 'the' coaching relationship or a client and coach relating to each other and enjoying rapport or trust, we should add from whose perspective this is the case. Is this what an observer seeing a recording registers? Is it what the coachee feels or what the coach experiences? These are likely all very different views on the same shared space, and they are not the same. Studies in psychotherapy have shown that clients' views of the relationship are more stable than their therapists' views (Martin *et al.*, 2000) and that successful clients experience generative ruptures during the work, so that they tend to go from a relatively high alliance, to a lower alliance, and back and forth, ending on a relatively high alliance again (Stiles *et al.*, 2004).

Controversy 5: what is the core of 'the' relationship?

Working alliances have been studied in many guises and under many aspects, and even though the proposed factors such as agreement, rapport, bonding, trust, etcetera, strongly correlate with each other, they do pick up different aspects of the relationship as well. The relationship between different aspects of the working-alliance scores and CE found in Grant (2014b), Gessnitzer and Kauffeld (2015), and De Haan *et al.* (2016) show that the bond aspect of the coach-coachee alliance (as measured by the amount of autonomy support experienced by the coachee) was a less powerful predictor of effectiveness than the agreement-focused aspects of the coach-coachee alliance.

Controversy 6: how to optimise the relationship factor

If I know the coaching relationship is important, what does that tell me about how to use it? Should I make it pleasant and smooth? Or can a modicum of challenge, a 'negative emotional attractor' (Howard, 2015), provided I maintain the positive relationship, also help to allow my client more perspectives? And how does the coaching relationship interact with the more 'relational' work that I do as a coach? What about making explicit use of the relationship by meta-communicating, about the here-and-now, about our contract (agreement on goals and tasks), or about our relationship (rapport, bond)? Is that a good thing? Or is it only good when I can do this in such a way that I also strengthen that relationship?

It is important to realise that even if we know that the coaching relationship predicts measurable outcomes of coaching, the learning for coaches is not straightforward. The client is saying that agreement on tasks, agreement on goals, and a positive rapport are important, but what that means for us coaches is not fully clear. Agreements on goals and tasks seem to point to contracting on these matters, and indeed meta-communicating on the nature of the goals and tasks as the client sees them. Importance of the working alliance may mean that we coaches should ask the client regularly what his or her expectations are, what would be a good outcome, which objectives for every session, etcetera.

Really unclear on the basis of existing statistics pertaining to the coaching relationship is whether 'relational' interventions can be helpful and important for the coaching relationship. Reviewing with the client what the here-and-now relationship feels like, what is happening between us in the moment in the room, may lead to further agreement and a better perceived relationship but it may also be unnecessarily challenging for clients. Unfortunately, so far, the value of 'relational' interventions has not been studied in quantitative outcome research.

Part B: what we need to know about this 'best predictor'

I would agree with Wampold (2001) that for the time being we need to stay with the contextual model and study broad common factors. Certainly at this time there is so little in coaching that we can specify and measure, in terms of specific 'techniques' – and even when we do and we measure 'technique' in coaching, we have mixed results for the specific techniques. So far, measurement of technique seems to point to the importance of a generally positive, dominant-friendly presence. If the coachee rates the relationship as positive, he or she seems to rate all techniques coming from the coach as equally positive (De Haan *et al.*, 2011).

A useful summary of all those general, contextual factors that one might study as part of the 'common factors' of coaching is as follows, following a classification by Grencavage and Norcross (1990):

1   Relationship-related factors

    a   development of a working alliance or helping relationship
    b   commitment to the relationship
    c   transference to the relationship

2   Coachee-related factors

    a   personal characteristics
    b   expectations of change ('hope')
    c   problem pressure and active contribution

3   Coach-related factors

    a   personal characteristics
    b   cultivation of the positive expectations of the coachee
    c   warmth, positive outlook, attention

4   Change-related factors

    a   possibility of expression and change
    b   acquiring new experiences and new behaviour
    c   acquiring a 'change rationale' inspired by ideology

5   Structure-related factors

    a   use of techniques, rituals and contracts
    b   focus on internal world and exploration of emotions
    c   commitment to a theory or ideology

94 Chapter 3: The coaching relationship as best predictor?

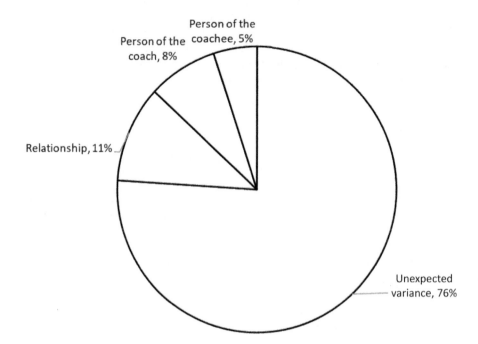

Figure 3.3 A first estimate of the 'Lambert pie chart' in coaching based on the estimates summarised in Chapter 2. Relationship aspects are on 11%, i.e. very similar to those found in psychotherapy.

Within the contextual model and those possible 'common factors,' Figure 3.3 shows the best estimate of active ingredients in executive coaching, based on the current effect sizes as summarised in the previous chapter (where I have added up personality, diversity, and preparedness factors for the coachee and converted to proportions of explained variance). The pie chart shows that for the time being we have a huge proportion of unexplained variance, which illustrates the many aspects of coaching that have not been sufficiently researched.

It seems from the evidence we have now that the relationship is the best predictor – not just in coaching; but also as briefly summarised earlier, in psychotherapy; and as we will see, in mentoring. Not only have we found the coaching relationship to be the most active ingredient, but it is perhaps the most useful as well for coach and coachee: unlike some of the other common factors it is always present and continuously evolving during a coaching conversation. Just like learning-, technique-, and change-related factors, it can be influenced at any moment of coaching, and it can be worked with explicitly by the coach, just by asking the coachee or by putting forward our own experience of the relationship.

Because it is such a fertile area for coaching, it is highly important now that we also establish causality. We need to demonstrate that the coaching relationship not only influences overall outcome, but also significantly impacts outcome from session to session. In the next section I will summarise new research into the coaching relationship that was designed to understand more about the impact from session to session.

Another area where work has already begun, is to see whether the coaching relationship can pick up demonstrable effects of other independent variables, through mediation. In Chapter 2 we have already seen six studies that showed that indeed the coaching relationship can pick up and mediate the predictions from coach-coachee demographics, coach psychological mindedness and techniques, and coachee self-efficacy, well-being, and perceived social support (Baron & Morin, 2009; Boyce *et al.*, 2010; Sonesh *et al.*, 2015; De Haan *et al.*, 2013, 2016, 2019).

Part C: overview of coaching relationship outcome research

1 A brief review of research on the coaching relationship

As we saw in Chapter 2, there is convincing evidence from nine independent sources that relationship factors have a significant relationship to outcome which is so strong that it tends to mediate other client-related ingredients such as coachee self-efficacy, well-being, and perceived social support, and client-coach matching. In different studies the working-alliance measures from the coachee, the coach, and an observer looking at video recordings of coaching sessions (Gessnitzer & Kauffeld, 2015) were found in a diversity of settings to correlate with effectiveness scores as measured by clients, coaches, and even line managers (De Haan *et al.*, 2019). There was a strong positive correlation between the coach-reported working alliance (WAI) and coaching effectiveness (CE) scores as measured by the coach, and the same for the coachees' experienced overall WAI and CE as measured by the coach. Moreover, the coachee's WAI also predicted CE as measured by the coachee at a much later time point. So, the working-alliance/coaching-outcome relationship seems to be robust to different sources and ways of measuring, even though we also know that there is little – yet consistently and significantly positive – correlation between working-alliance scores from coaches, coachees, and observers.

The older studies on the impact of the coaching relationship have recently been summarised in a meta-analysis (Graßmann *et al.*, 2020), which again shows consistently that working alliance (as measured by the Working Alliance Inventory, WAI) is linked to outcome. This is true for coachee-rated alliance (e.g. Baron & Morin, 2009; Boyce *et al.*, 2010; De Haan *et al.*, 2013), but also, to a lesser extent, for coach-rated alliance (Boyce *et al.*, 2010; Gessnitzer & Kauffeld, 2015; De Haan *et al.*, 2016, 2019), and even for observer-rated working alliance on the basis of video recordings (Gessnitzer & Kauffeld, 2015), so working alliance estimates seem to be powerfully related to outcome. Yet, they also seem to be independent between different stakeholders: coach, coachee, and observer ratings of WAI do not correlate significantly (e.g. Gessnitzer & Kauffeld, 2015; De Haan *et al.*, 2019).

2 A brief review of relevant mentoring outcome research

The previously discussed findings are further supported in the more extensive *mentoring* outcome literature reviewed by Allen *et al.* (2004), through a meta-analysis comprising 43 outcome studies of mentoring in the organisational and workplace domain. Taking only the studies with control groups they found generally small but significant effect sizes (e.g. $\delta = 0.67$ for the mentoring effect on number of promotions and $\delta = 0.41$ for the mentoring effect on career satisfaction). They also found the criterion measuring the mentoring relationship ('satisfaction with mentor') to be the best predictor of career outcomes ($\delta = 0.8$ for career mentoring and $\delta = 1.6$ for supportive or 'psychosocial' mentoring).

One thorough study of mentoring outcomes included by Allen et al. (2004), is Ragins et al. (2000) who studied a group of 1,162 professionals from a wide variety of organisations and looked at the effect of formal and informal mentoring relationships on a range of work and career attitudes. Of the respondents, 44% had an informal mentor, 9% a formal mentor as part of a mentoring programme, and 47% had no mentor. This last group was used as the control, which was therefore not randomised. Their results show that the crucial factor in effectiveness is the client's satisfaction with the mentoring relationship. In the absence of that factor, there were no demonstrable differences between professionals who were mentored and those who were not. If client satisfaction with the relationship is present, however, professionals clearly demonstrate more positive attitudes towards themselves (self-confidence), their work, promotion prospects, their organisation, and their career. These result patterns were again confirmed in a much larger meta-analysis, with $N > 10,000$ and including workplace, youth, and academic domains (Eby et al., 2008).

Gattellari et al. (2005) conducted an RCT study into 'peer coaching' (mentoring by more-educated peer doctors) focused on Australian general practitioners' use of evidence-based cancer screening and patient decision-making. There were 136 GPs in the intervention group and 140 GPs in the control group. When compared with the control group, those receiving mentoring were more likely to disclose to patients relevant facts previously identified by experts as essential to know before making a decision (some of these findings with four sigma accuracy; i.e. $p < 0.0001$). Moreover, GPs expressed greater confidence, lower levels of decisional conflict, and lower anxieties, so that patients could become more informed despite the risks and additional skills needed.

Vande Walle et al. (2020) recorded sessions of surgical coaching which were rated on effectiveness by experienced surgeons and coaches. In this study, coaches were much more senior in the same field, so I have ranked this study under 'mentoring.' They found some correlation between the coaching effectiveness and the MBTI similarity of coach and coachee and on the Life Style Inventory (which is based on the Leary, 1957, circle), the coach's 'constructive' style, but only for first sessions.

3 Longitudinal research on the coaching relationship

In a longitudinal RCT study reported on by De Haan et al. (2020), a group of 105 business-school students at a London university were coached by an equal number of qualified coaches, whilst another 105 students formed the control group. Data was collected over eight data points for all participants, enabling the researchers to establish the dose-effect change over the course of, and following the coaching sessions (see Figure 3.4). Responses were collected from both students and coaches, in order to overcome issues of purely self-reported measures. As reported in Chapter 1, effect sizes δ over the 6-month journey were between 0.9 and 1, indicating large effects.

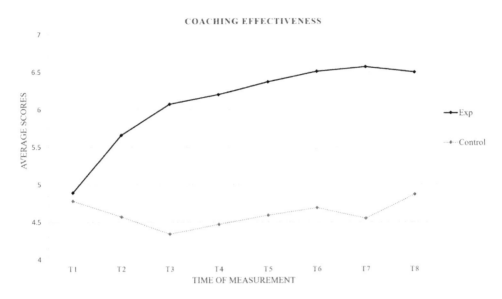

Figure 3.4 The first dose-effect curve in executive coaching, confirming clear benefits throughout the six coaching sessions and a diminishing return per session. Time T1 is before the first session, time T7 is shortly after the 6th session, and time T8 is a 3-month follow-up, which explains why the curve bends back.

Furthermore, in this study significant change was established on a range of parameters: coaching effectiveness, resilience, stress, and goal attainment scores. Again, there was unmistakable evidence for common factors contributing to this effectiveness, namely hope, outcome expectations, self-efficacy, perceived social support, and also the working alliance between coach and coachee.

However, there were also surprising findings. In this study and in the only other longitudinal study measuring the working alliance (Zimmermann & Antoni, 2020) it was only possible to detect significant predictions of working alliance ratings on the *levels* of effectiveness, not on the *change* in effectiveness during the course of coaching. This means it is now harder than before to associate working alliance with the effectiveness of coaching per se: working alliance did not correlate with the gains through coaching. I believe that this result, if replicated by still others, means that we will have to revise our thinking about coaching effectiveness profoundly.

In sum, *even though* coachee perceptions of the working alliance correlate with coaching outcome throughout; i.e. at different time points, even at much later time points, early working-alliance scores *do not correlate* with any *increase* in coaching outcome from the second session onwards (note: because coach and coachee need to have met and worked together before they can score their relationship, working alliance can only be measured after the first session). This can only be explained as working alliance being important in terms of a general readiness for coaching, i.e. for initial or average values of outcome, but not for the impact, the effectiveness of the coaching intervention itself.

There have been other doubts expressed about the use of working alliance over the years. There are different instruments and they measure different aspects of the alliance. In executive coaching there has been only correlational research into the impact of the alliance, involving only a single or a few measurements of WAI, and therefore causality is beyond the reach of most studies. One study in psychotherapy that did look into causality by measuring WAI and Outcome four times, found only a small yet significant link between working alliance and outcome (Zilcha-Mano *et al.*, 2014), just as we did.

4 An interpretation of these findings

I believe that working alliance has perhaps been misconstrued and misnamed as a relational variable, one that might tell us about the strength of the relationship in the coaching room. Instead, it is perhaps more justified to see it as a measure of a *coachee's propensity to relate*, i.e. not a relational variable but a client-related variable. The Working Alliance ratings by a coachee may tell us mostly about the coachee, about how disposed the coachee is, generally, towards a good working relationship, and how easily the coachee thinks s/he engages in a relationship that s/he rates positively (e.g. from the Agreement on Task, Agreement on Goal, and Bond perspectives). This picture is confirmed by the fact that coachee and coach scores of the working alliance only show a very limited correlation (De Haan *et al.*, 2016, 2019) and by the fact that observer scores behave differently from those of the coachee and coach (Gessnitzer & Kauffeld, 2015). It is like having observers or coaches estimating the coachee's self-efficacy, or well-being: they would struggle to do so in accordance with the coachee's own scores.

All earlier findings (summarised by Graßmann *et al.*, 2020) can now be understood in my view to show that coachees who say they 'relate' better also achieve better results in coaching, at least according to their own estimates, occasionally confirmed by their coaches and line managers. I think the Working Alliance Inventory may measure a relatively stable coachee personality 'trait,' because it seems rather stable and generalisable over time throughout therapy (Martin *et al.*, 2000; Crits-Christoph *et al.*, 2011), although it may also be measuring a more changeable aspect of personality, a 'state' (Zilcha-Mano, 2017). The fact that we found that working-alliance levels do tend to increase during the coaching journey (De Haan *et al.*, 2020)[1] confirms that there are movable, 'state'-like aspects present in WAI scores.

However, what is important for coaching outcome research is that the coachee's relationship scores *do not* seem to drive outcomes: the sense of relating well with their coach gives coachees a higher outcome over-all, but hardly impacts on further change by the sessions themselves (Zimmermann & Antoni, 2020; De Haan *et al.*, 2020). In fact, it was shown that the coachee's resilience scores are a much better predictor of outcome, to such an extent that most of the predictive power of other variables was picked up by Resilience which now seems to be a better 'mediator variable' for effectiveness than the relationship (De Haan *et al.*, 2020).

This helps to explain why so little evidence has been found for additional effectiveness to be had from particular 'matching' between coachee and coach (Boyce *et al.*, 2010; Page & De Haan, 2014; Bozer *et al.*, 2015): there are certain traits that give coachees an over-all increase in effectiveness (such as measured by working alliance, hope, self-efficacy, etcetera) but they are hardly further improved by the sessions themselves or by the coach match.

It appears that coachees rate their experience in coaching 'holistically,' or as some authors put it, with a 'halo effect' (Dion *et al.*, 1972): the coachee will rate all aspects of the experience as better or worse, in accordance with how useful the general experience was for them and their own optimism about these kinds of experiences (significantly influenced by coachee-based factors such as hope, expectancy, self-efficacy, resilience, mental well-being, and now, in my view, working alliance) and will then score all other aspects accordingly. Coachee personality aspects like 'Openness,' which are also known to correlate positively with outcome (Stewart *et al.*, 2008), might also be influenced by this halo effect. Part of the effect may be to do with 'cognitive dissonance reduction' (a form of 'placebo'): coachees may score any or all of these variables higher after coaching, just because they have gone through the whole effort of engaging with coaching and participating in six or more sessions. This may even be true for the coach- and line-manager-reported data, i.e. the controls for 'same-source' bias may not have been sufficient if we are only asking coaches, coachees, and their line managers.

This interpretation would explain why coachee ratings of effectiveness tend to correlate with self-scored working alliance, but also with *any* coaching technique as scored by the coachee on e.g. the Coaching Behaviours Questionnaire CBQ (see De Haan *et al.*, 2011, 2019). It also explains the high degree of 'reverse causality' which is often found, where coaching is not only impacted by but in turn improves aspects such as self-efficacy, working alliance, and resilience (see, e.g., Evers *et al.*, 2006; Baron & Morin, 2009). In our longitudinal study working alliance was significantly related to future coaching effectiveness (for most time periods), but there was no reverse causation of working-alliance scores.

It is still very early to say if these results are generalisable. In order to gain more certainty for or against this novel argument about the working alliance, we would need many more independent longitudinal trials studying executive-coaching outcomes (even in the larger research base of psychotherapy there is still controversy as there are also studies that do indicate a sustained impact of WAI on effectiveness, e.g. Falkenström *et al.*, 2013) Furthermore, there were constraints on generalisability, with both samples consisting of student coachees (De Haan *et al.*, 2020) and in one case also coaches in training (Zimmermann & Antoni, 2020). However, it is important to note that we have found no evidence of biases in comparing these samples to other recent samples in the coaching-research literature, such as the RCT sample of similar size with female business leaders in De Haan *et al.*, 2019.

5 *Future research: time to think differently about active ingredients*

In my view there is still a lot more work to do to discover what exactly makes coaching effective. Most of the factors found to date are coachee-related and not really related to anything that goes on in the sessions themselves. I believe it is important to start thinking differently in terms of predictors of outcomes. Specific techniques or approaches, specific common factors, are very difficult to demonstrate and may not be relevant. Although we should of course for the time being keep an open mind and test other self-scored relationship measures as well, particularly those that seem to refer more strongly to the actual coaching environment that is shared by both parties. In this regard there are some interesting studies that demonstrate alternative ways to measure a positive coaching relationship e.g. through fMRI, salivary cortisol samples, and coachee positive-emotion word counts: Jack *et al.* (2013) and Howard (2015).

It seems however that potential active ingredients in coaching are even more general than scholars have suggested so far with the 'common factors': they seem to point to a general optimism and stamina on the client's side (hope, self-efficacy, resilience) including generally positive feelings about techniques (CBQ) and the relationship (WAI). We will therefore have to look at more generalised and objective outcome measures, more longitudinal trials, and also at 'holistic' variables that can capture the whole experience in an integrated way, such as (1) around technique and behaviour, (2) around personality of coachee and coach, (3) around the 'in-between' or coaching relationship. The lattermost should perhaps focus more on the atmosphere in the room and the critical moments in sessions and should perhaps first be investigated through scoring by observers who are more likely to be objective about what they see in the conversation (following, e.g., Gessnitzer & Kauffeld, 2015; De Haan *et al.*, 2019).

Part D: what it means for coaching practice

Research such as presented in this chapter raises more questions than it answers. However, it does seem to indicate that for a coach's work from session to session the working alliance is not as important as was thought over recent decades. We need to be cautious not to interpret too much into a single paper or two (Zimmermann & Antoni, 2020; De Haan *et al.*, 2020), but we can try to draw some tentative conclusions here.

Coaches can trust that the working alliance is there as a 'background boost' to their work, as a very good client indicator that things are going well and that positive results are likely. Similar 'background boosts' on the client side are motivation or self-motivation or trust upon referral, or a positive impression from a client after a chemistry session.

At the moment, we cannot read much more into a good 'working alliance.' It may be that a 'good' alliance is not the main thing to aim for in coaching – the working alliance being only about getting to a good start. After that what is really important may be about improving the alliance or engaging in 'alliance rupture repair' (as Safran *et al.*, 2011, have shown in therapy). That would confirm the finding that good outcome also predicates a better alliance (De Haan *et al.*, 2020).

It is important for coaches to empathise with clients' experiences of the relationship and to be open to changing ways of working (tasks) and outcomes (goals). When in doubt, ask the coachee for expectations, goals, and outcomes.

Perhaps the coach can ignore working alliance from session to session and focus more on what is being presented, what is happening within the relationship, and how the coachee feels?

Summary of Chapter 3: 'The coaching relationship as "best predictor"?'

The coaching relationship in the form of the 'working alliance' between coach and coachee has been touted as the **best predictor** of coaching outcomes and the foremost active ingredient that coach and coachee can influence and optimise during their work together.

However, it turns out that this all-important working alliance – which in most formulations consists of agreement about tasks between coach and coachee, agreement about goals between the two, and the affective bond holding them together – is **not** really related to coaching outcomes after all.

From two recent studies, which are the only ones to have measured the working alliance over time, from both a coach and a client perspective (they measured coaching outcome longitudinally over at least four and up to 11 sessions of coaching in a dyad), we can see no correlation between 'working alliance' and 'outcome increase per session.' The same has been observed in several psychotherapy studies.

If this is true, then the working alliance is only related to overall outcome and may have much more to do with a response bias (through general trust or optimism) than with a driver or active ingredient of coaching outcomes.

It seems time to reconsider this active ingredient, and not to assume that it is a good predictor of coaching outcome:

- Either we need to find other, better ways of measuring the co-created relationship in the room, or
- We need to think about other aspects of the relationship that may matter more, such as rupture-and-repair cycles within the coaching relationship.

Note

1 We find that the three components of the working alliance go up from session to session by 1 to 2%. We also find that coachees' ratings of the working alliance components are 10% more stable than coaches' ratings, as expressed by the standard deviations.

An interlude before Chapter 4

In the next chapter we are going to inquire into what it is that coaching delivers. If we can demonstrate changes through coaching, what form do these changes take?

As a case analogy let me spend a few paragraphs thinking about what benefits coaching has brought me so far as a coachee. After my first experience of psychotherapy, I had three major journeys of coaching, each lasting around nine years and each now completed. The first was with a humanist counsellor (clinical psychologist). The other two were with psychoanalysts and they were each on at least a once-a-week basis. I stayed with each of them for a very long period, so I would regard them each as successful. So, what then did they deliver? What were they successful at?

To sum it up bluntly, I think the main benefit of all this work was entirely subjective and private to me. My inner deliberations and self-awareness were affected by the sessions in a myriad of ways. Often, I found solace and a form of confirmation of my thinking and decisions. More often, I found new perspectives and challenges to my existing mindset. I always felt deeply understood and that gave me a sense of safety, connection, and warmth.

Overall, I would certainly agree with those clients in the return-on-investment research who said that coaching gave them ideas and inspiration which earned them some six or seven times more money than they had invested in coaching. So, even though I clearly invested in many hundreds of sessions of coaching I still believe the investment was worth a multiple for me. However, I do realise that that is just a subjective sense of me feeling inspired and held, and feeling a growing resilience through coaching, the kind of thing that researchers investigate with the help of self-scores. In fact, I would say the thing each of my coaches helped me with the most was 'self-knowledge': understanding how my idiosyncrasies might have made sense at an earlier time but now took me in sometimes very unhelpful directions, harming my relationships with clients, colleagues, and bosses.

What about more objective benefits that I can recall? I called my first coach my 'mentor' because he introduced me to my new profession of organisational consulting and coaching, wherein he was himself already established. He certainly gave me advice as well as a good listening. For example he gave me suggestions for qualifying courses and business cards of colleagues he thought would be worthwhile for me to meet.

I have always enjoyed being coached, yet as noted in some of the other interludes it is impossible to say what would have happened if all those hundreds of sessions had not taken place. It is true that I was depressed in my late twenties, after which I was very much helped with 25 sessions of cognitive-behavioural therapy. My depression did not recur over the next decades and it feels that through my experience with my mentor and the two analysts I have been adding significant amounts of love, wealth, and meaning to my life; that I have become much more spontaneously myself and that I have had the feeling of expanding into a much more balanced and mature existence. But would that not have been the case anyway if I had just grown up, matured, and been as lucky as I have been in my life? We shall never know. Life – just like coaching – is famously an $N = 1$ experiment with no significance in any of the findings.

Chapter 4

Which outcomes does coaching actually deliver? What does executive coaching work on?

THE MULTI-OUTCOMES TAILORMADE COACH

This chapter will cover what it is exactly that executive coaching sessions may influence or change. We have already reviewed a great many experiments in this book, which have demonstrated measurable differences between coachees and control groups in similar circumstances. Up to now we have looked at the overall evidence base for coaching and the evidence for particular aspects or 'ingredients' within coaching, which may make the intervention more or less effective. Now, in this chapter, we are going to look again at this entire evidence base, asking a different question – namely, what kind of changes can one expect through coaching? In other words, what are the outcomes that we can hold coaching responsible for? We will pay the closest look at those changes that go beyond a basic positive feeling coming out of coaching conversations, i.e. we will go as much as possible beyond the 'self-scored' variables. I will try to discriminate 'hard evidence' from softer halo effects, that tend to be related to satisfaction and other self-scores. The 'hard outcomes' demonstrate something about executive coaching that would be noticeable by others than those who engage in coaching, i.e. more widely in the organisation, including independent or objective changes to do with the coachee's performance at work and also changes in other people who work with the coachee, such as changes in their productivity or behaviour.

Part A: some controversies

Perhaps it is useful right at the start of this chapter to select a few remarkable results reported on in earlier chapters which are probably beyond controversy because they are based on rather convincing experiments:

1. Coaching can help you with *efficiency*: in call centres, operators who have the benefit of regular coaching conversations with their line managers make net time savings of a couple of minutes on their 1,000 calls at the end of the day, despite the additional time that they need to be coached on the job (Liu & Batt, 2010). These small savings add up to very considerable ones over time, saving $18 per month per line manager over and above the additional cost for coaching.
2. Coaching can also help with *sales*: pharma reps achieve about 10% more of their goals on average, if their manager is objectively skilled at coaching (Dahling *et al.*, 2016).
3. Coaching can also help with *coping* when you are in transition: it has been shown that preventative coaching helps to increase life and work satisfaction but also helps to reduce absences through sickness days during the year, with around 15% reduction in those (Duijts *et al.*, 2008).

My own recent work has demonstrated coaching effectiveness through the eyes of senior managers, their coaches, and their line managers alike (De Haan *et al.*, 2019), as compared with the scores for our randomised control group. This research was done with senior female managers in a large pharma corporation.

Controversy 1: very high diversity of study methods

The just-quoted findings are based on four single studies of which only one, Duijts *et al.* (2008), was replicated. Four studies in four different industries with four different research designs and measures. One with senior managers as coachees, three others with client-facing employees. One making use of internal coaches, one making use of external coaches, and two with line managers hopefully (but not measurably) using coaching behaviours. They are all good quality and relatively large-scale studies with N from 150 to 2,350. Nevertheless, it is very hard to see how they can be lumped together for a statistical meta-analysis. In fact, we know from psychotherapy research (Wampold, 2001) that for a reliable meta-analysis we will need tens of thousands of cases (total N well above 10,000) with all individual studies coming from the same experimental design, ideally from a randomised controlled trial.

I think we are still at a stage where we need to understand the existing studies, explore where controversies lie, and how results from different studies can support each other, which is my intention in this chapter. However, this is controversial in itself, because meta-analyses have already been produced in coaching that have claimed that they can demonstrate effectiveness with great statistical significance. Moreover, they have excluded some of the best research such as the ones quoted earlier and have not been able to account for the tremendous differences in designs and sample sizes.

At the moment, in the absence of a large research base, we have to make do with many single studies which all define outcomes in a slightly different way. I will review many of those different specific outcomes in section C of this chapter. On the one hand, studies do not replicate each other because they are all set up very differently. On the other hand, they do provide evidence from many different perspectives that coaching has an impact. Having many independent creative attempts to demonstrate some sort of a significant relationship between variables is not all bad: it means we have a broad consensus that personal and organisational impacts can be expected. That is the state of play in the coaching outcome literature today.

Controversy 2: some contradictory findings

I do not want to gloss over contradictory findings – in fact, I find them the most interesting of all, because they can lead to a fresh hypothesis about the underlying phenomenon, something I have tried to show with regard to the coaching relationship in Chapter 3.

As another example, take multi-source feedback ratings. A lot of the coaching research base over many years has been showing enhanced 360-degree feedback scores: peers', managers', and self-scores tended to improve with coaching over and above 360-degree ratings for the control-group managers who did not receive coaching. However, there have been some important exceptions to this finding, and in particular in some of the more rigorous studies where the groups were both randomised: see Nieminen *et al.* (2013), Williams and Lowman (2018), and Jones *et al.* (2019) who all used 360-degree instruments and found only the self-ratings to be different between intervention and control groups.

A third example is technique. As pointed out in earlier chapters there is a strong coaching research tradition showing that a generally friendly, supportive, positive, solution-focused approach is beneficial (see, e.g., Grant, 2012; Ianiro *et al.*, 2013, 2015; Ianiro & Kauffeld, 2014; Jack *et al.*, 2013; Howard, 2015; Gessnitzer & Kauffeld, 2015; Gessnitzer *et al.*, 2016; Will *et al.*, 2016; Braunstein & Grant, 2016; Theeboom *et al.*, 2016; Grant & O'Connor, 2018; Will *et al.*, 2019; Jordan & Kauffeld, 2020). At the same time, we also have another longstanding and equally extensive tradition pointing out how beneficial coaching can be for performance when it is based on 360-degree feedback results which are communicated in coaching conversations (see, e.g., Hazucha *et al.*, 1993; Thach 2002; Luthans & Peterson, 2003; Seifert *et al.*, 2003; Orenstein, 2006). However, such coaching based on 360-degree feedback results is to a large extent critical, challenging, and confrontational, as is also recognized in some of the 'pro-friendly coaching' research articles (e.g. Howard, 2015, who uses the 'needs for improvement' condition coming out of 360-degree as an example of less friendly or supportive coaching).

This discrepancy could be explained by the observation that supportive, friendly coaching possibly improves with the coachee-ratings of the coaching and with coachee 'well-being,' whilst more challenging and confrontational coaching mostly helps with the coachee's performance towards others, as testified by the 360-degree results. So supportive coaching helps the coachee himself, whilst challenging coaching helps the coachee's colleagues. It is however still far too early to confirm such sweeping generalisations. At present I would prefer to keep seeing this as somewhat conflicting results in the literature that may be resolved in the future.

As a fourth example, we have had some contradictory findings in the area of personality as well, e.g. between the two studies that tested Big Five client personality factors (Stewart et al., 2008; versus Allan et al., 2018) or between those that tested MBTI factors (Scoular & Linley, 2006; versus De Haan et al., 2013 and later articles).

Controversy 3: the possibility of moderation

When managerial coaching is tested for different levels of structure or design, Wageman (2001) was able to show that if good structures are in place coaching does make a significant difference in the teams' performance: well-designed teams are helped more by effective coaching and they are also undermined less by ineffective coaching than are poorly designed teams. In short, the impact of leaders' coaching on their teams appears conditioned by the way in which they set the team up in the first place. Buljac-Samardzic and Van Woerkom (2015) took this a step further and showed that team coaching could be so moderated by a baseline level of team reflection, that it was not effective for teams that were already highly reflective – in which case high levels of team coaching could even be detrimental for the effectiveness of the team.

Similarly, when coaching is tested in combination with another developmental intervention, such as training or multi-source feedback, it remains difficult to attribute effectiveness solely to coaching because the coaching conversations could have been a *moderation* of the effectiveness of the other intervention. In some cases, executive coaching was shown to generate big increases on the impact of training (e.g. Olivero et al., 1997) or multi-source feedback (e.g. Smither et al., 2003; Kochanowski et al., 2010).

These experiments where executive coaching adds something substantial to another, different intervention are actually difficult to interpret. At face value the experiments may indicate that coaching is such an effective intervention that it generates substantial results over and above the other intervention. However, the same findings may instead indicate that coaching is more of a catalyst of learning: when you add coaching to the other intervention it makes the other intervention much more effective than it would be on its own. If coaching only moderates another process it is a much weaker intervention by itself. This may mean that one would advise to only make use of coaching in combination with that other intervention, and not on its own.

Obviously, in this case, we have data on stand-alone coaching too. Moreover, these other interventions (training and multi-source feedback) are indeed rather disparate interventions, which would strengthen the case for thinking that coaching is actually effective in and of itself.

Controversy 4: it's hard to see the wood for the trees, because of many weak results

All other controversies mentioned earlier in the book still apply when we think about the results listed in this chapter, e.g. the limited amount of very rigorous studies, the overabundance of self-scores, the generally low sample sizes, the rare occurrence of proper randomised controls, and the lack of truly objective outcomes in most studies. However, year after year we are getting better at this, and more and more research groups and PhDs in coaching are springing up all over the world, so it is certainly an exciting time to be a coaching researcher.

Many coaching studies report significant but weak results and small effects, e.g. the results regarding changes in the coachee's personality are not just contradictory, they are also weak. Weak results with a high p-value ($p < 0.05$) can also lead to false positives, i.e. the publication of a 'finding' or an 'outcome' where there would not be any if the experiment is repeated.

Part B: how to establish different coaching outcomes

There are a myriad of outcomes for coaching. In my own experience, every contract is different and lists a number of highly personal outcomes. If I look at my own contracts that I wrote for coaching over the past year then I can see a wide range of requests, such as:

- 'Your intention is to develop your division further: in addition to the technical improvements that you have managed to implement over the years, now is a time for more empowerment, involving your team more with your priorities, offering more clarity about roles and responsibilities of every team member, and working against a general defensiveness of your division.'
- 'You would like to define your role of Chair and determine what contribution is best for the various businesses and your own relationship with the executive team.'
- 'You would like to become a more rounded manager and complement your thorough understanding of numbers and finance with a usable understanding of people.'
- 'You would like to focus more on what is going well, the healthy state of the business and your own personal achievements, so that you increase your self-confidence.'
- 'You would like to transition away from the daily running of the business, so that you can surrender more of your "control" or "interference," in the knowledge and confidence that you brought in the right people to manage the business.'
- 'You want to be more attuned to the customers of your business.'
- 'You would like to work on becoming more strategic and inspirational for the three enterprises that you are responsible for.'
- 'You want to reflect deeply on your agenda and priorities at work and about whether your ways of working are conducive to the best realisation of your agenda.'
- 'Although you are experienced as visionary, likeable, and supportive, some of the feedback from your teams says that your communication can become muddled under stress or when you are lacking preparation.'
- 'You would like to become more deliberate in your communication with others, by managing to predict how others might react and then adapt your style more.'
- 'You know that the 'art of challenge' is a core aspect of your role and would like to challenge in a healthier way, without others feeling undermined or threatened.'

- 'You would like to look into your performance in your current roles and where you can improve your impact and effectiveness.'
- 'You want to look at longer-term career opportunities where you would like to take more ownership of your own career.'
- 'You wish to review your leadership offer with an eye towards finding your next role and becoming really successful in it, by demonstrating more "ownership," building more alliances, and becoming more politically astute in your leadership role.'
- 'You would like to become more effective by evening out your pace, allowing yourself to be less distracted, and becoming calmer overall.'
- 'The relationship with your own line manager: improve your balance between delivering on own priorities and empathising with your leader's changing priorities.'
- 'You aim to gain clarity on how you want to develop your career longer term.'
- 'Executive presence, Leadership, Delegation, and Self.'

Moreover, in my experience the contract changes from session to session, and is highly dependent on what the coachee chooses to bring to each session, what further emerges, and whether she or he is looking for a solution, a resolution, a deeper understanding of the issues, more self-understanding, new energy and resources to tackle the issues, or a combination of these. In earlier research I defined an effectiveness measure which tried to encompass all of these (De Haan et al., 2016, 2019, 2020):

'The outcome of my coaching objectives so far:

1 I have been successful in creating reflective space for me;
2 I have been successful in creating new insight for me;
3 Through coaching I have successfully engaged in new action or behaviour;
4 I would consider this coaching journey successful.'

This is a scale with four items which the coachee can rate independently and which can be shown to load upon one factor. But this is just measuring the outcomes for the coachee. There are of course many other outcomes that are relevant to coaching. Coachees are keen to achieve their own personal objectives as professionals or leaders, but their managers and the coaching commissioners may have other objectives for the coachee, which may be supporting or conflicting to the coachee's agenda and may be more related to the coachee's performance and that of others in the organisation.

What scientists need to demonstrate about coaching sessions can be summarised by the following:

1 Do coachees reach their goals?
2 Do coachees experience other benefits?
3 Do coachees perform better for the organisation generally?
4 Do others around the coachees experience other benefits from coaching?
5 Are there no contrary outcomes of coaching (negative side effects)? (We will return to this in Chapter 6.)

A thorough demonstration of these different groups of outcomes requires different research designs. The first two of these can be investigated by studying the coachees themselves, whilst the other outcomes may require more creativity from the researchers. I will give some examples of the more creative designs that I have come across.

As many authors show, it is important in research not just to have a prediction of a certain change or effect, but also a realistic model about how the change may come about. Good models with different variables impacting one another in complex, sometimes nonlinear ways, can give rise to important discoveries when validated – see, e.g., Wageman (2001), Atkins and Wood (2002), Carson *et al.* (2007), Buljac-Samardzic and Van Woerkom (2015) and Ebner *et al.* (2017).

Study designs for 'Do coachees reach their goals?'

The most straightforward design for this question is by making use of goal attainment scaling (Kiresuk & Sherman, 1968): all coachees in the sample can formulate a number of goals for coaching and are subsequently asked to indicate their own degree of attainment of each goal. Often the coachees are also asked to measure the degree of difficulty of their goal, on the same scale. In De Haan *et al.* (2020) we have done this both for coachees and for their peers in the randomised control group, after every session of coaching. One often finds clear improvements from session to session, significantly over and above the degree of improvement that the control group also achieves on their goals. This then means that the improvements found can be attributed to coaching and coaching alone.

However, an important caveat with this, as always, is that there may be a halo effect where the coachee judges everything to do with their coaching more positively simply because of a general feel-good factor or even because they have made the effort to be coached and want something to show for that. This kind of cognitive bias towards the coaching results may lead them to imagine that they have improved on their goals and to indicate a forward motion even if a colleague looking at their degree of goal attainment would disagree.

For this reason, one could widen the evidence base by asking the coachee to share his goals with others and then for others to rate the coaching goals as well. In De Haan *et al.* (2020) we have asked the coaches to also rate their coachee's specific goals, and we again found an improvement in the intervention group. Nevertheless, coaches are likely to experience the same biases in favour of coaching as the coachees.

Study designs for 'Do coachees experience other benefits?'

From the specifics of their goals with coaching, one can go on and ask the coachees wider questions about their coaching experience, related to the helpfulness of the coach (De Haan *et al.*, 2011), or the effectiveness of the sessions (De Haan *et al.*, 2013 and others), or about themselves (e.g. changes in their commitment, motivation, self-motivation, job satisfaction, well-being, resilience, stress, anxiety, and depression levels). All of these and more have now been investigated by several researchers, with the help of validated scales, as part of before-and-after questionnaires – and in distinction to control groups' levels of the same.

As stated before, general satisfaction with the coaching measured by a 'coaching helpfulness' or 'coaching effectiveness' questionnaire, tends to correlate very strongly with all of these general-preparedness or self-evaluation scores (e.g. if we look at the two recent publications that have collected data at the sessional level then we see that they both find a correlation amongst effectiveness and well-being variables of $r \approx 0.4$ with $p < 0.001$; see Zimmermann & Antoni, 2020; De Haan et al., 2020).

With some of the coachee-related effects one could go further than just measuring self-scores. For example, rather than measuring the impact of coaching on the coachee's job satisfaction as in Ellinger et al. (2003), one could measure job satisfaction rates more objectively and meaningfully by tracking retention rates over months and years. In this manner, Gardiner et al. (2013) appear to show that coaching impacts on longer-term retention rates, namely over a three-year period. Such research findings which are more difficult to collect, go way beyond self-scores in that they do not just demonstrate how the coachees will tend to experience a good feeling or good self-defined outcomes through coaching, but also shows that coaching can predict longer-term behaviours which are not consciously related to the coaching sessions by the coachees. The same can be done for job performance, by measuring the coachee's changing outputs – see next section.

Study designs for 'Do coachees perform better?'

Coaching is an organisational-development intervention that should not only have a beneficial effect on the coachee's personal goals and general well-being, optimism, or resilience, but also on the contributions of the coachee to his or her own organisation, work role, and practice. This may not be true for all coachees as coaching can be highly personal, and sometimes coaching even supports a coachee transitioning away from an organisation so that they start contributing less not more. Nevertheless, in statistical research encompassing high numbers of coachees one should expect a significant and positive impact of coaching on the performance of the coachee. This has indeed been demonstrated; most frequently through performance ratings by colleagues (peers, direct reports, and line managers) of the coachee.

Similar to coaching, multi-source feedback is an intervention that can wrap itself around highly individual and unique performance definitions, objectives, and measurements. Multi-source feedback tools involve a rating from those 'experts' that should know best about the performance of the coachee: his or her closest colleagues, because their own work is directly affected by the coachee's performance.

Many important contributions to coaching research have used multi-source feedback ratings and showed significant effects on the performance of coachees as rated by others: Thach (2002); Smither et al. (2003); Toegel and Nicholson (2005); Schlosser et al. (2007); Kochanowski et al. (2010); O'Connor and Cavanagh (2013); Ladegard and Gjerde (2014); Goff et al. (2014); Peláez et al. (2019, 2020), and Fontes and Dello Russo (2020), just to name a few. However, some of these results are only partial (e.g. Kochanowski et al., 2010; Fontes & Dello Russo, 2020). Some authors, despite doing multi-source feedback investigations, could only demonstrate performance increases for the coachee's self-ratings (Nieminen et al., 2013; Williams and Lowman, 2018; and Jones et al., 2019).

In some cases video feedback on recorded performance was used instead: Singh *et al.* (2015), Bonrath *et al.* (2015) and Niglio de Figueiredo *et al.* (2018). This could be argued as being a more objective and a better standard than ratings, because video assessments will be more specific and less dependent on 'the eye of the beholder.' Video feedback can also be arranged in the form of a dialogue and can then be supported by shared evidence.

Wageman (2001) used a range of technicians' service-level measurements and Latham *et al.* (2012) used mystery guests' feedback on the performance of restaurant waiters who were being coached; both strong, objective measures of performance.

Many other creative measurements of the coachee's performance itself have been undertaken in the coaching-outcome literature, as we will see in the next section: exposure to radiation levels, time spent handling calls, achievement of units of productivity, sales targets, customer satisfaction, service levels, job retention, handling of critical conversations, quantity and quality of health and safety measures, academic performance, etcetera. Looking at all these articles that show 'hard evidence' for the effectiveness of coaching conversations makes one realise that we can all do important research if we could simply measure the number of a company's coaching hours and a key performance indicator in the same period which ideally touches on the content of those coaching conversations: significant relationships between those variables are now to be expected.

Finally, the coaching performance of line managers was also significantly related to the coachee's performance, however this finding could be explained by a form of mutual idealisation: Ellinger *et al.* (2003), Shanock and Eisenberger (2006), Gregory and Levy (2011), Huang and Hsieh (2015), Kim and Kuo (2015), Weer *et al.* (2016), and Hsu *et al.* (2019).

Study designs for 'Do others around the coachees benefit from coaching?'

Obviously, if the performance of coachees improves through coaching then that in itself constitutes a beneficial effect on others in the organisation. They benefit from the increased performance of their colleague. However, other organisational benefits could also be measured more directly, e.g. by looking at the performance of others around the coachee. Precisely in this century of big data and network analysis, it is easy to see a lot of potential for this kind of research. See O'Connor and Cavanagh (2013) for a first paper that maps networks and network responses around the coachee and finds some interesting predictions as discussed in the next section.

Part C: overview of what we know about outcome measures

Here is an overview of all the outcomes that have been demonstrated in the coaching literature, starting from the most objective ones that are in large part beyond criticism of subjective bias. From those independent objective outcomes, we then continue with the multi-source outcomes which confirm the results subjectively but from a multitude of perspectives, and then with the self-rated outcomes, after which we end with any beneficial effects that have been demonstrated for the coaches themselves. Experience says that coaches also benefit from undertaking coaching conversations, not just because they get paid for them, but also because they practice their talents for listening, care, and support. There is already some evidence in support of the idea that not just coachees and their organisations but also the coaches themselves benefit from the coaching conversations.

1 Changes to objective measures

There is mounting evidence that coaching makes a difference on objective measures, which cannot be influenced so easily by a general good feeling during coaching, i.e. the coach or the coachee or the researcher building up a 'good feeling' or halo effect around coaching. Such objective evidence, independent from self-scores, is what executive and workplace coaching will be judged by in the future.

We can make a distinction between productivity and achievement, job retention and promotion, and demonstrable personal changes.

1 A great many different demonstrable changes in productivity

In managerial coaching several studies have shown improved objective performance with more coaching:

- Wageman (2001) showed that, provided the right team structure is in place, coaching can be linked to a higher performance of the (Rank Xerox) customer service in terms of customer satisfaction, expenses, response times, service and repair times, and also machine reliability.
- Liu and Batt (2010) showed that coaching time with the direct line manager reduced overall call-centre time per call, even clearly above the extra time taken to be coached.
- Latham *et al.* (2012) showed higher server performance and a higher customer count in three restaurants during the period when specific coaching conversations based on mystery shopper feedback were provided daily. There was some evidence for a long-term effect of the coaching with post-coaching customer count remaining higher for around six months. By the end of the experiment it was easy to calculate a substantial growth of revenue through the mystery shoppers and the resulting feedback and coaching sessions, over and above the payment for the agency and the mystery shoppers themselves.
- Deane *et al.* (2014) showed an (objectively assessed) better implementation of a new service model amongst care workers who received transformational coaching as compared to skills coaching.
- Dahling *et al.* (2016) showed that coaching by managers who are skilled in coaching helps to achieve the pharma reps' sales targets.
- Kines *et al.* (2010) show convincingly that safety standards objectively increase through external coaching of foremen in the construction industry.
- Many of the health coaching RCTs (as covered in Chapter 1) also achieve objective outcomes for patients; e.g. Fischer *et al.* (2019) show that telephone coaching can have a lasting impact on physical activity levels, and are still significant a year after ending the coaching.

- Carson *et al.* (2007) found that external team coaching developed shared leadership in consulting teams with MBA students, which in turn predicted third-party client ratings of the quality of the consultancy. Teams with an unsupportive internal team environment were still able to develop the first of these: high levels of shared leadership, so long as they received a high level of coaching.
- Olivero *et al.* (1997) and Poluka and Kaifi (2015) also demonstrate improved (objectively measured) productivity through executive coaching.
- Passmore and Rehman (2012): driving instructors who coach deliver candidates with better objective results in terms of number of hours driving that pupils needed to pass the test, the number of tests taken by pupils before passing, and the likelihood of pupils to pass on the first attempt.

There are several other studies taking academic achievement in students as outcome variable: Franklin and Doran (2009) found improvements in academic marks for one of their two co-coaching samples ($\delta = 0.61$; $p < 0.01$). Vandekerckhove (2010) found similar improvements in marks both for tutor-coaching and online coaching. Andreanoff (2016) found objective module grades on two measures of those who received coaching were higher than for the control group ($\delta = 0.35$; $p < 0.01$), an effect which was mostly still there in the next semester and led to a better retention in the coached group of students. However, Tee *et al.* (2019) does not replicate this with a smaller group. Academic procrastination was shown to be significantly lower in individual coaching (Losch *et al.*, 2016). Both Sue-Chan *et al.* (2012) and Theeboom *et al.* (2016) show that 'promotion' coaching and 'solution-focused' coaching respectively give better results for undergraduate students on a cognitive problem-solving exercise.

The next three articles are medical improvements, i.e. doctors achieving higher standards through coaching.

Gattellari *et al.* (2005) showed GPs receiving mentoring were more likely to disclose relevant facts previously identified by experts as essential to know for patients before making a decision (some of these findings with four sigma accuracy; i.e. $p < 0.0001$). Moreover, GPs expressed greater confidence, lower levels of decisional conflict, and lower anxieties.

Niglio de Figueiredo *et al.* (2018) show statistically significant improvement ($\delta = 0.45$, $p = 0.01$) in oncologists' interaction with patients after just three additional sessions of coaching, with most of the difference in more straightforward areas of communication such as asking the patient's perspective; with nonsignificant change on more subtle skills such as dealing with emotions. Personal coaching was also shown to improve significantly upon training alone. Singh *et al.* (2015) and Bonrath *et al.* (2015) convincingly demonstrate that a series of just four or five coaching sessions based on video recordings can help student-surgeons increase their dexterity and success in operations. Slegers *et al.* (2015) show on-the-spot coaching almost halves exposure to radiation for experienced physicians. George *et al.* (2020) summarise their own earlier work that shows that coaching of nurses leads to better adherence to safe childbirth protocols, as observed independently.

2 A variety of changes in job finding, retention, and promotion rates

Improved (objectively measured) retention and promotion rates through coaching have also been demonstrated: Gardiner *et al.* (2013), Reyes Liske and Holladay (2016), Andreanoff (2016).

For homeless clients, being supported by a job coach created significantly higher chances of gaining employment and of successfully sustaining their current employment (Hoven *et al.*, 2014).

Less objective sick-leave absence (difference of 2.5 days a year between intervention and control group; with an overall sickness leave average in the company of 14 sickness leave days a year): Duijts *et al.* 2008 although only as a partial result and Telle *et al.* (2016) could not replicate it.

Viering *et al.* (2015) found significant results for employment rates and number of new jobs obtained in the field of labour market reintegration ($p < 0.01$).

Hui *et al.* (2013) shows guidance coaching is objectively better for similar tasks, and facilitation coaching is objectively better for dissimilar tasks which require creativity.

Here is one example of a large-scale study where objective change through executive coaching could not be demonstrated: Oberschachtsiek and Scioch (2015).

3 A few objective changes in personal physiology and behaviour

Unconscious, physiological changes through coaching on nuclear magnetic resonance scans (Jack *et al.*, 2013) and on the frequency of coachee positive-emotion words (Howard, 2015) have also been demonstrated.

Miller *et al.* (2004) show that coaching helps to maintain the improvement achieved during training of clinicians, in terms of the behaviour of the clinicians and their clients (independently) as analysed from recorded sessions.

Further micro-discoveries about how explicit observer-rated coach behaviours can elicit explicit observer-rated client behaviours in the Braunschweig studies. These changes are all observed during the sessions which were video recorded:

- Ianiro *et al.* (2015) showed how dominant-friendly coaching behaviour significantly evoked dominant coachee behaviour and vice versa, whilst other dominant coach behaviour, namely both neutral and hostile, in fact evoked dependent coachee behaviour.
- Will *et al.* (2016) showed how paraphrasing and naming coachee feelings induced a positive response in coachees.
- Gessnitzer *et al.* (2016) showed that open questions and offering support by coaches led to more 'self-efficient' coachee statements.
- Jordan and Kauffeld (2020) showed that solution-focused questions led to more clients' solution statements.
- Will *et al.* (2019) showed that coaches' positive-supportive statements yielded explicit client-intentions to change.

2 Changes to multi-source performance measures

Firstly, coaching seems to be able to improve the impact of the 360-feedback as such:

Hazucha *et al.* (1993) showed that various developmental activities including coaching could increase 360-degree feedback scores after 24 months. Luthans and Peterson (2003) show after just three months others' ratings increased significantly when 20 managers in a manufacturing organisation had only one feedback cum coaching session plus a few informal follow-ups. Seifert *et al.* (2003) show that even a 'feedback workshop' can enhance the impact of 360-degree feedback. However, Ebner et al. (2020) do not seem to find such effects.

Next, coaching also seems to increase 360-degree feedback ratings:

Firstly, coachee-rated managerial coaching can increase managers' performance ratings for the coachee: Ellinger et al. (2003), Shanock and Eisenberger (2006), Gregory and Levy (2011), Huang and Hsieh (2015), Hui and Sue-Chan (2018), Weer et al. (2016), and Hsu et al. (2019) showed how in an industrial setting, on the shop floor of warehouses or retail outlets, employees' perceptions of coaching skills of their line managers were correlated with their performance, as rated independently by those same line managers. Building on these results, Sue-Chan et al. (2012) and Jarzebowski et al. (2012) show that employees and coachees, respectively, increase their motivation if their coaching shares the same principles as their own implicit person theory (i.e. if they think of people as fixed and less changeable, then a 'prevention' coaching style receives higher ratings; and if they think of people as incrementally changeable, then a more supportive 'promotion' coaching style is received as being more effective). Buljac-Samardzic and Van Woerkom (2015) also found team-member-rated coaching to impact manager-rated effectiveness, but only in certain circumstances.

Secondly, many more studies focus on the fact that coaching can also increase the ratings for the coachee in the organisation:

> Kochanowski et al. (2010) did a field experiment with 30 store managers in a supermarket organisation (a group of 15 with only feedback and then another 15 with feedback plus 6 short coaching sessions by the author) and show that subordinate ratings increased only for the coached leaders ('collaboration' dimension only).

> Goff et al. (2014) demonstrated that school principals who were coached could respond significantly to actions communicated by teachers in termly multi-source feedback data. In fact, Goff et al. found effect sizes of $\delta = 0.15$ per coaching session ($p < 0.05$) in the teachers' ratings on principals' leadership dimensions extracted from their own suggested actions earlier in the year, rated at the end of the school year.

To summarise this entire literature, Smither et al. (2003), Finn et al. (2007; only direct-report rated), Goff et al. (2014), and Reyes Liske and Holladay (2016) all demonstrate that personal coaching of various kinds improves the 360-degree ratings from self, peers, line managers, and reports. Kochanowski et al. (2010; direct-report ratings only) showed more collaboration in the eyes of subordinates. Cerni et al. (2010; direct-report ratings only) showed that hundreds of staff rated the eight principals in the intervention group significantly higher on transformational leadership skills. Peláez et al. (2019, line-manager ratings only; 2020, line-manager and direct-report ratings) and Fontes and Dello Russo (2020; peer and supervisor ratings only) offer more recent evidence that coaching improves line-manager-, peer-, and direct-report-rated leadership performance. It is important to note that the results by Finn et al. (2007), Goff et al. (2014), and Fontes and Dello Russo (2020) are only partial, i.e. on a few competences only. Teemant (2014) found the same for observer-ratings of teachers.

Peterson (1993), Thach (2002), Luthans and Peterson (2003), Orenstein (2006; with only a single client), corroborate this evidence but without the use of control groups. In Luthans and Peterson (2003) coaching can also be found to affect the job satisfaction ratings of direct reports significantly and positively.

Toegel and Nicholson (2005) measured changes in multi-source feedback for 89 investment bank managers over ten months after a group feedback workshop and a single executive coaching session. There was a significant improvement in ratings for the coachees from their direct reports ($p < 0.001$).

Nieminen *et al.* (2013) and Williams and Lowman (2018) could only demonstrate significant results for self-ratings and failed to find a significant result for ratings by others. Likewise, Jones *et al.* (2019) found that coaching had a significant effect only on self-rated performance and not on the line-manager-rated performance.

There is some other evidence as well that coaching can have a wider impact in organisations:

> O'Connor and Cavanagh (2013) did a broader 'network' measurement of the effects of coaching 20 leaders within a wider group. Whilst the coaching intervention did appear to improve the quality of communication from the coachees' perspectives, this quality of communication was perceived by those around the coachees to have become less positive, initially. However, those observed to have increased their psychological well-being the most over the intervention period were people in the network most closely connected to the coachees (as measured through closeness centrality in the coachees' neighbourhood networks). In other words, coaching seems to significantly increase the well-being of others beyond the coachees themselves.

It is interesting to see in this paper an example of a pattern that many coaches know: the first response to coaching may actually be negative, rather than an improvement. When a coachee is challenged or manages to communicate his or her own profound challenge for the first time to a supportive outsider, 'disclosure remorse' may occur and there may be a distinct sense in the room that things are not getting better but actually worse. Similarly, when a coachee starts improving their performance or changing their communication with direct colleagues (e.g. the coachee becomes more assertive), the first responses from those that work with the coachee may not be positive either. As we see in O'Connor and Cavanagh (2013), the sense from the direct environment of the coachee may be that things have worsened, or that communication has become more difficult, whilst at the same time the performance on other measures is greatly improving. Coaching challenges are very subtle and highly personal, they negotiate a route between wishes and needs, and they find new compromise solutions for intractable problems. All this may mean that successful coaching can 'make matters worse' in some respects, and there is room for much more creative research on this in the future.

3 Changes to self-rated personality measures

Personality is regarded as relatively stable and is not directly affected by the halo effect because it describes an underlying continuity in the nature of self-experiencing and in one's 'reputation' with others. Of all the subjective outcome measures personality is probably the most interesting one if it shows effects, because it will be noticed by others in the workplace and touch on deeper levels than just being ready or motivated for coaching.

There are now some first significant indications that personality and career derailment aspects may show demonstrable improvement through coaching, from studies by Allan et al. (2018), Zanchetta et al. (2020), and De Haan et al. (2019; $\delta = 0.5$; $p < 0.05$). De Haan et al.'s (2019) findings relate to two out of 28 personality aspects measured with the Hogan personality suite, namely Prudence which went significantly up and Excitable which went significantly down only in the intervention and not in the control group (although if one applies the Bonferroni correction as they should have done, these effects become only near-significant). The effect seems consistent because Prudence negatively correlates with Excitable (with $r = -0.32$ according to the Hogan statistical guide). It seems therefore that effective coaching has a small but significant calming, balancing, and responsibility-enhancing effect on personality. Because they used a measure that stretches over both time points, we know that the significant correlations found indicate causality; that is, executive coaching progressively makes a difference to these personality measures.

Allan et al. (2018) showed that regardless of the facets chosen by coachees to work on, Neuroticism significantly decreased ($p < 0.001$), and Conscientiousness ($p < 0.05$) and Extraversion ($p < 0.01$) increased in coachees.

Zanchetta et al. (2020) showed that impostor tendencies and fears of negative evaluations were significantly reduced through coaching, as well as tendencies to cover up errors; moreover, significant increases were found in self-enhancing attributions.

4 Changes to self-rated preparedness or well-being measures

There is a lot of evidence now that coaching has a measurable impact on the coachee's 'preparedness' or 'psychological capital,' including optimism, well-being, and self-motivation.

Even a single short series of coaching questions, i.e. much less than a full coaching session, seems to make a significant and replicable positive difference in a student's affect, self-efficacy, goal orientation, and cognitive flexibility (Grant, 2012; Neipp et al., 2016; Theeboom et al., 2016; Braunstein & Grant, 2016; Grant & O'Connor, 2018; Grant & Gerrard, 2020).

Self-efficacy

A number of authors have found significant and positive changes in self-efficacy and outcome expectancies, and for the intervention cohort only: Evers et al. (2006) showed that coaching significantly changes self-efficacy beliefs ('setting one's own goals') and outcome expectancies ('acting in a balanced way'). Baron and Morin (2009), Anthony et al. (2013), Hunt et al. (2019), and Zanchetta et al. (2020) likewise demonstrated significant effects on self-efficacy as their outcome variable. McDowall et al. (2014) found a higher increase of self-efficacy for the 'feedforward' condition. Finally, Moen and Skaalvik (2009) demonstrated small but significant increases on their self-efficacy instrument, where the intervention group had a year of coaching.

Well-being

Willms (2004) found a significant impact on positive affect. Green *et al.* (2006 and 2007), Spence and Grant (2007), Grant *et al.* (2009, 2010), and Poepsel (2011) found that coaching led to greater goal commitment, workplace well-being, cognitive hardiness, resilience, and hope.

Employees in the intervention group significantly reported improved health, less distress, less burnout, less need for recovery, and increased satisfaction with their lives (Duijts *et al.*, 2008). Telle *et al.* (2016) also found a significant reduction in depressive symptoms, a heightened ability of the participants to distance themselves from work, more experience of work-related success, less depletion of emotional resources, and a greater satisfaction with life compared to the control group. Other studies that demonstrate less self-reported stress are Taylor (1997), Grant *et al.* (2009, 2010), Gardiner *et al.* (2013), Junker et al. (2020) and De Haan *et al.* (2020). Significant effects on burnout were also found by McGonagle *et al.* (2014, 2020) and Dyrbye *et al.* (2019) – on work engagement also by Peláez *et al.* (2019, 2020) and McGonagle *et al.* (2020).

However, in a smaller group, Gyllensten and Palmer (2005) could not demonstrate a significant effect on stress, depression, or anxiety.

Resilience

McGonagle *et al.* (2014) showed significantly improved work-ability perceptions, core self-evaluations, and resilience as compared with the control group, and these changes were still there in a 12-week follow-up measurement. Peláez *et al.* (2020) also see self-reported changes in hope, resilience, optimism, and self-efficacy. De Haan *et al.* (2020) also show self-reported changes in resilience, well-being, and self-efficacy. Dyrbye *et al.* (2019); Fontes and Dello Russo (2020) and McGonagle *et al.* (2020) likewise report strong effects on psychological capital, consisting of hope, optimism, self-efficacy, and resilience.

Jones *et al.* (2006) found some weaker evidence for increasing flexibility (including resilience) through coaching over and above the waiting-list control group.

Job satisfaction and leadership

In Luthans and Peterson's experiment (2003), the coachee's job satisfaction went significantly up and turnover intentions significantly down, and even the coachees' direct reports' job satisfaction went up significantly after the single session of coaching plus 'some follow-up.' Bowles and Picano (2006) show that more involvement with coaching according to the coach was correlated with greater work satisfaction. In a small-scale RCT, Fontes and Dello Russo (2020) replicate this by significant predictions of coaching on self-scored job satisfaction and organisational commitment in the coachee (a weak effect also reported by McGonagle *et al.*, 2020; but not found by Dyrbye *et al.*, 2019, in a similar RCT design).

Ellinger *et al.* (2003), Shanock and Eisenberger (2006), Gregory and Levy (2011), Huang and Hsieh (2015), Hui and Sue-Chan (2018), Kim and Kuo (2015), Weer *et al.* (2016), and Hsu *et al.* (2019) also showed that line-management coaching behaviour as perceived by employees was a highly significant predictor variable for employee citizenship, job satisfaction, team commitment, and motivation. Mackie (2014) and Nieminen *et al.* (2013) show significant effects of coaching on self-scored leadership attributes.

Effects of group coaching

Jordan *et al.* (2016) show that self-scored career planning, self-efficacy, and decision status increase with coaching, significantly more than in the control group. Ebner *et al.* (2017) show that group coaching increases self-efficacy and self-management compared with the control group, and reduces stress-enhancing coping strategies (namely rumination).

5 Changes to self-rated goal-attainment measures

Goal attainment measures were introduced by Kiresuk and Sherman (1968) and they have often been used in coaching research. The basic idea is to select a few goals and then ask the coachee for each goal to rate the degree of achievement and the degree of difficulty on a scale from 1 to 100.

Willms (2004), Grant *et al.* (2009), and Grant *et al.* (2010) found that coaching significantly enhanced goal attainment. McDowall *et al.* (2014) and Zimmermann and Antoni (2018) also show an enhance in goal attainment through coaching, the first mostly in 'feedforward' coaching and the second without a control group comparison. De Haan *et al.* (2020) shows a significant impact on goal attainment, both self-scored and scored by coaches, over and above the control group. Goal attainment was also significantly higher only for the individual coaching condition in Losch *et al.* (2016) and Zanchetta *et al.* (2020), but not in Junker *et al.* (2020).

Burke and Linley (2007) showed that coachees' self-reported 'self-concordance' of their goals, alignment of their goals with their personal values and their own commitment to their goals had significantly increased after a single session of GROW coaching.

Moen and Skaalvik (2009) show significant effects on self-scored goal-setting behaviours and self-attributions of success and of need satisfaction.

6 Changes for the coach rather than the coachee

Mukherjee (2012) has looked at the effects on managers of their coaching training and early experience, from the perspective of internal coachees, and he found a difference in interaction style before and after. In Passmore and Rehman (2012) a similar effect is reported for driving instructors.

Jordan *et al.* (2017) also study the effect of training on coaches and found that coaches' occupational self-efficacy, goal orientation, and career adaptability significantly increased during their train-the-coach course which consisted in part of extensive coaching practice. One could explain this as the students benefiting from 'doing' coaching rather than 'receiving' the benefits of coaching.

Finally, one could argue that through the 'mutual idealisation' in coaching relationships, or just the shared pleasure in achieving results, coaches are benefiting just as much as coachees. Some evidence has already been found that this may be the case – if an employee judges a manager a good coach, there is an increased chance that the manager will see the performance go up (Ellinger *et al.*, 2003; Shanock & Eisenberger, 2006; Gregory & Levy, 2011; Huang & Hsieh, 2015; Kim & Kuo, 2015; Hui & Sue-Chan, 2018; Weer *et al.*, 2016; Hsu *et al.*, 2019). It seems these ratings go further up if the coaching style is in accordance with the implicit person theory of the coachee, i.e. the way the coachee thinks about change. If a coachee is critical about personal change, then critical ('prevention'/'guidance') coaching is more appreciated, whilst supportive ('promotion'/'facilitation') coaching is more appreciated overall, and particularly if a coachee is more convinced of personal change (Sue-Chan *et al.*, 2012; Jarzebowski *et al.*, 2012; Hui *et al.*, 2019).

Part D: what it means for coaching practice

If we look at the objective outcomes of executive coaching conversations that have already been found in the samples in the literature, then we can appreciate the breadth and depth of the (measurable) improvements that have been shown to ensue from coaching. Coaching is a highly personal and 'holistic' intervention, which should flex seamlessly around the wide-ranging needs, challenges, and objectives of the coachee and even the coachee's organisation. Through reflection these needs, challenges, and objectives are explored in terms of meanings, origins, and still deeper-lying issues and needs. For this reason alone, one would hope for coaching results of great variety, stretching from practical to insightful, from quantitative to qualitative outcomes, from enhancement of the coachee's effectiveness to improving the coachee's efficiency. Such variety is indeed what has been found:

- Efficiency improvements: call time reduction in call centres (Liu & Batt, 2010)
- Efficiency improvements: number of units of production per day (Olivero *et al.*, 1997; Poluka & Kaifi, 2015)
- Effectiveness improvements: improved sales conversion rates (Dahling *et al.*, 2016) plus technicians' (Wageman, 2001), waiters' (Latham *et al.*, 2012), and mental-health workers' (Deane *et al.*, 2014) service levels
- Effectiveness improvements in complex medical interventions (related to sensitive conversations with patients: Gattellari *et al.*, 2005; Niglio de Figueiredo *et al.*, 2018; to precision in surgery: Singh *et al.*, 2015; Bonrath *et al.*, 2015; Slegers *et al.*, 2015; and to adherence to childbirth protocols: George *et al.*, 2020)
- Quality improvements: improved health and safety standards (Kines *et al.*, 2010; Slegers *et al.*, 2015; Fischer *et al.*, 2019)
- Quality improvements: academic and practice learning grades and progression (Franklin & Doran, 2009; Vandekerckhove, 2010; Andreanoff, 2016; Passmore & Rehman, 2012)
- Employment transitions: higher rates of return to work and job retention (Hoven *et al.*, 2014; Viering *et al.*, 2015)

Another example of the wide range of outcomes of coaching are the findings by Hui *et al.* (2013): certain coaching interventions were shown to allow coachees to learn more creatively and transfer learning to other tasks, whilst other coaching interventions are more useful for repeat tasks.

These are important results that coaches can take to heart: coaches can continue to flex their interventions and confidently support a very wide range of organisational and personal development issues.

One might add to these important findings (1) the encouraging results regarding goal-attainment on a multitude of self-set goals as summarised in the previous section, and (2) results from research using multi-source feedback instruments, i.e. the improvements to a coachee's leadership or work contribution as assessed by others in his or her organisation, particularly where it could be shown that the coaching condition did better than just giving 360-degree feedback alone (Kochanowski *et al.*, 2010; although Nieminen *et al.*, 2013, contradicts this for their sample), training, or the no-treatment control condition (Goff *et al.*, 2014; Reyes Liske & Holladay, 2016; Fontes & Dello Russo, 2020). Both the goal-attainment and multi-source feedback results underline again the flexibility of significant coaching outcomes, since they can flex around different goals and different job expectations from colleagues, clients, direct reports, and bosses.

O'Connor and Cavanagh (2013) also found increases in well-being in colleagues most closely associated with their coachees in the organisational networks. In other words, executive coaching seems to generate positive 'ripple' effects beyond the coachee, as it should do.

Another exciting development are the first indications that coaching may impact the coachee in deep and rich ways: recently, Allan *et al.* (2018), Zanchetta *et al.* (2020), and De Haan *et al.* (2019) all show an impact of coaching on the coachee's personality. Reductions of neuroticism, general anxiety and fears, impostor tendencies, and excitability may be the consequence of coaching, as well as an increase in conscientiousness, prudence, and responsibility-taking. Even an increase in extraversion is shown in one of these studies: Allan *et al.* (2018).

If we look at the meaning of these measures, we find that the leaders being coached are becoming more self-disciplined, responsible, or conscientious whilst becoming less fearful, moody, annoyed, hard to please, insecure, or emotionally volatile. Executive coaching seems to have a demonstrable calming or containing effect, which is exactly what it sets out to do in being a supportive, conversational, reflective practice. This result is comparable to what was found in psychotherapy. Compare e.g. Roberts *et al.* (2017), a large-scale meta-analysis study into the effect of psychotherapy on similar personality traits (such as emotional stability and extraversion), which has reported midsize effects ($\delta = 0.37$) that persist over substantial periods after treatment. At this point, it is far too early to say if coaching does have the capacity to change the bright or dark sides of personality, or if coaching only affects mood states in such a way that the coachee only 'feels' better or calmer.

We also do not know which aspects of the coaching relationships help most to produce the measured changes. All we know is that measurable adjustments on 'hard' productivity criteria, 360-degree feedback, and rigorous psychometrics do occur in these samples. Regarding the personality changes, the case could be that coachees are generally calmer, happier, or uplifted following the coaching sessions; however, in that case, we would have expected more effects on other personality dimensions as well. Moreover, Roberts *et al.* (2017) make a plausible case that in their very large sample ($N = 20{,}024$), personality traits have been changed substantially and robustly, a change that could not be explained by mood changes. Another possibility is that coachees may have received new insight that sensitized them to their habitual responses, so that they became more self-aware, adaptive, or self-regulated in general ways, without fundamentally changing their deeper 'personalities.'

I would argue this would still change the coachees' reputation in the workplace in a positive manner, so at least their personalities as perceived by others would be affected positively. Moreover, the tools that have been used, the Big Five and Hogan personality models, are well known for measuring lasting reputations in the workplace.

Another area for speculation, and in the future for more research, is the question what exactly contributes to the realised changes in these 'personality derailers'? I would conjecture that to make an impact on these deeper levels of personality in such a short time frame, a combination of substantial safety, trust, and intimacy with direct, frank, and robust challenge would have been required. This may help us to conceptualise coaching for leaders as both a deeply supporting (or, more technically, 'containing') and a robustly challenging intervention. If support and challenge are indeed important, that finding would argue against purely facilitative coaching approaches such as those promoted by prominent coach associations and coaching handbooks.

All other findings about outcome are coachee improvements on certain scales, e.g. those to do with their objectives, their self-motivation, or their well-being or stress. They could be attributed at least in part to a halo effect coming from the coaching, where the coachee just feels good about having been coached and therefore makes all sorts of self-assessments improve on questionnaires related to the coaching.

Summary of Chapter 4: 'Which outcomes does coaching generate?'

In this chapter we have looked much more closely at the changes or 'results' demonstratively generated by executive coaching. This chapter reports on the significant outcomes that coaching has yielded according to the full, current research base. Taking all these sources together, a number of wide-ranging objective outcomes have been found:

- Efficiency savings: call time reduction in call centres
- Efficiency savings: increase of the number of units of production per day
- Effectiveness improvements: improved sales reps' conversion rates and technicians', waiters', and mental-health-workers' service levels
- Effectiveness improvements in complex medical interventions: regarding sensitive conversations with patients and precision in surgery
- Quality improvements: improved health, physical activity, and safety standards
- Quality improvements: better academic and practice learning grades and progression
- Work/Life transitions: higher rates of return to work and of job retention

Moreover, coaching has consistently been found to improve the coachee's 360-degree feedback ratings, not just his or her own ratings but from all parties in the organisation, over and above default improvements from repeat measurement.

Various studies also show an impact of coaching on the coachee's personality. Reductions of neuroticism, of general anxiety (e.g. fears of negative evaluations), of impostor tendencies, and of excitability are shown to be the consequence of engaging with coaching, as well as increases in conscientiousness, prudence, and responsibility-taking.

Apart from this there is overwhelming evidence that coachees do better than control groups on self-rated goal commitment and goal achievement, hope, self-motivation, well-being, resilience, and stress.

These various improvements are self-rated and could therefore be attributed at least in part to a halo effect coming from the coaching. Nevertheless, they are consistent and emerging from a high number of studies.

From all these results we can now safely conclude that coaching is an effective intervention on a very wide variety of results (related to highly tailored coaching objectives), ranging from personal well-being and work efficiencies to organisational effectiveness.

An interlude before Chapter 5

Self-awareness is very much the business of coaching. Many have argued that coaching can only ever change perspective, insight, or outlook – and from that understanding it is the client who will change decisions, ways of being, and performance, quite independent from the coaching.

Some coachees seem to want to use coaching to uphold positive ideas about the self and they fight any critical observations even though at a deeper level they know they may need self-criticism the most. Other coachees seem to critique themselves to such an extent that they come to coaching looking for more self-confidence. In still other cases, both tendencies exist at the same time: rigidly holding on to a frail positive self-image whilst internally suffering from surges of self-doubt.

As coaches we help to offer and collect new observations and together with our clients we work towards more realistic ideas about the self and the coachee's competences. Coachees and organisations ask us to work on self-confidence or self-awareness directly, helping to raise self-belief or to work against self-aggrandizement. We are either employed to scrutinize low self-belief accompanied by rumination or to question overblown ideas about the self. Both overblown and underwhelmed ideas about the self may lead to 'impostor' tendencies which coaching might address. Sometimes the self-belief is already so undermined by rumination and anxiety that the self-awareness that is craved or seems needed is only about positives.

Let me give two slightly extreme examples both heard recently in supervision and disguised: (1) a VP has recently started being coached and has requested some 360-degree soundings by the coach, so as to identify more objectives for the coaching. The coach calculates the extra budget needed and when the VP, Paul, goes back to his CEO for that budget, the CEO suggests that he will save him the additional expense and do the 360-degree interviews for his direct report himself. Somewhat exasperated Paul comes back to the coach, confessing that he did not have much trust in his manager, the CEO, in the first place, so he is now worried that in this way the whole thing may become a rather biased and negative sample of 360-degree observations. The coach explores Paul's trust issues and together they look at various alternatives. Paul decides to go back to his CEO to renegotiate. Perhaps he can do the interviews himself or still obtain some budget for his coach doing a smaller number of 360-degree interviews. Then, a couple of weeks later, there is a request from the CEO to speak with the coach directly. They speak over the phone and the CEO alleges to the coach, 'Paul tells me that you think that I will manipulate the interviews if I do them. Please could you refrain from saying such things. We already have trust issues between us.

I am trying to build higher levels of trust between Paul and me and this is not helpful at all.' The coach states that because of confidentiality he cannot say very much about the coaching, and so the CEO continues, 'Why don't the two of you speak again and feel free to ring me at any time. It would be good if you can work to bring us more together rather than divide us.' The coach obviously feels upset, disappointed, even annoyed with Paul that a normally helpful tool to increase self-awareness is now being politicised and apparently contributing to a further loss of trust between CEO and direct report. He admits to his supervisor to a veritable cocktail of emotions, because he feels guilty for this turn of events and at the same time extremely cautious, almost inhibited in going forward. Can he open this up with Paul? Or will that only lead to more escalation? How could he use these experiences and the acrimony on the recent phone call in Paul's interest? After all, Paul wanted to increase his self-awareness and develop accordingly. The first thing I noticed on hearing this experience from the coach is how he struggled to trust his client Paul now – and how he trusted the CEO even less. We agree that the trust issues which were present from before the coaching started had come out into the open and even spilled into the coaching relationship. In the organisation self-awareness appeared to be lower than before, because self-preservation had taken over.

The coach realised that his slight annoyance with Paul about blaming his coach for the accusation towards the CEO would influence the way he might raise this with him, and that his feelings were moving him away from more deeply trusting Paul and his CEO. He was somewhat taken aback by how much annoyance had seeped into the relationship with his client. Building up his own awareness of the situation and his options helped him in stating the need to build trust for all parties (including himself) so as to create a client relationship in which to be able to work on self-awareness again.

Limited self-awareness leading to higher and higher self-protection, and even to a 'protection racket' around senior executives in a company, is one form in which self-awareness issues can play up in coaching. Organisationally, several individuals spend large quantities of time and energy to protect and maintain their distorted self-beliefs, i.e. to maintain their high self-confidence in the face of critical reports or other evidence to the contrary.

The opposite is also fairly common in my view, where our clients become highly critical of themselves, sometimes over-expose themselves to critical self-awareness and lower their self-ratings to placate their own anxious ruminations. Here is a case in point.

(2) A coach has been working with Madeleine, a highly educated top civil servant who was spending most of the sessions worrying about 'when I will get found out.' She reported with a strong 'inner critic' and repeated time and time again how much she hates making mistakes; in fact, to such an extent that she does not dare to take any risks at work. Her female coach was now, after several sessions, beginning to think she was not doing such a good job as a coach, and perhaps getting too involved with her client. She had already been helping her to rephrase some of her emails so that Madeleine could come across more confidently. Another example was the regular occurrence of Madeleine accusing herself of 'procrastination,' taking many days to answer simple emails. After some exploration by the coach it turned out that the

procrastination was actually a form of perfectionism: Madeleine agonized over every single message, to get it 'right.'

I view these and many similar cases as two instances of the 'impostor syndrome.' One case is often found amongst the dominant nationalities, male and white leaders in organisations. And the other, a self-punishing variety, is encountered more amongst leaders from relative minority groupings, but not at all always. For example, I have occasionally worked with owners in very successful family-held businesses who present in the same way, with very low confidence. However, in those cases they often had had the experience of 'being kept small' by their elders in the business from early childhood.

Both examples are instances of excessive care around whether one is 'good enough' as a leader, even if in some cases one does not trust oneself to give a good rating, whilst in other cases one does not trust others. Put differently, in one scenario the harsh superego is directed internally, at one's one sense of self-worth and serenity, whilst in the other scenario the equally fierce superego is directed externally and becomes grandiosity and judgement of others. Ultimately, in both scenarios we may end up as not feeling trusted or not being very trustworthy. We may become more similar to those 'impostors' we fear that we are, because we are leading a kind of a 'double life' in an increasing number of work relationships. According to research as summarised in the next chapter, it appears that coaches on the whole are more of the former variety than the latter, protecting their high self-regard as 'professionals.' In other words, it appears coaches have distortions of self-awareness towards being more 'coaching' than they really are.

Chapter 5

What perceptual biases may be at play? Can we trust a coach's perceptions of coaching?

In this chapter I will explore what we now know about the perceptual biases of coachees and coaches and how such biases are relevant for research in the coaching field. Interestingly, highly subjective biases can be researched quantitatively if they behave in predictable ways. I will show some such predictable patterns related to the way coaches construct their own interventions and contributions, e.g. where they may have blind spots in their work with their coachees.

Part A: some controversies

I have mentioned many times in this book that so much of our measurement of coaching outcome, and therefore so much of our evidence base in executive coaching, is based on self-perception (mostly by coachees but also by coaches and line managers). Serious questions need to be asked about whether coachees or individual employees can judge the benefit of an organisational-change intervention that should ultimately benefit the shareholders and clients of the organisation. Even though this change intervention is directed at individuals, ultimately how these individuals will act for the organisation and influence others is what matters in judging effectiveness. Moreover, change is in the eye of the beholder. What looks and feels like a very impressive, deep personal change for one person may not amount to much for another and be entirely invisible for a third.

Most of our evidence in executive coaching is based on a change in self-scores by coachees, when coachees rate their state of mind or their experience of coaching. Some ratings are of effectiveness or helpfulness of the coaching, some are ratings of their own goal attainment or even others' goals, some are more about their mood or state of mind, and finally some are on a range of deeper-rooted personality attributes. Beyond these self-scores, coachees have also rated their own productivity. Yet despite all these fine distinctions in the ratings, we know that self-perception has immense biases and that all of these various aspects when measured at the same time point, are likely to correlate strongly with one another giving an impression that they are to a large extent the same for the coachee. A lot of the research summarised so far (not the 'objective' findings listed in the previous chapter, but all other findings summarised there) may have been strongly affected by biases towards 'satisfaction' with coaching or 'post-hoc rationalisation' of coaching, and therefore not truly about 'outcomes' of coaching.

Not only is self-perception in organisations limited and biased, coming from only a single perspective, there is great intrinsic value in bringing in other perspectives or correcting self-perceptions where possible. This is where multi-source feedback plays a key role for executives.

Multi-source feedback has been shown to be an effective intervention (Hazucha *et al.*, 1993; Walker & Smither, 1999; Heslin & Latham, 2004) and works by the grace of different people having a different perspective on the same executive, as measured on a range of scales that are relevant for his or her performance or contribution in the role. It is often surprising for individuals to see how differently they are being viewed by others – that others see them as far less anxious, or as less effective leaders, or as less motivated, or as more insightful and humorous, than they see themselves (and vice versa of course). These 'other-perceptions' open our eyes to our real impact in the workplace.

Executives' performance improves substantially if they receive regular feedback regarding aspects of performance from those they work with most closely, and the performance improves even more if they have a conversation with the feedback giver on the basis of the feedback given (see Walker & Smither, 1999). One way to understand the helpful impact of multi-source feedback is as a way to widen our perspective and to calibrate our own rather limited self-observations.

Some studies show that out of all multi-source feedback our own self-ratings are the worst for predicting our performance whilst the ratings by our direct reports are the best. Atkins and Wood (2002) found that self-ratings were negatively and nonlinearly related to assessment-centre performance, with some of those who gave themselves the highest ratings having in fact the lowest performance on the same competences. Other research also shows self-ratings by executives to have a much lower correlation with performance than direct-report and peer ratings (Gentry *et al.*, 2007). It seems as if ratings by superiors correlate more with the technical competence of the leader and less with the leadership aspects of the role such as the leader's impact on the performance of the team; whilst peer ratings are contaminated by the organisation's politics. Nevertheless, co-worker ratings of self-awareness predict the risk of derailment (Gentry et al., 2009) and of getting fired up to five years later (Gentry et al., 2007). Gentry et al. (2007) also show that the 'self-awareness gap' widens for more senior leaders, due to more inflated self-ratings.

An executive coach is often seen as another important resource which can help to calibrate and adjust self-perceptions in organisations, by exploring them in depth, looking at the evidence for them, and even transforming them by introducing different assumptions or points of view. A coach may even organise a tailored version of multi-source feedback by engaging in short interviews with stakeholders about the coachee, and then bringing the information gathered back to the coachee.

However, coaches themselves are also biased in their perceptions, and that is what the rest of this chapter is about. This chapter is about the limited self-awareness of coaches – something that also plays into the research and may cause additional biases. As we will see, coaches have a very different view of their own skills and their own effectiveness as their clients do. Commissioners, i.e. the bosses of the coachees or else their colleagues, may have very different perceptions and perspectives still.

Controversy 1: what is so bad about the biases in self-scores?

Perceptual biases are not necessarily harmful. They are probably there for a good reason. Having perceptual biases which give a rosier view of oneself can help with our self-confidence and our ability to act even when we have limited data at our disposal. Also, our post-hoc rationalisations keep us happier and more motivated, because they explain to ourselves that we have done well and made the right decisions, whenever that argument can be made plausibly (to ourselves!).

Controversy 2: what is so bad about using self-scores for research?

Some people might say (I am not one of them), what is so bad about self-scores in research? It is well known that self-scores can pick up smaller effects and amplify the effect size, so they may be seen as a more sensitive antenna for the effects of coaching. On the other hand, the over-estimation of effects is arguably not due to the effectiveness of coaching, but rather due to halo effects, common-methods biases, and post-hoc rationalisations, as explained before, and therefore will not necessarily correlate with more objective variables measured by another source.

Controversy 3: is the distinction between self- and other-scores not artificial?

By splitting into self and other scores we may forget that these 'selves' and 'others' are in relationship, whether they are the leader and their team in multi-source feedback, or the coach and the coachee engaged in the coaching sessions. Perceptions are co-created and in fact coach and client need positive self- and other-ratings to flow back and forth in order to do their work well. Technically this is called the establishment of a positive transference, or one might call it 'mutual idealisation': an ongoing, positively validating process, which helps for working together well and for working effectively towards the results of coaching. This mutual affirmation is possibly not what we should measure if we want to inquire into coaching results and outcomes, because it is only a base for good collaboration as a necessary condition to work towards those results. It leads to an increase in alignment between the views of the coach and the coachee on their mutual collaboration, such that their ratings may become similar (for an overview of qualitative research on how the views of the coachee and coach and the commissioner on the coaching sessions themselves differ, see De Haan, 2019b).

Quantitative research that makes use of coachee- or coach-ratings of the relationship or the results runs the risk of inquiring into process rather than outcome, and mistaking a general 'optimism' or 'good rapport' for the achievement of change and objective positive outcomes.

Part B: how to establish coaching self-perception outcomes

1 Research showing coaching changes personal ratings of performance

There are now many studies that compare and disentangle perceptions from different participants in the coaching process (coachees, coaches, colleagues, commissioners) and even outside observers (e.g. researchers looking at videos). See the previous chapter (Chapter 4, section C.2) for an overview of those studies. It was concluded there that coaching generally seems to have the power to improve 360-degree ratings from self, peers, line managers, and reports (Smither *et al.*, 2003; Finn *et al.*, 2007; Kochanowski *et al.*, 2010; Goff *et al.*, 2014; Reyes Liske & Holladay, 2016) although there were several counter-examples too (usually smaller-size studies), where ratings by others around the coachee had not significantly changed and only self-ratings improved.

Client and coach ratings of relationship and performance often correlate with ratings of coaching outcome from other sources (e.g. Smither *et al.*, 2003; De Haan *et al.*, 2019); however, not always. One example is Gessnitzer and Kauffeld (2015) where only observer-rated working-alliance behaviours correlated with coaching outcomes, *not* working-alliance ratings by coach or coachee which did not correlate much with one another either. In fact, it seems the coach is often wrong about their own coaching: Ellinger *et al.* (2003) have found widely differing management coaching perceptions between line managers and employees: 'whereas line managers perceive that they are serving in a developmental role and are engaging in coaching behaviours, their respective employees only moderately perceive that this is the case' (Ellinger *et al.*, 2003, p. 449).

2 Research showing the coach's mindset about change is an important predictor of outcomes

The coach's mindset does seem to matter though for coaching outcomes. Heslin *et al.* (2006) have shown that managers' implicit person theories (IPTs) about the malleability of personal attributes (e.g. personality and ability) affect their willingness and ability to coach others. Specifically, individuals holding an 'entity theory' that human attributes are innate and unalterable are disinclined to invest in helping others to develop and improve, relative to individuals who hold the 'incremental theory' that personal attributes can be developed. Three studies examined how managers' IPTs influence the extent of their employee coaching. The first longitudinal field study found that managers' IPTs predicted employee evaluations of their subsequent employee coaching. This finding was replicated in a second field study. The third experimental study found that using self-persuasion principles to induce incremental IPTs increased entity theorist managers' willingness to coach a poor-performing employee, as well as the quantity and quality of their performance improvement suggestions.

3 Research showing that mindsets of coach and coachee about change strengthen one another

Finally, one could argue that through the 'mutual idealisation' in coaching relationships, or just the shared pleasure in achieving results, coaches are benefiting just as much as coachees. Some evidence has already been found that this may be the case – if an employee judges a manager a good coach, there is an increased chance that the manager will see the performance of that employee go up (Ellinger et al., 2003; Shanock & Eisenberger, 2006; Gregory & Levy, 2011; Huang & Hsieh, 2015; Hui & Sue-Chan, 2018; Weer et al., 2016; Hsu et al., 2019). It seems these ratings go further up if the coaching style is in accordance with the implicit person theory of the coachee: if a coachee is critical about personal change, then critical ('prevention') coaching is more appreciated, whilst supportive ('promotion') coaching is more appreciated generally, and particularly if a coachee is more convinced of personal change (Sue-Chan et al., 2012; Jarzebowski et al., 2012).

Dello Russo et al. (2017) have shown that employees find their organisation less political when they think their manager is a good coach. Ianiro et al. (2013) show that mutual perceptions of dominant-friendly behaviour strengthen the results of coaching.

4 Research showing that coaches develop perceptual biases in looking at their own skills

In order to start investigating coaching skills, one needs a basic tool measuring the full range of interventions that is general and broad enough, not too detailed and complex, and with a limited number of classes of interventions, so that reliable measurements can be made. The model should have high validity as well: both clients and coaches need to be able to recognize each of the classes of intervention from a short description, and their ratings should conform to their intuitive appreciation of the interventions. We have found such a model in the Coaching Behaviours Questionnaire[1] which has 72 items and is an adaptation of Heron's well-known model of counselling interventions (Heron, 1975). Summarising in brief, it has three "push", coach-centred (directive) sets of behaviours – *Prescribing*, *Informing*, and *Confronting* – and three "pull", client-centred (nondirective) sets of behaviours – *Exploring*, *Supporting*, and *Releasing* (see Figure 5.1).

The next section of this chapter will give more insight into the analysis we undertook. This study shows that we can now reliably measure a wide range of coaching interventions and make comparisons between samples of coaches and between the

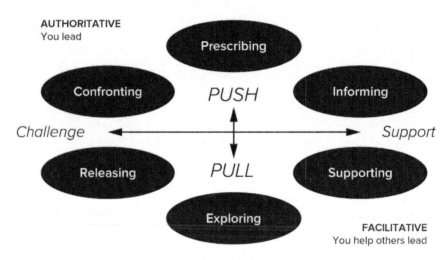

Figure 5.1 The so called 'Heron Model' of counselling and coaching behaviours (after Heron, 1975), stretching from highly directive to highly facilitative interventions, and from challenging to supporting alternatives.

client- and coach-perspective on those same interventions. One might think of the patterns we found as indicative of development and adaptation, with older and professional coaches perceiving more 'typical' pull and client-centred coaching behaviours over time and as they specialize more as coaches. We have found some indications that these are mainly self-perceptions of the professional coaches, which are not shared by their clients. We have found some evidence of coaches adapting to their national cultures and becoming more confrontational, direct, or explorational in cultures where that is more the norm.

It turns out that coaches are not the coach they think they are. Coaches have a different view from coachees about how they are using their coaching skills with them.

Part C: overview of what we know about perceptual biases in coaches about their own coaching

1 A brief review of research on coaching interventions

One of the first to measure coaching behaviours was Hein (1990), using a 'survey of coaching activity' listing six specific coaching behaviours (providing positive feedback, providing negative feedback, providing direction in the coaching conversation, emphasizing facts or concepts, adhering to schedules, and identifying employee development needs) taken by manager and direct report from 90 middle-management relationships in a US national 'high-tech' corporation. He found that the managers' Myers-Briggs Type Indicator (MBTI) personality preferences for Extraversion and Intuition correlated significantly with giving more positive feedback. Also, managers with Judgement preferences placed more emphasis on tight scheduling, and those with preferences for Intuition and Thinking spent more time on identifying development needs. Higher scores on the Extraversion and Intuition dimensions were associated with higher scores (from both managers themselves and their subordinates) for coaching effectiveness. Finally, just like in the later study by De Haan *et al.* (2011), Hein found significant relationships between *all* the coaching behaviours and coaching effectiveness. In his case as well as ours this could very much be the result of same-source bias.

David Noer (2005) developed a 'triangular' coaching-behaviours inventory measuring 'Supporting' (including attending, inquiring, reflecting, affirming behavioural components), 'Challenging' (including confronting, focusing/shaping, reframing, empowering/energizing behavioural components), and 'Assessing' (including data-gathering, gap analysis, goal-setting, measurement/feedback behavioural components), each with ten items. This coaching-behaviours inventory was later used to explore national differences in self-reported coaching styles with a sample consisting of 71 US and 80 Saudi managers from the same petrochemical corporation (Noer *et al.*, 2007). Results indicated that Saudi managers scored significantly higher on 'Supporting' ($\delta = 0.57$; $p < 0.01$) and 'Challenging' ($\delta = 0.35$; $p < 0.05$) dimensions. Moreover, US managers exhibited significantly more variance in their responses on both those scales, so they appeared to be a more heterogenous group with regard to these behaviours. One interesting finding was that self-reported differences in style were not always confirmed on observation of videotaped sessions (Noer, 2005, with regards to 'Supporting' behaviours).

Newsom and Dent (2011) developed an instrument consisting of 152 items of 'work behaviour of executive coaches' which was taken by 130 senior coaches working for a single global consultancy organisation. Factor analysis yielded three main clusters: generic 'professional coach activities,' conversational 'goal setting and attainment activities,' and more intimate 'relationship activities.' They then showed that female coaches self-scored significantly higher on both goal setting and attainment, and on relationship behaviours ($\delta = 0.4$; $p < 0.05$) and more experienced coaches scored themselves significantly higher on goal setting and attainment behaviours ($\delta = 0.49$; $p < 0.05$).

Chen *et al.* (2014) reconstructed Noer's triangular coaching behaviours inventory for Chinese managers with 11, 15, and 20 items on the 'Assessing,' 'Challenging,' and 'Supporting' scales, showing Cronbach Alphas of around 0.9. They looked at self-reported coaching behaviours for a group of 145 Chinese managers from three different sectors, demonstrating that

- women have a significantly higher score than men on the 'Supporting' ($p < 0.05$) dimension and no difference on other dimensions;
- more senior managers self-report significantly more 'Challenging' ($p < 0.01$) and 'Supporting' ($p < 0.05$) behaviours;
- hospital managers report significantly more 'Challenging' ($p < 0.01$) and 'Supporting' ($p < 0.01$) behaviours;
- 'Challenging' and 'Supporting' scores also correlate with age, with older managers reporting significantly more 'Challenging' ($p < 0.01$) and 'Supporting' ($p < 0.05$) behaviours;
- 'Assessing' ($p < 0.05$) and 'Challenging' ($p < 0.01$) coaching behaviour scores also correlate positively with 'pleasure' in their 'orientation to happiness' scale (the scale consists of 'pleasure,' 'meaning,' and 'engagement').

The effect sizes are all of small to medium size: δ between 0.18 and 0.55.

De Haan *et al.* (2011) examine how various executive-coaching interventions make a difference to clients. A total of 71 coaching clients, senior managers from nearly as many organisations, reported on the various interventions of their accredited external coaches with a predecessor of the Coaching Behaviour Questionnaire (CBQ), and these ratings were compared with their evaluations. De Haan *et al.* (2011) found a strong relationship between perceived coaching behaviours and client-reported effectiveness (δ = 1.1 for the combined model; $p < 0.001$), but no distinction among specific coach interventions: just as in Hein (1990), clients did not appear to prioritise any one category of behaviour above others, except for some individual items such as 'Playing the devil's advocate' and 'Converting objections into opportunities,' where no significant link with effectiveness was found. Same-source bias was likely to play a role here. Nonetheless, in the eyes of clients the helpfulness of their coach is experienced almost indiscriminately across all coaching behaviours, corroborating the suggestion that factors common to all coaching, such as the relationship, empathic understanding, and positive expectations are important for effectiveness (De Haan, 2008).

Ianiro *et al.* (2013) analysed executive-coaching outcomes on the basis of genuine interaction data from videotaping 33 initial coaching sessions with trainee psychologists as coaches and young professionals as clients, in terms of both the client's and the coach's interpersonal behaviour over two basic dimensions: Affiliation and Dominance (the well-known Leary, 1957, model). Findings suggest that both (1) the coach's Dominance behaviour and (2) similarity of Dominance and Affiliation behaviour between coach and client predicted positive client ratings of goal-attainment after 5 more sessions; whilst (2) also predicted positive client ratings of the relationship quality after 5 sessions. Similarly, Will *et al.* (2016) analysed videotapes of 19 one-off sessions in terms of coaches' empathetic behaviour as perceived by both clients and coaches. They found that coaches' and clients' ratings of empathy did not correlate and that 'paraphrasing' behaviours of coaches were indeed correlated with clients' perceived empathy and were also significantly followed by affirmative client responses.

2 Research on coaching interventions using the Coaching Behaviours Questionnaire

The fourth version of our Coaching Behaviours Questionnaire (CBQ) was used in a large-scale study of coaching behaviours, amongst 537 professional-coaches, 196 consultant-coaches, and 559 manager-coaches from a total of 54 countries, and also 221 clients of coaching. The study demonstrated significant differences in perceived behaviour by coaches who differ in gender, age, and nationality. Significant differences are also found for those that identify themselves as 'managers' versus 'consultants' versus 'coaches.' Finally, we found that client-reported behavioural profiles are systematically different from their coaches' own profiles. Here is a summary of that research; details can be found in De Haan and Nilsson (2017).

The model was proposed by John Heron (1975; see figure 5.1) and looks at coaching skills and behaviours in a broad sense, through six classes of interventions that a coach may use:

1 *Prescribing* (PR): giving directions, advice, and recommendations to the learner/coachee. The coach directs the learning experience in some way, taking a degree

of responsibility for coaching goals, learning methods, the design and possible solutions within the coaching experience, and the learning review and assessment process.
2   *Informing* (IN): giving information and knowledge to the learner/coachee. The coach gives information to the learner; this could be technical, professional, business, or organisational knowledge. It could also be 'feedback' about the content of coaching or about the potential consequences of different courses of action. The coach might offer this spontaneously or might be asked for it by the learner.
3   *Confronting* (CO): challenging the learner/coachee's assumptions; stimulating their awareness of their own behaviour, attitudes, or beliefs. The coach uses confrontation to help the learner to gain a deeper awareness of something that appears (to the coach) important to his or her learning.
4   *Releasing* (RL; or, in Heron's own terms, *cathartic* interventions): helping the learner/coachee to release tension, and to discharge or come to terms with emotions that are blocking progress. The coach helps the learner to express and to deal with emotions that are holding him or her back in the learning activity.
5   *Exploring* (EX; or, in Heron's own terms, *catalytic* interventions): helping the learner/coachee to self-discovery, to self-directed learning, and to owning and solving his or her own problems, without becoming involved in the learning or change oneself as a coach. Skills used within EX are active listening, summarising, paraphrasing, echoing, and inquiring more deeply through open, coachee-led questioning.
6   *Supporting* (SU): building the learner/coachee's self-esteem, self-confidence, and self-respect. Self-esteem is strengthened by welcoming and offering specific support, appreciation, and praise; expressing confidence or agreement; or by appropriate self-disclosure and sharing.

We used Heron's summaries of relevant behavioural categories to redesign the CBQ as a circumplex model with six opposite pairs that can be mapped on two orthogonal axes. These axes reflect choices that have long been recognized to be important in helping conversations (De Haan & Burger, 2005): directive versus nondirective interventions ('push' versus 'pull') and challenging versus supporting interventions ('addressing weaknesses' versus 'supporting strengths'). The circumplex structure suggests that coaching behaviours are distributed in a two-dimensional circular space, spanned by dominance (push versus pull) and appreciation (pessimism versus optimism) dimensions, a bit like Timothy Leary's circumplex model of interaction, which is spanned by dominance and affiliation (Leary, 1957). Dominance represents the vertical axis and appreciation represents the horizontal axis, whilst the centre of the circle represents a neutral level of both and so ultimately a vanishing of the coaching relationship. The model implies that the best coaches are those whose repertoires can flexibly and nimbly use the full range of behavioural presence at the right time.

The six classes of intervention illustrate that as a coach you have a dizzying range of interventions at your disposal. At any point in time in a coaching conversation, you will have the options of:

1   not doing anything, devoting your energy to following the coachee and to listening;
2   offering a piece of direction, either by means of an advice or suggestion (*Prescribing*) or by means of information that might help the coachee (*Informing*);

3   offering a challenge to the coachee, a different way to look at his or her issues (*Confronting*);
4   offering facilitative interventions, by offering warmth and support (*Supporting*), an effort to summarise and inquire more deeply into the issues at stake (*Exploring*), or an invitation to open up emotional undercurrents to the issues and the conversation itself (*Releasing*).

Each of these can have very different effects on your coachee and the conversation. One might argue that a truly skilful coach would be able to:

- have a view and careful consideration on when to lead and when to follow, choosing an appropriate balance between direction and facilitation;
- select and apply intervention styles appropriate to particular learners in particular situations;
- use a range of skills and interventions within each style for maximum effectiveness;
- use the styles consistently in terms of meta-communication and nonverbal support; and
- move cleanly and elegantly from one intervention to another as required.

Coaches, consultants, managers, and clients participated in this survey-based study, and data collection took place between December 2013 and March 2017. In that period a total of 1,302 participants completed the survey. However, demographic information was only available on 1,292 of participants, which excludes the remaining participants from demographic comparisons. The distributions consisted of 559 professional coaches, 196 consultants, and 537 managers. Gender distribution consisted of 755 females and 537 males. The mean age belonged to the age group 41–50 ($SD = 1.34$ on a 9-point scale). The sample consisted of 54 different nationalities and the largest samples were from the Netherlands ($N = 475$), the United Kingdom ($N = 348$) and Belgium ($N = 132$). Also, 234 coaching clients participated in this research with 13 incompletes, which rendered 221 complete client questionnaires.

3 Significant differences found for gender, age, job, and nationality of the coach

Here are the systematic differences on the six classes of coaching behaviours that we found in our sample, between various groups of coaches and also between those coaches and their clients:

Firstly, women score themselves higher on the pull interventions and lower on the push interventions than their male counterparts, whilst they do not differ significantly in the amount of 'challenge' and 'support' they think they give their coachees (δ between 0.38 and 0.53; $p < 0.001$).

Secondly, older coaches/consultants/managers score significantly lower on push interventions than their younger colleagues (δ between 0.41 and 0.67; $p < 0.001$), particularly if the under-40s are compared with the over-40s. They also reported giving less active support whilst their emotionally *Releasing* interventions are more prevalent in their self-scores.

Thirdly, job role influences the scores on the questionnaire as well. Manager-coaches, consultant-coaches, and 'professional' coaches self-score progressively lower on push and supportive interventions whilst they score themselves progressively higher on pull (*Exploring* and *Releasing*) interventions (δ between 0.20 and 0.41; p < 0.01). In other words, participants who describe their role as 'coaches' report a more 'coaching' (pull) profile in their scores. This may be the influence of progressive 'acculturation' in the consulting and coaching professions, where coaches learn to think about their interventions progressively in terms of more 'typical' coaching interventions, i.e. the 'pull' behaviours within *Exploring* and *Releasing*. In fact, we find that if client scores are compared to all three categories, the discrepancies are largest for professional coaches, which indicates that coaches may be changing their self-perceptions more than their actual coaching behaviours.

Fourthly, there are significant differences in scores when measured against country of origin. We first took the three largest countries in the sample: the Netherlands (N = 475), United Kingdom (N = 348), and Belgium (N = 132). We found self-scored coaching behaviours from Belgium and the Netherlands are higher on *Confronting* and lower on *Exploring* behaviour than those from the United Kingdom (with the former effect size δ = .70, a medium-sized effect, and the latter δ = .28, a small effect; p < 0.001). This result gives us confidence that over time more national differences can be demonstrated with this questionnaire.

We have also checked the conclusions on national differences from the Noer *et al.* (2007) article. Even though datasets from 'Northern America' (United States plus Canada, N = 39) and from the 'Middle East' (14 different Middle Eastern countries, N = 64) were small, we still found significant results. Self-reported *Prescribing* and *Informing* were higher in Northern American coaches, whilst self-reported *Releasing* and *Exploring* were higher in Middle Eastern coaches (with effect sizes δ between .67 and 1.0; i.e. large effects; p < 0.001). On the other hand, there were only small and contrarily significant differences in *Confronting* and *Supporting*, as would have been expected on the basis of the Noer *et al.* (2007) results. Similar to those results, however, the variance in our Northern American sample was higher than in the Middle Eastern sample, although only significantly so for the *Prescribing* dimension. Any differences may be due to sample biases. Noer *et al.* (2007)'s dataset consisted entirely of manager-coaches, whilst our Middle East dataset is dominated by professional coaches and has proportionally more female and older coaches than the North American dataset. Nevertheless, it is interesting to see that both regions' average scores are widely differing from the European averages (e.g. much more *Prescribing* in North America and much more *Exploring* in the Middle East), confirming that substantial national differences are to be expected around the world.

Fifthly, clients of executive coaches are scoring their own coaches significantly higher on push interventions than the coaches themselves do, whilst they score them significantly lower on some pull interventions. We believe this shows that coaches may be more central in their interventions than they themselves realise. They may be giving more advice (*Prescribing*) and information (*Informing*) – at least in the eyes of their clients – than they think.

Moreover, they do not go as deeply into the client's inner world and emotions (*Releasing*) as they perceive themselves doing (δ between 0.61 and 0.77; p < 0.001). We do not know if any of this 'general feedback for coaches' is related to skill; however, it is tempting to think that the coaches are sometimes so busy with their own ideas and suggestions that they attend less to their clients' emotional process and so become less effective coaches. Certainly, their clients are saying demonstrably that the coaches are placing themselves more central with their advice and information than the coaches themselves think.

Sixthly, we have found evidence that the differences in self-perceptions of coaches are not replicated by their clients, namely for the 'gender' and 'job description' dimensions where this could be tested. The fact that these coach differences are not confirmed by the client scores provides strong indications that the differences found, at least on the 'gender' and 'job description' dimensions, are mainly due to self-perception of the coaches. It seems therefore that self-identification of female and professional coaches is more 'pull,' whilst this does not show up as different behaviour towards the clients.

4 An interpretation of these findings

As briefly summarised here, De Haan and Nilsson (2017) show that there are systematic differences in their sample between various groups of coaches and also between coaches and their clients. Women score themselves higher on the nondirective interventions and lower on the directive interventions than their male counterparts, whilst they do not differ significantly in the amount of 'challenge' and 'support' they think they give their coachees. Executive coaching has often been called a 'female profession' since it is geared towards receiving the client, nurturing the ideas and development of the client, and helping to look after the client's agenda. These are perceived to be traditionally and biologically more female roles (see, e.g., De Haan, 2008). It is therefore interesting if these self-perceptions can also be picked up as different behaviour in practice. There is already some evidence that female coaches are slightly more effective in the eyes of clients than their male counterparts (De Haan *et al.*, 2016).

Similar to the gender differences, older coaches/consultants/managers score significantly lower on directive interventions than their younger colleagues. They also reported giving less active support whilst their emotionally *Releasing* (cathartic) interventions are more prevalent in their self-scores.

Job role influences the scores on the questionnaire as well. Manager-coaches, consultant-coaches, and 'professional' coaches self-score progressively lower on directive and supportive interventions whilst they score themselves progressively higher on nondirective (*Exploring* and *Releasing*) interventions. In other words, participants who describe their role as 'coaches' report a more 'coaching' (nondirective) profile in their scores. This may be the influence of progressive 'acculturation' in the consulting and coaching professions, where coaches learn to think about their interventions progressively in terms of more 'typical' coaching interventions, i.e. the 'pull' behaviours within *Exploring* and *Releasing*. In fact, we find that if client scores are compared to all three categories, the discrepancies are largest for professional coaches, which indicates that coaches may be changing their self-perceptions more than their actual coaching behaviours.

There are some significant differences in scores when measured against country of origin. We found substantial differences in terms of how many *Confronting* interventions have been reported: highest in the Netherlands, mid-level in Belgium, and lowest in the United Kingdom. There are significant differences in terms of how many *Exploring* interventions have been reported as well: highest in the United Kingdom, and lower in Belgium and the Netherlands. Similar contrasts of 'directness' and 'nonavoidance' were reported by Van Meurs (2003) in her PhD thesis on negotiations between Dutch and UK managers. From personal experience and studying cultural assessments of national cultures (e.g. the dimension of internal versus external control in Trompenaars's well-known 7-dimensional model), we can recognize the progressive increase in *Confronting* from the UK, to Belgium, and then to the Netherlands.

Clients of workplace coaches are scoring coaches significantly higher on directive interventions, whilst they score them significantly lower on some nondirective (*Releasing*) interventions. Three effects are significant, which show that clients see their coaches do more *Prescribing* and *Informing* and less *Releasing* than coaches are scoring themselves. We believe this shows that coaches may be more central in their interventions than they themselves realise. They may be giving more advice (*Prescribing*) and information (*Informing*) than they think. Moreover, they do not go as deeply into the client's inner world and emotions (*Releasing*) as they perceive themselves doing. We do not know if any of this 'general feedback for coaches' is related to skill; however, it is tempting to think that these coaches are sometimes so busy with their own ideas and suggestions that they attend less to their clients' emotional process to be truly effective coaches. Certainly, their clients are saying to some significant extent that the coaches are doing this more than they themselves think. It would be worth testing if clients also *wish* their coaches to be less advisory, informing and more in tune with their own highly personal emotional experience. We know from other studies that clients may perceive the empathic behaviour of coaches differently from coaches themselves (Will et al., 2016) and that they perceive effectiveness of coaching quite differently from their coaches (De Haan et al., 2016). Given that the client sample is still small and the effects are nonetheless large, we believe more research needs to be done and are looking forward to replicating this analysis with larger samples.

We have also found evidence that the differences in self-perceptions of coaches are not replicated by their clients, namely for the 'gender' and 'job description' dimensions where this could be tested. The sample is still relatively small so we need to be cautious in drawing conclusions; however it seems that perhaps self-identification of female and professional coaches is more nondirective, whilst this does not show up as different behaviour towards the clients. It is clearly possible that such perhaps more sophisticated coaches change something about their behaviour that the client does not even notice whilst still being impacted; however there is no evidence yet for such a differential impact on clients.

Coaches, consultants and managers may have answered in the direction of 'how they want to become' rather than 'how they see themselves right now' (although the questionnaire asks specifically not to do that). Similarly, coaches, consultants, and managers may have answered in the direction of 'how they ought to coach' rather than 'how they coach right now' (social-desirability bias).

In addition, coaches, consultants, and managers may experience difficulty in observing their own interventions (same-source bias), or they may be unsure, self-critical, or defensive in sharing their self-observation. They may have interpreted the descriptions of interventions more or less extremely and may have had a 'central-tendency' bias on all dimensions (although the ipsative nature of the questionnaire has a considerable mitigating effect on such response biases). Coaches, managers, and consultants may have interpreted the descriptions through different cultural, linguistic, or educational-background lenses. Coachees may also adopt a different cultural standard for the observation of female coaches, which could explain why they do not see them as 'nondirective' as they see themselves.

These reporting biases may make it difficult to attribute results to the independent variables that we have measured. There could also well be other underlying variables that we have not measured directly, which moderate the effects that we have found, such as to do with meta-communication, relational orientation, or attachment styles.

Another limitation of this research is the relatively low volume of feedback scores from clients of coaching. The matched $N = 91$ sample seems however large enough to compare coach and client scores in the same coaching relationship, detecting both significant correlations and significant biases.

Part D: what it means for coaching practice

Regarding the scoring of relevant variables for coaching we have first learned that ratings coming from the coach-coachee pair tend to behave in unexpected ways:

1 When coach and coachee independently rate the same common aspect of their collaboration, such as the working alliance, we find surprisingly low agreement: $\delta \approx 0.23$ ($p < 0.05$; Gessnitzer & Kauffeld, 2015; De Haan *et al.*, 2016).
2 When on the other hand the coachee – and presumably also the coach – rates highly disparate variables at the same time, such as well-being, perceived stress, coaching effectiveness, resilience, self-efficacy, and satisfaction of needs, we find surprisingly high agreement: $\delta \approx 0.87$ ($p < 0.001$; Zimmermann & Antoni, 2020; De Haan *et al.*, 2020).

Despite the proud independence of coach and coachee in determining ratings on their collaboration, we have also seen some evidence for *co-creation* of ratings, namely when coachees rate their coach (manager) as very competent they are also being rated competent by their coaches (Ellinger *et al.*, 2003; Shanock & Eisenberger, 2006; Gregory & Levy, 2011; Huang & Hsieh, 2015; Hui & Sue-Chan, 2018; Weer *et al.*, 2016; Hsu *et al.*, 2019).

We have also seen evidence for a subtle *co-creation* of the need for coaching which leads to the finding that similar effect sizes are found for different 'doses' of coaching (i.e. for different numbers of sessions; see Anthony *et al.*, 2013; Goff *et al.*, 2014; and in the realm of psychotherapy: Stiles *et al.*, 2015).

This chapter has added to these remarkable findings the *creation* of the nondirective coach: how with increasing age, increasing specialisation in coaching, and also for female coaches, we see a greater self-reported use of nondirective 'coaching' styles. De Haan and Nilsson (2017) show that we can now reliably measure a wide range of coaching interventions and make reliable comparisons between samples of coaches and between the client and coach perspective on those same interventions. There seem to be systematic scoring patterns in terms of directive and nondirective coaching styles; and also in terms of the amount of support or challenge provided by the coach, consultant, or manager. One might think of the patterns we found as indicative of development and adaptation, with older and professional coaches perceiving more 'typical' nondirective and client-centred coaching behaviours over time and as they specialize more as coaches. We have also found some indications that these are mainly self-perceptions of the professional coaches, which are not shared by their clients. We also found some confirmation that one can see coaching as more a 'female' profession with female coaches and more experienced coaches perceiving more 'typical' coaching skills in their own work. Finally, we have found some evidence of coaches adapting to their national cultures and self-describing as more confrontational, direct, or explorational in cultures where that is more the norm. However, the systematic patterns we have found still need to be linked back to measurable behaviours and skills – since this is not yet the case, we have only found evidence for patterns in the *perceptions* of coaching skills.

Clearly there are predictable, demonstrable (significant) patterns in those perceptions – e.g. that coaches usually over-rate their coaching skills precisely when they are formally and officially, coaches. Their clients tend to see less 'coaching' skills than the coaches are imagining there to be.

In this chapter we have learned that future researchers need to be wary about coachee self-reported changes but also about coach-reported changes and coach self-perceptions of their own skills.

However, coaches also need to be wary – especially as they are becoming more experienced – about their listening skills. They may think they are deepening them and progressing to being ever more *exploring* and *releasing* coaches (or, as John Heron would have said: cathartic and catalytic coaches), since chances are that their clients are not recognising such progress in them. Even this could be post-hoc rationalisation: after completing so many hours of training and many more of supervision, after passing certain exams and accreditation, why would they not be simply 'better' coaches using more typical coaching styles and interventions?

As coaches we need to keep checking our skills, with our clients and supervisors, and by practicing our coaching in supervision groups, collecting feedback on how we work. Moreover, we need to keep an open mind as to how we may be perceived by our clients: we may think we are a good listener and a very nondirective coach, but our clients may perceive that very differently.

It may be that some self-doubt in this regard is a good thing. It is well known that inexperienced coaches do experience a lot of self-doubt, but their more experienced colleagues much less (De Haan, 2019a). Even though as a coach you may have many doubts about your client's issues, your work with your clients, and your own interventions, you are not immune to perceptual bias regarding both your client's issues and your own coaching skills.

Summary of Chapter 5: 'What perceptual biases may be at play?'

In this chapter we have looked much more closely at what is behind 'ratings' of coachee and coach on various instruments. How trustworthy is the (self-) perception of these partners in a change process, and how does their perception get swayed by participating in research about coaching?

We found evidence that when coach and coachee independently rate the same common aspect of their collaboration, such as the working alliance, we find a surprisingly low overlap of scores: in fact, nearly no overlap.

When on the other hand the coachee – and presumably also the coach – rates highly disparate variables, such as their well-being, perceived social support, resilience, self-efficacy, satisfaction of needs, or the coaching effectiveness, all also at the same point in time, we find surprisingly high overlap of scores: i.e. large correlations.

We found some evidence as well for the *co-creation* of ratings, namely when coachees rate their coach as very competent they are also being rated competent by their coaches, a process of mutual idealisation.

Furthermore, we have seen evidence for a subtle *co-creation* of the need for coaching which leads to the finding that similar effect sizes are found for different 'doses' of coaching.

Coach ratings are also saying as much about their own ideas about self as about their skills in the eyes of others:

- Female coaches report that they are more nondirective than male coaches, although their clients do not confirm this.
- The same for specialised coaches: they report more *Releasing* and *Exploring* than their consultant and manager colleagues – however, their executive-coaching clients do not recognise this difference.
- Older coaches also self-report more *Releasing* and *Exploring* than younger coaches.
- Cultural differences come through in the self-reports as well, with more *Confronting* in Holland and Belgium than in the United Kingdom; and relatively more *Prescribing* in North America with generally more *Exploring* in the Middle East.
- Coachees are scoring their own coaches significantly higher on directive interventions than the coaches themselves do, whilst they score them significantly lower on some nondirective interventions.

Note

1 The first version of the questionnaire was created and used by Richard Phillips in 1994, and subsequent versions were developed with help from Alex Davda, Helen Lockett, John Pateman, and Judy Curd at Ashridge.

An interlude before Chapter 6

It strikes me that many of the positive as well as the negative outcomes of coaching are linked to the experience of *being seen* in coaching. Seeing leads to noticing, valuing, rating, being seen for who you are, a personal distinction, shining a light, reaching new insight on challenges, acquiring new perspectives, etcetera. But seeing can equally lead to exposing, prying (e.g. prying behind a mask or a false-self presentation), discovering, shaming, and critiquing – experienced as an inquisitive, judging, or critical glance.

I remember one client, Susan, who began with very high expectations and a strong idealisation of me and the coaching, with high-flown objectives despite a rather chaotic, almost transient life and career. Having grown up in a sectarian environment, she was finding it very difficult to trust, both to trust herself and to trust others. She was still living the experience of the ostracised, the 'outcast,' the black sheep of the family, someone who had left the sect to go out into the 'worldly world' where she had found great personal and business success. From the beginning of our work there were references to sadness and conflict, e.g. 'I wasted a decade of my life,' but overall, the beginning of our relationship was strong, hopeful, even jolly and somewhat flirtatious. I felt I was being put on a pedestal and into a position of authority. I think I made the mistake with this client to assume that she wanted to be 'seen' by me and that she would value exploration and hypothesis like so many other coachees. I slowly learned that this was not really the case with Susan. As I was coming close with what I thought was my positive regard and my empathetic understanding I was actually frightening her and slowly turning her away. Since this time, I have occasionally noticed the same with other clients.

Let me briefly sum up my work with Susan. In the first sessions we managed to formulate and progress several of her objectives which included her difficulties in trusting others and showing those that she felt suspicious towards more than a rather sweet and lovely but somewhat shallow style of collaboration. We noticed how she was offering me as a coach a similar kind of interaction at times. Three or four explorative sessions ensued.

There was a significant moment when I observed how she often talked about major events and decisions in a rather casual way, as if wanting to move onwards straight after telling me. As if they were not major events that stirred up major feelings. Susan confirmed my observation, when I put it to her, by becoming very moved and blushing. She said, 'Clearly, I like to think and talk, but I'm not good at feeling what I feel.'

Susan was doing well with her organisational targets and becoming more confident as a leader. I experienced her as still idealising me and being very tolerant of my mistakes, very accommodating, gracious, and apologetic. Large parts of sessions became quite animated, although drifting off from our objectives and where the learning might be, at least in my view. Every time I tried to bring our work back to those overall objectives, there was largely a cognitive response. I wrote in my session notes, 'It all seems so easy, so smooth and so uneventful. Really difficult to point to a single moment of importance.'

In a symbolic way the topic of indoctrination which she knew so well from her childhood became part of our work. One day, she had just sat down and then pulled two books out of her bag that she had just bought on her way in, both handbooks of coaching. I was struggling to respond. My client was bringing in books on helping conversations, books about *my* profession, books by other coaches. Was she just expressing her curiosity in me and my profession, or was there a veiled criticism in bringing those books, as if they described what I was failing to offer? If I had said something about what I thought about the books, I could accuse myself of trying to indoctrinate my client, which is not what I wanted, so I kept quiet despite her invitations to comment. I felt us slowly drifting apart in that moment. Almost an hour into the session, Susan was in my view just chatting away about life, opportunities and missed opportunities. After trying to deepen the 'chat' by referring to loss, disappointment, grief, and mourning, I took the session head-on and suggested we would 'work on' something, and I also suggested that we explored what she was expressing by bringing the books. Straightaway I thought that I was being too directive, informed mostly by my own needs and sentiment that the session was not going anywhere nor delivering anything. Did I want to show my own 'manual,' show how I could also achieve things in coaching?

After spending two or three sessions trying to trust the process whilst dancing around the objectives, Susan started postponing and cancelling sessions and even failed to turn up once. My efforts to speak about how this might be meaningful and how we had perhaps got stuck or not delivered for her and we might look into that, etc., did not meet much of a response and failed to improve this pattern. What turned out to be our final meeting was the one before the last agreed session. I am used in my practice to encountering critical moments around endings, so I was hypothesising that the difficult ending was also somehow to do with the coaching. By this time even though she turned up for the session Susan was not really engaging with it. She did make one telling remark in that final hour, suggesting that perhaps I had only gone 'the extra mile' with her because of my fees. After this session she did not come back, and she did not pay the last invoice which I thought was expressing a disappointment with the coaching most of all.

The work with Susan made me explore the potential for pain in being seen. Maybe I as a coach had to engage in a transformation similar to what Rilke described in *Wendung*, his famous poem that marked an important turning point in his career. In the poem Rilke concludes that although 'seeing' can feel very helpful and powerful and yields beautiful poetry, 'seeing' also degrades and objectifies. He affirms that the power of his look could force nature and inanimate objects to submit to him: 'stars collapsed on their knees,' and towers were 'filled with terror' such that they had to be rebuilt. There were strong benefits as well, a landscape could 'rest in his calm perception,' animals and birds trusted him, imprisoned lions 'stared into his regard as if in unfathomable freedom,' and flowers returned his gaze as they did to little children. The very rumour of such an observer, a seer, stirred up women. The turning point of 'Turning' (*Wendung*) comes when the poet realises the limits of his former successes, when he realises how scatterbrained and grumpy he has become and how he is even shamefully avoiding his own image in the mirror. He realises he cannot go forward with himself and his poetry because he is lacking love. From there he concludes the known world wants to be nourished in love. He asserts therefore that the 'work of the eyes is done,' and he must now go forth and 'do heart-work' on the very images his gaze has brought him, yet he still does not truly know. He decides to connect to this trace within himself and learn from another, more feminine side within him. That is the vision that ends the poem.

I believe this poem carries a truth for coaches as well. Coaching geared towards seeing, empathising, and observing runs the risk that we deplete ourselves and hurt our coachees: our seeing can be felt as valuing and judging. So maybe our work should be more about connecting with our own hearts, our own inner feeling which somehow connects in a deeper, fuller way with the other person. Being in close communion with ourselves can help us to ground ourselves, ignite and sustain personal 'heart work' which goes beyond the kind of negative side effects I have experienced in the work with Susan.

Chapter 6

What about negative side effects of coaching? Are there risks? Can coaching do harm?

This chapter is best seen as a 'final check' on all the results summarised in this book, a final check on the rather strong case for coaching being an effective intervention with a rich variety of significant impacts for coachees and their organisations. We will now look at the case that can be made *against* coaching, based on all the inconclusive and contrary findings in this book, and also based on the case *for* negative side effects which has been made by a few researchers. We will introduce some new (mainly qualitative) research in this chapter, and we shall look through a new lens at the research already covered in this book. At the end of the chapter we will have to conclude that the case *for* coaching is still robust even if very incomplete and tentative, and we finish with some recommendations for future coaching researchers.

Part A: some controversies

In a rigorous book about coaching outcome research we do need to tell the 'counter narrative' to the dominant findings that have been summarised already. Are there any cases where coaching does not deliver or even has an adverse effect? Or else, with such a lot of evidence that coaching can be helpful and effective (as found earlier, in Chapters 1, 2, and 4), does coaching nevertheless come with adverse side effects, or risks, or losses to the coachee's functioning and competence?

That is what this chapter will look into. What evidence do we have to the contrary? What costs or risks or downsides of coaching have been found through the same rigorous research methods that have been demonstrating those positive changes? Are there patterns within the less favourable results that we need to be aware of? What 'null hypotheses' do we need to accept about coaching?

The standard of new evidence will be lower in this chapter, since there have not been that many research groups actively looking for negative outcomes of coaching. What we have is mainly (correlations between) survey data – no control groups, not even measurement of outcomes. When this work reaches the same significance, it should probably be reviewed together with and alongside the studies that have looked for positive outcomes, so it would have to be reviewed in Chapters 1 and 2.

The main reason for dedicating a special chapter to 'negative outcomes' is that there has not been much research into this, and there has not been much evidence of negative outcomes. This critical voice would be snowed under if it did not receive a chapter of its own. Moreover, it is good science to amplify that voice: give one's opponents or the single 'counterexample' the maximum amount of space and time. After all, their voices are the only chance that we might all be spurred on to greater levels of certainty: a single, convincing counter example can make a whole theoretical edifice crumble and perish, according to the lauded principle of 'falsifiability.'

Before summarising all the evidence we can muster *against* coaching, let us look at a few controversies first and then in the next section, I will look at the research methods and first indications of possible negative side effects from qualitative research.

Controversy 1: can we actually treat 'negative' outcomes separate from 'positive' ones?

Researching 'negative (side) effects of coaching' presupposes that we all agree on what negative side effects *are*, e.g. that we would all agree for any outcome that it is either a positive one or a negative one. But the world of coaching is not as simple as that: one person's negative outcome can very well be another's victory lap. The assumption that we know what 'negative outcomes' are in an absolute sense can and should be questioned. We might even question the whole underlying mindset that endeavours to split off the negative from the positive effects. 'Splitting' often seems a convenient process, for it brings us two neatly separated piles of results, a blanket of security amidst a confusing and sometimes terrifying world. A pile of 'good things' (i.e. 'us') and a pile of 'bad things' (i.e. 'them'). We feel that we have brought some order to the world and we can start embracing the positives and pushing away the negatives, so that we can live a 'good life.' Coaches however know better; they know about the presence of the shadow within the good and the silver lining surrounding the negative. Ever since the times of Melanie Klein have analysts and coaches helped to expose and counter the illusions and false dichotomies of 'splitting and projecting' in our clients' minds.

Therefore, as in so many other areas of life, coaching outcomes are not either positive or negative. If coaching works, then coaching can positively strengthen good as well as bad management, healthy as well as relatively toxic organisations, e.g. coaching can strengthen authoritarian leadership to become even more powerful and oppressive, which may have serious negative consequences for minorities or vulnerable groups in the organisation. There are 'very real dangers' within executive coaching (Berglas, 2002), even if so much of it is geared towards the good in organisations and there are so many positive outcomes of coaching to report.

I would go further and say that negatives and positives are hard to distinguish, just as main effects and side effects, because within every positive effect there can be an unavoidable negative consequence. Classical is the case where a line manager describes the increase in self-confidence of their direct report as a real gain from the coaching contract, yet adds that in meetings this very same employee has now become too assertive and dominant (e.g. one of the sponsors of the research in De Haan *et al.*, 2016, wrote in the open question: 'Positive: opening the mind-set to emerging organisational development. Negative: being coached on self-confidence issues which resulted in some relationship issues').

In the hurly-burly, dynamic, antagonistic, political world of large organisations it is arguable that within every positive outcome a negative outcome of coaching can be found. And conversely, anyone's negative side effect is another colleague's palpable gain from the same coaching assignment.

It is best for research to focus on the ability of the collaborative work in coaching to produce *changes* for the individual and their organisation, without perhaps being able to comment on whether these changes are actually positive or negative, certainly not in an absolute sense. So, a researcher may find that coaching leads to significantly higher sales performance (e.g. Dahling *et al.*, 2016) or increased self-confidence (e.g. Gattellari *et al.*, 2005; McDowall *et al.*, 2014), whilst the report refrains from claiming that this is a 'good' thing in itself. Higher sales of faulty products could in fact be a bad thing, and arrogantly overblown self-ratings compared to peer-ratings could be quite damaging for a leader's effectiveness.

Controversy 2: is there an assumption that reported experiences are significant outcomes?

Inventories of negative mentoring and coaching experiences have been created and they have informed questionnaires, so that we can now explore such negative side effects in a rigorous way (e.g. Graßmann *et al.*, 2019). Examples of negative client experiences in coaching are, 'My job/life satisfaction/motivation decreased,' 'I experienced my work as less meaningful,' 'My original goals were modified without my approval,' 'In-depth problems were triggered that could not be dealt with,' 'My work-life balance worsened,' 'My job performance fluctuated more strongly,' and 'Relationship quality with my manager decreased.' These are in fact the most frequent negative events coachees have reported, according to Graßmann and Schermuly (2016). However, they are just negative, subjective *experiences*, they cannot count as *evidence* that coaching is any less effective. Learning sometimes hurts and challenging feedback or actions from coaches can lead to quite negative experiences. Still, those negative experiences may subsequently be seen by clients and others as necessary pain to come through highly formative pressures which have changed their lives (and jobs) for the better. So, the simple reporting of negative experiences does not mean that there are negative effects, unless a predictive link can be made to those (which has not been done yet).

Client reports cannot count as a demonstrable negative consequence of executive coaching just as very similarly positive reports cannot demonstrate positive outcomes of coaching either. For a veritable demonstration we need to do rigorous statistics on many such client reports, linking them to objective outcomes. We know that 'feel good' experiences do not demonstrate that coaching is helpful, and neither do painful, challenging experiences prove that an intervention is unhelpful. When it comes to highly challenging conflict or the experience of learning from one's mistakes at work, explored through the help of tools like 360-feedback or a few coaching sessions, a 'negative' coaching relationship can be the accompaniment of an otherwise extremely beneficial assignment. I remember how I once interviewed workers and foremen in a factory setting and uncovered all sorts of abuse and bullying, which I reported back to the board of the manufacturing company. On the very same day they appointed me as the executive coach to the Technical Director who was in charge of that factory, the one who had been in post for nearly 20 years and was held most responsible by my interviewees for all the issues and transgressions that I had uncovered. In retrospect it was a master stroke not to fire him but to force him to work with me. Nevertheless, I could make very long lists of negative side effects of both my collecting feedback and me coaching the Technical Director, especially from his perspective. I remember him being so emotional that initially he could not sit down in the same room with me, reported on me to the company's management, and then filled up several hours of our precious time with fierce accusations to me and others on the shop floor. I think now more than 25 years later he and I, and more importantly the factory workers, would probably agree that this was nevertheless one of the most effective interventions that had happened at that manufacturing plant in several decades.

When I briefly covered the ROI studies in coaching in Chapter 2, we could already see that simply reporting a *perceived* positive effect is not going to bring us any nearer to significant quantitative findings, even if those perceptions are averaged out over large numbers of clients. Such perceptions would be interesting and worth researching (as has been done extensively; see my summary in De Haan, 2019b), but they would not be part of effectiveness or outcome research, because every perception is only an *opinion* about coaching, not a criterion for effectiveness; let alone evidence of a change or an effect.

Controversy 3: there seems to be a difference between the coaching and mentoring literature

In mentoring – where there is generally a larger power differential between mentor and mentee – there seems to be more overlap between negative side effects as observed by both parties than in coaching (see section C). We probably need more evidence to understand this. Mentors and mentees are often part of the same institution so perhaps that increases their mutual understanding. Nevertheless, the research findings in these helping professions normally support one another more than here, when it comes to negative side effects.

This observation is only based on single articles (Eby *et al.*, 2008; versus Graß-mann & Schermuly, 2018); however the latter article analyses data from more experienced students 'coaching' less experienced students, i.e. something very close to 'mentoring,' which is why one would expect these two groups of researchers to report more similar results. It has to be added though that there were 80 matched mentoring pairs and only 29 matched coaching pairs, possibly too small a group to pick up a correlation.

Part B: how to establish negative side effects of coaching

As argued in the previous section it is probably not such a good idea to set out to find negative effects per se. It is probably best to just try to establish 'change' through coaching (as most researchers summarised in this book have done) and then to analyse any 'changes' found, for better or worse. To understand possible side effects one would have to do this analysis in great depth, since arguably any demonstrated 'change' can have a beneficial as well as an adverse effect, or at least one of each on the coachee and also more widely on the organisation that has commissioned the coaching. We will do a first analysis of this kind with the existing articles in the next section.

Let us try a simple thought experiment: suppose a certain small dose of 'C' makes a great majority of people 'P' feel significantly happier. Then one would have demonstrated a 'happiness effect,' at least for most of the 'C' users, and possibly also for some other people in their direct surroundings (or potentially, it could have also some adverse effects, say on their 'rivals' at work). Of course, there could be other adverse effects to such a potent elixir, e.g. 'P' may become addicted to it, or their teeth might fall out, or their liver could stop functioning after ten years of using 'C.' But even if this were not the case, if there are no adverse or side effects whatsoever, it is important to remember that 'P' would have to pay to obtain 'C' (and in some classic tales happiness cures have been notoriously expensive – for example Mephistopheles' cure). 'P' would agree to a cost in time or money or other expenses to obtain or engage with 'C' and these costs should also be listed under negative side effects for 'P' or for 'P's organisation that pays for 'C.'

Back to coaching. Arguably, all the many studies in this book that have not demonstrated a beneficial effect for coaching on the intervention group or others in the organisation have demonstrated by default a net negative effect of coaching. After all, coaching is costly both in terms of the fees that need to be paid to the highly qualified professionals and in terms of the time investment and the demands of the contract, which may include thinking about clear objectives, being open and vulnerable about what you have tried already towards those objectives, and finding the resilience of dealing with the challenges from the conversations, from the homework or from the 'aporia' and other frustrations of not (yet) finding answers to your quest. Psychological costs could also be the loss of secondary gains or the deep pain, loss, and uncertainty felt when consciously working through trauma and tackling or tearing down natural defences. Every single coaching study that does not find positive results will at the same time be a testament of these types of costs and could therefore be argued to have a negative net effectiveness result. It is fortunate that such coaching studies without demonstrable findings are in a tiny minority and seem to be decreasing as better research standards are being introduced in the coaching literature.

The following studies into negative side effects, undertaken by Eby, Schermuly, and others, asked both parties (mentees/mentors and coachees/coaches respectively) whether they had experienced any negative side effects in their most recent mentoring/coaching experience. They can serve as an inspiration for quantitative researchers, because they may point to potential changes through helping conversations which are worth investigating quantitatively. For example, if these parties report 'relationship with spouse decreased' as some have indeed done, then this could trigger a randomised controlled trial into the effects of helping conversations on spouses: positive as well as negative effects.

The qualitative study of negative side effects started earlier in the mentoring literature, where Eby et al. (2000) studied negative mentoring experiences for 277 mentees and Eby and McManus (2004) did the same for 90 mentors. Eby et al. (2008) were able to collect perspectives from both mentors and mentees in 80 matched mentor-mentee pairs in two large universities. They found that mentors' perceptions of negative mentoring experiences were related to both mentors' and mentees' perceptions of relationship quality and fair exchange. Burk and Eby (2010) also investigated the consequences of these negative side effects on mentees, their decisions to leave the mentoring relationship, and what stops them from leaving, e.g. lack of perceived mentoring alternatives and fear of mentor retaliation.

Schermuly and others similarly started out with three explorative, qualitative studies, investigating:

- 104 coaches' perceptions of negative effects of coaching for themselves in their most recent assignment (Schermuly, 2014), where the coaches reported the usual effectiveness ratings for their own coaching but also that 90% of cases had negative side effects for them;
- 123 coaches' perceptions of negative effects of coaching for their most recent coachee (Schermuly et al., 2014), with 57% of coaches reporting negative side effects for their coachees;
- 111 coachees' perceptions of negative effects of coaching for themselves in a recent assignment (Graßmann & Schermuly, 2016), with 68% of coachees reporting negative side effects.

Further measurements over a time period of eight weeks based on self-scores only and no controls, showed that

1. for coachees the number of negative effects was inversely proportional to relationship quality at both measurement times and also to the coach's expertise at Time 1 (Graßmann & Schermuly, 2016) and
2. for coaches the number of negative effects was inversely proportional to the relationship quality and to their own feelings of competence as a coach, and also led to them perceiving more stress and impaired sleep eight weeks later (Graßmann et al., 2019).

Graßmann and Schermuly (2018) conducted an experiment with 29 coach-client dyads (masters students who were coaching bachelor's students) of which a randomised

16 coaches received two 2-hour group supervision sessions during the period of coaching. After the first coaching session, coaches took a questionnaire on neuroticism. After coaching completion, coaches and clients evaluated negative effects of coaching for clients. There was no correlation between these two estimates (contrary to Eby et al., 2008, in the mentoring domain). Coaches additionally evaluated negative effects of coaching for themselves, and these turned out to strongly predict the negative effects they saw for their clients. Coaches' neuroticism also predicted the amount of negative side effects they themselves saw ($p < 0.01$) but not the number of negative side effects that their clients experienced. The presence or absence of supervision made no difference in the amount of negative side effects reported.

Part C: overview of what we know about side effects

Let us first examine a few studies that did find adverse effects or negative side effects (which of the two it is depends on what one would choose to see as the main effect of coaching, i.e. the distinction is slightly arbitrary).

The worst news for coaching that I have been able to find were five (clusters of) studies where an adverse effect was found instead of the anticipated beneficial effect:

1   In an excellent independent study of a single consulting intervention, Aust et al. (2010) show how not to implement organisation-development in a hospital. Many consulting interventions including leadership coaching failed and resulted in better results for the no-intervention control group participants. It appears that firstly, hospital employees did not have time to organise and conduct group meetings and despite the fact that consultants repeatedly offered their help, employees only contacted them twice during the entire project; and secondly, leaders were unsure about their role in the intervention project and therefore never fully took ownership of it.
2   Bozer et al. (2013) showed that in their experiment the control group performed better in terms of line-manager-rated task performance than the intervention group which had no fewer than 10 to 12 coaching sessions. It is important to note, however, that (a) the control group was not random: they were recruited as peers of the coachees, and (b) these peers had a much lower (manager-rated) performance initially, after which (c) the peers' performance scores only climbed up to the same level as that of the coachees, which had not moved significantly despite the 10 coaching sessions. With a much smaller nonrandomised control group one can never be sure that the 'Hawthorne' effect in that group outweighed the coaching effect in the other group.
3   Ebner et al. (2020) also find a negative impact of the single one-to-one coaching session that they offered – it significantly reduced the coachee's life satisfaction. That seems quite a powerful result of a single session, and contrary to the direction expected. Moreover, it is interesting to note that 'decrease in life satisfaction' is one of the top coachee negative side effects that Graßmann and Schermuly (2018) found – a few places below the most frequent one, 'decrease in job satisfaction.' Again, group assignment was not random in a similar way as in Bozer et al. (2013): participants chose which experimental group they wanted to belong to. Moreover, Ebner et al. (2020) tested only a single coaching session so the lack of satisfaction could have come from scarcity of the offer.

4 Building on Wageman's (2001) result that coaching does not help much if a proper team structure is not in place, Carson et al. (2007) and Buljac-Samardzic and Van Woerkom (2015) show that it is possible to coach too much in some teams. They showed that although it was possible to demonstrate a correlation between team coaching now and team effectiveness a year later, this relationship was only significant when team reflection (Buljac-Samardzic & Van Woerkom, 2015) or the team's supportive environment (Carson et al., 2007) had been low. There was indeed a detrimental effect on efficiency when team reflection was high, something they labelled 'excessive managerial coaching.' It is perhaps understandable that there is a case for 'excessive' reflection and coaching, e.g. at those moments where action is needed. An executive coach who does not pick up the fact that a client is bringing something that s/he has to act on immediately and is looking for an immediate outcome, but carries on inviting the client to engage in deep and abstract reflection, could be a similar and understandable example of ineffective coaching. At the very least we should as executive coaches make it explicit that we notice the urgency, and contract around an immediate deliverable if that is what our client wants from the session.

5 Another interesting finding was that coaching needs the addition of instruction to make a difference on objective academic marks (Franklin & Doran, 2009) and otherwise does not do very much beyond increasing self-scores. Hui et al. (2013) and Zanchetta et al. (2020) also explicitly show that in some cases guidance and training are better suited for certain outcomes, such as cognitive acquisition. However, they did also find that facilitative coaching had better results for *new* tasks. One can understand this as a particular application for coaching (towards new strategies and more creative tasks) but also as a negative result, namely when it comes to academic achievement, cognitive acquisition, and repeat tasks. Similarly, Deane et al., 2014 found that 'transformational' coaching had a more lasting impact on productivity than 'skills' coaching had.

I would argue that none of these studies demonstrates a strong case for an adverse effect of the use of executive coaching: for the first one the overall intervention seems to be doomed from the beginning (and in fact one can argue that precisely the coaching element for the leaders was indeed successful, more successful than the rest of the project, because it was entirely voluntary and still all leaders took up the offer and took seven hours of coaching on average); for the next two, one doubts the significance especially given the fact that there are many other studies which do show a positive effect on the same outcome dimensions (see Chapter 4) and the latter two studies specify very specific circumstances where coaching might not work or not work so well – namely in those circumstances wherein reflection is already high and there are perhaps other expectations of the helper, e.g. to help move the team to action (Buljac-Samardzic & Van Woerkom 2015) or for the coachee to learn more facts (Hui et al., 2013; Zanchetta et al., 2020).

Now let us look at the studies that failed to demonstrate any effects (beyond self-scored) where positive change had been expected. I will skip the studies with 'null' effects that were so small in scale that one would not necessarily have expected much significance in terms of effectiveness, such as Miller (1990), Deviney (1994), Grant et al. (2010), Tee et al. (2017, 2019), Junker et al. (2020), and Ebner et al. (2020).

To begin, we can go back all the way to the first studies described in this book. We started in Chapter 1 by looking at 'health coaching' studies. That was a bit of a detour away from our core topic, workplace and executive coaching, which is why I haven't referred to those studies again. However, we did see that those health coaching experiments that are used to support medical treatment demonstrated high significance, with the main effect sizes δ between 3 and 6 on average, indicating that nearly all patients in the coached group were better off than those in the control group. But we also learned that health and wellness coaching applications in the work setting fared a lot worse: Bennett et al. (2005) only found one small effect; Strijk et al. (2013) and Van Berkel et al. (2014) found that coaching combined with yoga training and mindfulness training, respectively, did not make a significant difference for hospital and research-centre workers on a range of health and vitality determinants. Moreover, Emmons et al. (2014) found that telephone coaching did not add any more significance over self-coaching on five health determinants for a large sample. Additionally, Geraedts et al. (2014) could not show that health coaching helped employees with their high depression scores, although this finding could be due to low attendance (leading to attrition), which is a problem in psychotherapy for depression as well. Finally, in driving-instructor coaching, Passmore and Velez (2012) found exactly the same occurrence of speed convictions, their main outcome variable, in the intervention and control groups.

In most of these examples a good rationale for what was a labour-intensive, high-intensity intervention could not be demonstrated (with the exception of Passmore & Velez, 2012; Emmons et al., 2014: their intervention consisted of only one and two sessions of telephone coaching, respectively).

There are several studies, starting from the early Green et al. (2006, 2007) and Grant et al. (2009, 2010) studies wherein a significant effect was demonstrated on coachee scores but *not* on peer ratings. The same was found again on coach scores (Schermuly et al., 2020), direct-report scores (Finn et al., 2007), manager scores (Williams & Lowman, 2018; Jones et al., 2019), peer, direct-report, and manager scores (Nieminen et al., 2013), and some objective measures (e.g. physiological responses: Schermuly et al., 2020; Howard, 2015; and business viability: Oberschachtsiek & Scioch, 2015). These studies do stand apart as a warning to coaches and researchers alike. They show that demonstrating universally agreed, objective results from coaching is still a difficult job, and that several who have set out to do so have failed (and can only report significant findings on self-scores which we know are notoriously biased towards false positives).

Oberschachtsiek and Scioch (2015) studied a large-scale ($N > 418,000$), historic dataset of German support structures for new business owners over five years, which should be very relevant for commissioners and decision makers in the field of executive coaching because it makes a good link between expense and return on investment in coaching. They focused on three different coaching programmes provided along with a financial subsidy to entrepreneurs who started a business whilst they were unemployed. Their results show that the coaching effects tended to be low and did not make a meaningfully significant difference in the viability of their businesses. On the basis of timings in their data of foreclosing businesses they can argue that some of the coaching is likely to have led to better insight about the viability of the business and therefore, despite the businesses of these coached entrepreneurs floundering, some entrepreneurs may have gotten out earlier thanks to the coaching.

Oberschachtsiek and Scioch (2015) seems a very rigorous study and although entirely historical, it is perhaps one of the strongest arguments we have against coaching, since this work clearly makes it difficult to argue for coaching as part of the subsidies for new entrepreneurs. However, the authors argue that possibly coaching did help the entrepreneurs in many cases, namely by clarifying for them when to bow out of their fledgling enterprises, before giving up comes too late and too costly.

Part D: what it means for coaching practice

1 What do coaches need to know about negative (side) effects in coaching?

In the previous section we have found some clear results on negative effects in coaching. Sometimes it has not been possible to prove a positive objective result such as on (reduction of) stress hormones or the viability of businesses. Sometimes it is not possible to show positive results on peer, line-manager, and direct-report ratings. And sometimes even self-scores do not show significance between intervention and control group. It is worth mentioning that there are now around twelve studies in which such null results have been found, as opposed to the 148 other quantitative studies in this book that were mostly more rigorous and did show significant effects in workplace and executive coaching (summarised in the first two chapters). As mentioned in the previous section, a few of those 'negative' studies showed that only specific applications of coaching work towards the intended target, i.e. they seem to say that sometimes there is no need for still more reflection or that directive 'skills' coaching has its limits when it comes to dealing with new challenges and the need for creativity.

It seems that the case *against* coaching remains weak for the time being with mostly evidence for clear circumstances wherein coaching might not add much or even be 'too much,' i.e. circumstances wherein more reflection is not called for. The case against coaching nevertheless still has strong arguments in its favour. Firstly, it is well known that in social sciences and psychology only around 20% of 'null results' actually get published. This is not so much due to journals not being interested in null results but more due to stubbornness of researchers who often stick with their models against evidence and tend to conclude that their 'experiment did not work out' and is therefore not worth publishing (see Franco et al., 2014). This means that if we have 12 or so negative and null results this is more likely to signify 60 independent studies that showed a null result of which 48 were not published. Secondly, the other 148 articles in Chapters 1 and 2 do not all demonstrate coaching effectiveness, since many of those studies only compare conditions. There are maybe only around 110 studies that do provide evidence of effectiveness, which means that the odds would be around 1:2 to find a null result, which is still too high to be sure of effectiveness.

In sum, a provocative summary of this chapter for coaches can be that focusing on the negatives in coaching research has given us more confidence for the efficacy of coaching, i.e. only a stronger case for executive and workplace coaching. Certainly, the analysis of potential adverse effects in coaching deserves further work and needs to be taken up with the help of new models for positive and negative change through coaching. For the time being we can conclude that 92% of the studies published to date show at least a few significantly positive outcomes.

Now that we have come to the end of this 'systematic review of coaching studies,' it is worth asking the question, what do coaches need to know about doing research in coaching? How can readers help to further increase the quantitative research base in executive coaching?

2 What expert advice can we give to coaches who want to do quantitative research?

If you have come this far in the book you will agree that the following 'ten commandments for undertaking coaching research' make sense and give you the best chances of getting a good (i.e. a significant finding or a clear null-hypothesis confirmation) result with your sample, a good chance of getting published and of getting a large academic audience for your undertaking:

1. Go for the largest N as you possibly can, which means in some cases preparing longer or keeping data collection open longer: it is better to forestall disappointments through attrition or weak significance by giving yourself the best start for data analysis.
2. Make an estimate of how many tests you want to do beforehand, so you can estimate your sample size, using other research with similar samples. Generally, there is a logarithmic relationship between sample size needed and the number of tests you will be able to do and safely reach the same significance level, so if you are able to add some $N = 50$ to your sample size you can do twice as many tests on your sample, with the same estimated level of significance p. That is another very valid reason to go for large samples: you do not always know in advance which tests you might like to do.
3. Although arguably (see Chapter 4 section B) it is helpful to have a model of what you might find, to structure your hypotheses – do not be dogmatic about your model: too many projects have been designed just to prove a highly naïve, simplistic model of coaching such as a 'coaching approach' developed by the researcher, which leads to a lot of researcher bias (the same is true of course with medicine studies designed 'just' to demonstrate effectiveness of an existing pill rather than understand the dynamics of a natural process).
4. When deciding your sample, make it as coherent (uniform) and representative as you can, with practitioners and clients that can really be representative of the profession.
5. Do not ask only one group in your sample to complete questionnaires – ask other parties as well if you can, or even better, make objective measurements of physiological or organisational changes.
6. Do not only compare the sample to themselves: have a control group or at least an alternative intervention group. The science of coaching has now matured to such an extent that 'mixed methods' and 'pre-post' measurements of single groups are no longer needed.
7. For your measurement of self-scores, use recognised and validated instruments and if you have a choice, always use the same instrument as other coaching researchers have used, so that you can compare with your peer-researchers and the extant literature.

8   Do not open up your data to analysis before you have fully collected it. Think of the very strong 'placebo' effect in research, also from the researcher side – so if you begin to see trends in your data, or you build your hopes on finding some significance, you might nudge the data collection in that direction, even if unconsciously.
9   Have someone analyse your data who has not designed the experiment, so that they can have a critical look at the findings – they may also see new patterns that you had not anticipated.
10 Do not revert to data slicing by splitting out your data to publish more than one article. This may risk self-plagiarising or upsetting editors who need to know that your article uniquely refers to a single experiment. You can always write more interpretative or accessible articles later – or even a whole book following your projects, as in the case of this book.

Much more guidance can be found in the standard handbooks on doing research in business, e.g. David Gray's wonderful (2019; 2nd edition) book *Doing Research in the Business World* (as a researcher I should come clean here about the fact that I am probably biased because David was a dear researcher friend).

3 What moral advice can we give to coaches who want to do quantitative research?

In the companion volume about qualitative research in the coaching field (De Haan, 2019a) I already reminded readers of the five important foundations which support integrity in coaching and research:

1   *Independence* – guarding the client's autonomy. It is important for coaches and researchers alike to be able to pursue their work wholly independently of influence from financial backers, sponsors, or funding providers. And a crucial degree of independence must be maintained with regard to clients themselves and their issues, and those of other stakeholders. This is why it is so important that coaches (or researchers) do not enter into any partnerships or relationships with their clients (or research participants) other than a pure coaching (or research) relationship.
2   *Informed consent* – from the outset, the client must have a reliable idea of what s/he is getting involved in and what will be asked of him/her. This is why a written contract containing defined agreements is important, as well as a first informal meeting to discuss potential cooperation. If traceable information is to be cited in other forums, consent must be sought in advance and the client must feel truly free to say no.
3   *Confidentiality* – all information obtained in connection with the work must be treated with absolute confidentiality. There may be an option of conducting research jointly, in which case traceable attributions can be made in sharing the original dataset (although in quantitative research this can usually be avoided), provided the client has given his/her explicit consent and is free to say no.
4   *Respect and diversity* – coaching should allow for multiple voices and perspectives, and treat at-risk groups or vulnerable parties with respect. This applies

equally to research. Good coaching and research strengthen diversity and show respect for even the softest dissenting voices and tiniest notes of discord, if only because a single counterexample can revive an entire research programme or even professional field. Special attention should be paid to the fact that the coachee is an active and relatively vulnerable participant in the coaching sessions. In participatory research, this also applies to the research participants.

5   *Integrity and trust* – this covers various aspects such as compliance with legislation, including personal data protection laws, but also integrity in a broader sense in the areas of data handling, data analysis, and the publishing process. Finally, it includes fairness towards clients and striving for a high quality of service, supported by regular supervision or (in the research field) independent peer review.

I would like to end this book with some more specific advice when it comes to doing quantitative research:

1   You are going to proclaim a 'truth' about coaching, so be as clear as you can not only about the 'evidence base' for your truth but also about your allegiances. Are you being funded by a coaching institute or association? Then come clean about this in the report. A lot of medical research was funded by pharma companies and that does have a huge impact on what is being researched and what is being reported, so it needs to be made explicit by law.
2   Informed consent is less important in quantitative research because you are not normally going to divulge any information about a single client: only averages of quantifiable variables that all subjects in the research share. Nevertheless, data protection is still important and it is good practice to have only one person (e.g. an administrator) who is not likely to know any names in the sample, to keep the record of names and translate all subjects into 'numbers' for representations of the data, such as in comprehensive spreadsheets of responses.
3   It is important to have a 'Limitations' section in your report where you really try to list all the flaws of your research design and sample. Although you might do 'marketing' of your particular project in the Abstract, Introduction, Methods, Results, and Discussion sections, it is important in this Limitations section to truly play the devil's advocate and expose all the many flaws in your case, such as self-scoring, same-source bias, nonrepresentativeness of your sample, etcetera. You can then still tell the reader why you think these many flaws do not take away the significance of your main reported findings, but they have to be listed comprehensively for ethical reasons.
4   Be open about your data and respond to requests to see your raw data, instruments, or detailed calculations. This means that such details – which are impersonal – need to be stored much longer than personal data, namely for as long as you possibly can. Be open and supportive also in doing some work as a peer reviewer for others, to keep the review and publication standards in your field as high as possible.
5   Do not (self-) plagiarize, which is a temptation that may be strong, e.g. if you publish a second or third article with a new, similar experiment including a new sample.

Summary of Chapter 6: 'What about negative side effects of coaching?'

In the extensive research literature, we can spot only a few negative or adverse effects of coaching:

- When managerial coaching is rife for teams that are already reflecting enough, then the coaching can become 'too much' or perhaps, too solipsistic, i.e. 'navel-gazing.'
- When more directive 'skills' coaching is offered but more facilitative, 'transformational' coaching is needed.
- When coaching is not the main need but 'business viability' is at stake.

Other than these, there are also examples of studies that could not demonstrate an effect and therefore had to uphold the 'null hypothesis.' Often this appeared to be due to the scale of the study, where for example self-ratings became significant but ratings by others did not.

Overall, less than 8% of published studies in coaching report a negative or null effect, whilst the overwhelming majority of 92% did report an effect, which they could demonstrate on a variety of instruments and scales.

This can be qualified though if we take into account that four fifths of 'null results' studies are not published in the social sciences: that would lead us to conclude that around 33% of coaching effectiveness studies deliver a 'null result' – so there is still room for debate about effectiveness in this profession.

So, at the moment, even though a lot of good work has been done to explore and survey what potential negative side effects may result from coaching, we need more research. However, we also conclude that the case for an adverse effect of this intervention is rather weak. Positive effects are not just abundant but they are also closely aligned with the objectives of the coaching, so it appears that coaching – through careful contracting – delivers on a wide variety of measures, measures that can usually be cast appropriately to the occasion and the goal of coaching.

This chapter ends with some expert and moral advice for future researchers in the outcome-research science of workplace and executive coaching.

References

Agarwal, R., Angst, C. M. & Magni, M. (2009). The performance effects of coaching: A multilevel analysis using hierarchical linear modeling. *International Journal of Human Resource Management, 20*, 2110–2134.

Alameddine, M. B., Englesbe, M. J. & Waits, S. A. (2018). A video-based coaching intervention to improve surgical skill in fourth-year medical students. *Journal of Surgical Education, 75*(6), 1475–1479.

Allan, J., Leeson, P., De Fruyt, F. & Martin, S. (2018). Application of a 10 week coaching program designed to facilitate volitional personality change: Overall effects on personality and the impact of targeting. *International Journal of Evidence Based Coaching and Mentoring, 16*(1), 80–94.

Allen, T. D., Eby, L. T., Poteet, M. L., Lentz, E. & Lima, L. (2004). Career benefits associated with mentoring for protégés: A meta-analysis. *Journal of Applied Psychology, 89*, 127–136.

Andreanoff, J. (2016). Issues in conducting quantitative studies on the impact of coaching and mentoring in higher education. *International Journal of Evidence Based Coaching and Mentoring, 10*, 202–216.

Anthony, A., Gimbert, B. & Fultz, D. (2013). The effect of e-coaching attendance on alternatively certified teachers' sense of self-efficacy. *Journal of Technology and Teacher Education, 21*(3), 277–299.

Athanasopoulou, A. & Dopson, S. (2018). A systematic review of executive coaching outcomes: Is it the journey or the destination that matters the most? *The Leadership Quarterly, 29*(1), 70–88.

Atkins, P. W. & Wood, R. E. (2002). Self-versus others' ratings as predictors of assessment center ratings: Validation evidence for 360-degree feedback programs. *Personnel Psychology, 55*(4), 871–904.

Aust, B., Rugulies, R., Finken, A. & Jensen, C. (2010). When workplace interventions lead to negative effects: Learning from failures. *Scandinavian Journal of Public Health, 38*(Suppl. 3), 106–119.

Bandura, A. (1997). *Self-efficacy: The exercise of control*. New York: Cambridge University Press.

Baron, L. & Morin, L. (2009). The coach-coachee relationship in executive coaching: A field study. *Human Resource Development Quarterly, 20*(1), 85–106.

Baron, R. M. & Kenny, D. A. (1986). The moderator – Mediator variable distinction in social psychological research: Conceptual, strategic, and statistical considerations. *Journal of Personality and Social Psychology, 51*, 1173–1182.

Behrendt, P. (2006). Wirkung und Wirkfaktoren von psychodramatischem coaching – Eine experimentelle Evaluationsstudie. *Zeitschrift für Psychodrama und Soziometrie, 5*(1), 59–87.

Bennett, J. A., Perrin, N. A., Hanson, G., Bennett, D., Gaynor, W., Flaherty-Robb, M., Joseph, C., Butterworth, S. & Potempa, K. (2005). Healthy aging demonstration project: Nurse coaching for behavior change in older adults. *Research in Nursing & Health*, 28(3), 187–197.

Berglas, S. (2002). The very real dangers of executive coaching. *Harvard Business Review*, June, 86–92.

Blackman, A., Moscardo, G. & Gray, D. E. (2016). Challenges for the theory and practice of business coaching: A systematic review of empirical evidence. *Human Resource Development Review*, 15(4), 459–486.

Bonrath, E. M., Dedy, N. J., Gordon, L. E. & Grantcharov, T. P. (2015). Comprehensive surgical coaching enhances surgical skill in the operating room. *Annals of Surgery*, 262(2), 205–212.

Bordin, H. (1979). The generalizability of the psychoanalytic concept of the working alliance. *Psychotherapy: Theory, Research and Practice*, 16, 252–260.

Bowles, S. V., Cunningham, C. J. L., De La Rosa, G. M. & Picano, J. J. (2007). Coaching leaders in middle and executive management: Goals, performance, buy-in. *Leadership and Organization Development Journal*, 28(5), 388–408.

Bowles, S. V. & Picano, J. J. (2006). Dimensions of coaching related to productivity and quality of life. *Consulting Psychology Journal: Practice and Research*, 58(4), 232–239.

Boyce, L. A., Jackson, R. J. & Neal, L. J. (2010). Building successful leadership coaching relationships: Examining impact of matching criteria in a leadership coaching program. *Journal of Management Development*, 29, 914–931.

Bozer, G., Baek-Kyoo, J. & Santora, J. C. (2015). Executive coaching: Does coach-coachee matching based on similarity really matter? *Consulting Psychology Journal: Theory and Practice*, 67(3), 218–233.

Bozer, G., Sarros, J. C. & Santora, J. C. (2013). The role of coachee characteristics in executive coaching for effective sustainability. *Journal of Management Development*, 32(3), 277–294.

Bozer, G., Sarros, J. C. & Santora, J. C. (2014). Academic background and credibility in executive coaching effectiveness. *Personnel Review*, 43, 881–897.

Braunstein, K. & Grant, A. M. (2016). Approaching solutions or avoiding problems? The differential effects of approach and avoidance goals with solution-focused and problem-focused coaching questions. *Coaching: An International Journal of Theory, Research and Practice*, 9(2), 93–109.

Bright, D. & Crockett, A. (2012). Training combined with coaching can make a significant difference in job performance and satisfaction. *Coaching: An International Journal of Theory, Research and Practice*, 5(1), 4–21.

Briner, R. B. 2012. Does coaching work and does anyone really care? *Occupational Psychology Matters*, 16, 4–11.

Buljac-Samardzic, M. & Van Woerkom, M. (2015). Can managers coach their teams too much? *Journal of Managerial Psychology*, 30(3), 280–296.

Burk, H. G. & Eby, L. T. (2010). What keeps people in mentoring relationships when bad things happen? A field study from the protégé's perspective. *Journal of Vocational Behavior*, 77(3), 437–446.

Burke, D. & Linley, P. A. (2007). Enhancing goal self-concordance through coaching. *International Coaching Psychology Review*, 2(1), 62–69.

Burt, D. & Talati, Z. (2017). The unsolved value of executive coaching: A meta-analysis of outcomes using randomised control trial studies. *International Journal of Evidence Based Coaching and Mentoring*, 15(2), 17.

Carson, J. B., Tesluk, P. E. & Marrone, J. A. (2007). Shared leadership in teams: An investigation of antecedent conditions and performance. *Academy of Management Journal*, 50, 1217–1234.

Caulat, G. & De Haan, E. (2006). Virtual peer consultation: How do virtual leaders learn? *Organisations & People*, 13(4), 24–32.

Cerni, T., Curtis, G. J. & Colmar, S. H. (2010). Executive coaching can enhance transformational leadership. *International Coaching Psychology Review*, 5(1), 81–85.

Chan, Y. H. (2003). Randomised controlled trials (RCTs) – Sample size: The magic number? *Singapore Medical Journal*, 44(6), 172–174.

Chen, G. H., Ai, J. & You, Y. (2014). Managerial coaching behaviours and their relations to job satisfaction, life satisfaction and orientations to happiness. *Journal of Human Resource and Sustainability Studies*, 2, 147–156.

Chinn, A. T., Richmond, J. P. & Bennett, J. L. (2015). Walking a mile in an executive's shoes: The influence of shared client-coach experience on goal achievement. *International Coaching Psychology Review*, 10(2).

Cohen, J. (1988). *Statistical power analysis for the behavioural sciences*. Hillsdale, NJ: Lawrence Erlbaum.

Cooper, M. (2008). *Essential research findings in counselling and psychotherapy: The facts are friendly*. London: Sage.

Crits-Christoph, P., Gibbons, M. B. C., Hamilton, J., Ring-Kurtz, S. & Gallop, R. (2011). The dependability of alliance assessments: The alliance – Outcome correlation is larger than you might think. *Journal of Consulting and Clinical Psychology*, 79, 267–278.

Dahling, J. J., Taylor, S. T., Chau, S. L. & Dwight, S. A. (2016). Does coaching matter? A multilevel model linking managerial coaching skill and frequency to sales goal attainment. *Personnel Psychology*, 69, 863–894.

De Haan, E. (2005). From stigma to status: Coaching comes of age. *The Ashridge Newsletter*, Summer, 4.

De Haan, E. (2008). *Relational coaching – Journeys towards mastering one-to-one learning*. Chichester: Wiley.

De Haan, E. (2019a). *Critical moments in executive coaching: Understanding coaching process through research and evidence-based theory*. London & New York: Routledge.

De Haan, E. (2019b). A systematic review of qualitative studies in workplace and executive coaching: The emergence of a body of research. *Consulting Psychology Journal*, 71(4), 227–248.

De Haan, E. & Burger, Y. (2005). *Coaching with colleagues: An action guide for one-to-one learning*. Basingstoke: Palgrave Macmillan.

De Haan, E., Culpin, V. & Curd, J. (2011). Executive coaching in practice: What determines helpfulness for clients of coaching? *Personnel Review*, 40(1), 24–44.

De Haan, E. & Duckworth, A. (2013). Signaling a new trend in coaching outcome research. *International Coaching Psychology Review*, 8(1), 6–20.

De Haan, E., Duckworth, A., Birch, D. & Jones, C. (2013). Executive coaching outcome research: The contribution of common factors such as relationship, personality match, and self-efficacy. *Consulting Psychology Journal: Practice and Research*, 65(1), 40–57.

De Haan, E., Grant, A., Burger, Y. & Eriksson, P.-O. (2016). A large-scale study of executive coaching outcome: The relative contributions of working relationship, personality match, and self-efficacy. *Consulting Psychology Journal: Practice and Research*, 68(3), 189–207.

De Haan, E., Gray, D. E. & Bonneywell, S. (2019). Executive coaching outcome research in a field setting: A near-randomized controlled trial study in a global healthcare corporation. *Academy of Management Learning and Education*, 18(4), 1–25.

De Haan, E., Molyn, J. & Nilsson, V. O. (2020). New findings on the effectiveness of the coaching relationship: Time to think differently about active ingredients? *Consulting Psychology Journal*, 72(3), 155–167.

De Haan, E. & Nilsson, V. (2017). Evaluating coaching behaviour in managers, consultants and coaches: A model, questionnaire, and initial findings. *Consulting Psychology Journal: Practice and Research*, 69(4), 315–333.

Deane, F. P., Andresen, R., Crowe, T. P., Oades, L. G., Ciarrochi, J. & Williams, V. (2014). A comparison of two coaching approaches to enhance implementation of a recovery-oriented service model. *Administration and Policy in Mental Health and Mental Health Services Research, 41*(5), 660–667.

DeBar, L. L., Ritenbaugh, C., Aickin, M., Orwoll, E., Elliot, D., Dickerson, J., Vuckovic, N., Stevens, V. J., Moe, E. & Irving, L. M. (2006). YOUTH: A health plan – Based lifestyle intervention increases bone mineral density in adolescent girls. *Archives of Pediatrics & Adolescent Medicine, 160*(12), 1269–1276.

Dejonghe, L. A. L., Becker, J., Froboese, I. & Schaller, A. (2017). Long-term effectiveness of health coaching in rehabilitation and prevention: A systematic review. *Patient Education and Counseling, 100*, 1643–1653.

Dello Russo, S., Miraglia, M. & Borgogni, L. (2017). Reducing organizational politics in performance appraisal: The role of coaching leaders in appraising age-diverse employees. *Human Resource Management, 56*, 769–783.

Deviney, D. E. (1994). *The effect of coaching using multiple rater feedback to change supervisor behavior* (Doctoral dissertation). Nova University, DAI-A 55/01, p. 114.

Digman, J. M. (1990). Personality structure: Emergence of the five-factor model. *Annual Review of Psychology, 41*(1), 417–440.

Dion, K., Berscheid, E. & Walster, E. (1972). What is beautiful is good. *Journal of Personality and Social Psychology, 24*(3), 285–290.

Duijts, S. F. A., Kant, I., Van den Brandt, P. A. & Swaen, G. M. H. (2008). Effectiveness of a preventive coaching intervention for employees at risk for sickness absence due to psychosocial health complaints: Results of a randomized controlled trial. *Journal of Occupational Environmental Medicine, 50*(7), 765–776.

Dyrbye, L. N., Shanafelt, T. D., Gill, P. R., Satele, D. V. & West, C. P. (2019). Effect of a professional coaching intervention on the well-being and distress of physicians: A pilot randomized clinical trial. *Journal of the American Medical Association Internal Medicine, 179*, 1406–1414.

Ebner, K., Schulte, E., Souček, R. & Kauffeld, S. (2017). Coaching as stress-management intervention: The mediating role of self-efficacy in a framework of self-management and coping. *International Journal of Stress Management, 25*, 209–233.

Ebner, K., Souček, R. & Kauffeld, S. (2020). Incongruities between values, motives, and skills: Exploring negative effects of self-exploration in career coaching. *British Journal of Guidance & Counselling*, 1–23.

Eby, L. T., Allen, T. D., Evans, S. C., Ng, T. & DuBois, D. L. (2008). Does mentoring matter? A multidiscinplinary meta-analysis comparing mentored and non-mentored individuals. *Journal of Vocation Behaviour, 72*, 254–267.

Eby, L. T., Durley, J. R., Evans, S. C. & Ragins, B. R. (2008). Mentors' perceptions of negative mentoring experiences: Scale development and nomological validation. *Journal of Applied Psychology, 93*, 358–373.

Eby, L. T. & McManus, S. E. (2004). The protégé's role in negative mentoring experiences. *Journal of Vocational behavior, 65*(2), 255–275.

Eby, L. T., McManus, S. E., Simon, S. A. & Russell, J. E. (2000). The protege's perspective regarding negative mentoring experiences: The development of a taxonomy. *Journal of Vocational Behavior, 57*(1), 1–21.

Edelman, D., Oddone, E. Z., Liebowitz, R. S., Yancy, W. S., Olsen, M. K., Jeffreys, A. S., Moon, S. D., Harris, A. C., Smith, L. L., Quillian-Wolever, R. E. & Gaudet, T. W. (2006). A multidimensional integrative medicine intervention to improve cardiovascular risk. *Journal of General Internal Medicine, 21*(7), 728–734.

Egan, T. & Song, Z. (2005). A longitudinal quasi-experiment on the impact of executive coaching. Paper presented at the 20th Annual Conference of the Society for Industrial and Organizational Psychology, Los Angeles.

Ellinger, A. D., Ellinger, A. E. & Keller, S. B. (2003). Supervisory coaching behaviour, employee satisfaction, and warehouse employee performance: A dyadic perspective in the distribution industry. *Human Resource Development Quarterly, 14*(4), 435–458.

Ely, K., Boyce, L. A., Nelson, J. K., Zaccaro, S. J., Hernez-Broome, G. & Whyman, W. (2010). Evaluating leadership coaching: A review and integrated framework. *Leadership Quarterly*, 21(4), 585–599.

Emmons, K. M., Puleo, E., Greaney, M. L., Gillman, M. W., Bennett, G. G., Haines, J., Sprunck-Harrild, K. & Viswanath, K. (2014). A randomized comparative effectiveness study of healthy directions 2 – A multiple risk behavior intervention for primary care. *Preventive Medicine*, 64, 96–102.

Evers, W. J. G., Brouwers, A. & Tomic, W. (2006). A quasi-experimental study on management coaching effectiveness. *Consulting Psychology Journal: Practice and Research*, 58, 174–182.

Eysenck, H. J. (1952). The effects of psychotherapy: An evaluation. *Journal of Consulting Psychology*, 16(5), 319–324.

Falkenström, F., Granström, F. & Holmqvist, R. (2013). Therapeutic alliance predicts symptomatic improvement session by session. *Journal of Counseling Psychology*, 60, 317–328.

Finn, F. A. (2007). *Leadership development through executive coaching: The effects on leaders' psychological states and transformational leadership behavior* (Unpublished doctoral thesis). Queensland University of Technology, Brisbane.

Finn, F. A., Mason, C. M. & Bradley, L. M. (2007). *Doing well with executive coaching: Psychological and behavioural impacts*. Paper presented at the Academy of Management Annual Meeting Proceedings, Philadelphia.

Fischer, X., Kreppke, J., Zahner, L., Gerber, M., Faude, O. & Donath, L. (2019). Telephone-based coaching and prompting for physical activity: Short- and long-term findings of a randomized controlled trial (movingcall). *International Journal of Environmental Research and Public Health*, 16(140), 2626.

Fisher, E. B., Strunk, R. C., Highstein, G. R., Kelley-Sykes, R., Tarr, K. L., Trinkaus, K. & Musick, J. (2009). A randomized controlled evaluation of the effect of community health workers on hospitalization for asthma: The asthma coach. *Archives of Pediatrics & Adolescent Medicine*, 163(3), 225–232.

Flückiger, C., Del Re, A. C., Wlodasch, D., Horvath, A. O., Solomonov, N. & Wampold, B. E. (2020). Assessing the alliance – Outcome association adjusted for patient characteristics and treatment processes: A meta-analytic summary of direct comparisons. *Journal of Counseling Psychology*.

Fontes, A. & Dello Russo, S. (2020). An experimental field study on the effects of coaching: The mediating role of psychological capital. *Applied Psychology*.

Franco, A., Malhotra, N. & Simonovits, G. (2014). Publication bias in the social sciences: Unlocking the file drawer. *Science*, 345, 1502–1505.

Franklin, J. & Doran, J. (2009). Does all coaching enhance objective performance independently evaluated by blind assessors? The importance of the coaching model and content. *International Coaching Psychology Review*, 4(2), 128–144.

Gan, G. C. & Chong, C. W. (2015). Coaching relationship in executive coaching: A Malaysian study. *Journal of Management Development*, 34(4), 476–493.

Gardiner, M., Kearns, H. & Tiggemann, M. (2013). Effectiveness of cognitive behavioural coaching in improving the well-being and retention of rural general practitioners. *Australian Journal of Rural Health*, 21(3), 183–189.

Gattellari, M., Donnelly, N., Taylor, N., Meerkin, M., Hirst, G. & Ward, J. E. (2005). Does 'peer coaching' increase GP capacity to promote informed decision making about PSA screening? A cluster randomised trial. *Family Practice*, 22, 253–265.

Gentry, W. A., Hannum, K. M., Ekelund, B. Z. & de Jong, A. (2007). A study of the discrepancy between self- and observer-ratings on managerial derailment characteristics of European managers. *European Journal of Work and Organizational Psychology*, 16, 295–325.

Gentry, W. A., Katz, R. B. & McFeeters, B. (2009). The continual need for improvement to avoid derailment: A study of college and university administrators. *Higher Education Research and Development*, 28, 335–348.

George, E. R., Hawrusik, R., Delaney, M. M., Kara, N., Kalita, T. & Semrau, K. E. (2020). Who's your coach? The relationship between coach characteristics and birth attendants' adherence to the WHO safe childbirth checklist. *Gates Open Research*, 4(111), 111.

Geraedts, A. S., Kleiboer, A. M., Twisk, J., Wiezer, N. M., Van Mechelen, W. & Cuijpers, P. (2014). Long-term results of a web-based guided self-help intervention for employees with depressive symptoms: Randomized controlled trial. *Journal of Medical Internet Research*, 16(7), e168.

Gessnitzer, S. & Kauffeld, S. (2015). The working alliance in coaching: Why behaviour is the key to success. *Journal of Applied Behavioural Science*, 51(2), 177–197.

Gessnitzer, S., Schulte, E. M. & Kauffeld, S. (2016). "I am going to succeed": The power of self-efficient language in coaching and how coaches can use it. *Consulting Psychology Journal: Practice and Research*, 68(4), 294–312.

Goff, P., Goldring, E., Guthrie, J. & Bickman, L. (2014). Changing principals' leadership through feedback and coaching. *Journal of Educational Administration*, 52(5), 682–704.

Goldberg, S. B., Rousmaniere, T., Miller, S. D., Whipple, J., Nielsen, S. L., Hoyt, W. T. & Wampold, B. E. (2016). Do psychotherapists improve with time and experience? A longitudinal analysis of outcomes in a clinical setting. *Journal of Counseling Psychology*, 63(1), 1–11.

Grant, A. M. (2002). Towards a psychology of coaching: The impact of coaching on metacognition, mental health and goal attainment. *Dissertation Abstracts International Section B*, 63, 6094 and downloadable at http://files.eric.ed.gov/fulltext/ED478147.pdf.

Grant, A. M. (2012). Making positive change: A randomized study comparing solution-focused vs. problem-focused coaching questions. *Journal of Systemic Therapies*, 31(2), 21–35.

Grant, A. M. (2014a). The efficacy of executive coaching in times of organizational change. *Journal of Change Management*, 14(2), 258–280.

Grant, A. M. (2014b) Autonomy support, relationship satisfaction and goal focus in the coach – Coachee relationship: Which best predicts coaching success? *Coaching: An International Journal of Theory, Research and Practice*, 7(1), 18–38.

Grant, A. M. & Cavanagh, M. (2007). The goal-focused coaching skills questionnaire: Preliminary findings. *Social Behaviour and Personality*, 35(6), 751–760.

Grant, A. M., Curtayne, L. & Burton, G. (2009). Executive coaching enhances goal attainment, resilience and workplace well-being: A randomized controlled study. *The Journal of Positive Psychology*, 4(5), 396–407.

Grant, A. M. & Gerrard, B. (2020). Comparing problem-focused, solution-focused and combined problem-focused/solution-focused coaching approach: Solution-focused coaching questions mitigate the negative impact of dysfunctional attitudes. *Coaching: An International Journal of Theory, Research and Practice*, 13(1), 61–77.

Grant, A. M., Green, L. S. & Rynsaardt, J. (2010). Developmental coaching for high school teachers: Executive coaching goes to school. *Consulting Psychology Journal: Practice and Research*, 62(3), 151–168.

Grant, A. M. & O'Connor, S. A. (2018). Broadening and building solution-focused coaching: Feeling good is not enough. *Coaching: An International Journal of Theory, Research and Practice*, 11(2), 165–185.

Graßmann, C. & Schermuly, C. C. (2016). Side effects of business coaching and their predictors from the coachees' perspective. *Journal of Personnel Psychology*, 15, 152–163.

Graßmann, C. & Schermuly, C. C. (2018). The role of neuroticism and supervision in the relationship between negative effects for clients and novice coaches. *Coaching: An International Journal of Theory, Research and Practice*, 11(1), 74–88.

Graßmann, C., Schermuly, C. C. & Wach, D. (2019). Potential antecedents and consequences of negative effects for coaches. *Coaching: An International Journal of Theory, Research and Practice*, 12(1), 67–88.

Graßmann, C., Schölmerich, F. & Schermuly, C. C. (2020). The relationship between working alliance and client outcomes in coaching: A meta-analysis. *Human Relations. Human Relations*, 73(1), 35–58.

Gray, D. E. (2019). *Doing research in the business world*. 2nd Edition. London: Sage.

Gray, D. E. & Goregaokar, H. (2010). Choosing an executive coach: The influence of gender on the coach-coachee matching process. *Management Learning*, 41(5), 525–544.

Green, L. S., Grant, A. M. & Rynsaardt, J. (2007). Evidence-based life coaching for senior high school students: Building hardiness and hope. *International Coaching Psychology Review*, 2(1), 24–32.

Green, L. S., Oades, L. G. & Grant, A. M. (2006). Cognitive-behavioural, solution-focused life coaching: Enhancing goal striving, well-being, and hope. *The Journal of Positive Psychology*, 1(3), 142–149.

Greenson, R. R. (1965). The working alliance and the transference neuroses. *Psychoanalysis Quarterly*, 34, 155–181.

Gregory, J. D. & Levy, P. E. (2011). It's not me, it's you: A multi-level examination of variables that impact employee coaching relationships. *Consulting Psychology Journal: Practice and Research*, 63(2), 67–88.

Grencavage, L. M. & Norcross, J. C. (1990). Where are the commonalities among the therapeutic common factors? *Professional Psychology: Research and Practice*, 21(5), 372–378.

Grover, S. & Furnham, A. (2016). Coaching as a developmental intervention in organizations: A systematic review of its effectiveness and the mechanisms underlying it. *PLoS One*, 11(7), 1–41.

Gyllensten, K. & Palmer, S. (2005). Can coaching reduce workplace stress? A quasi-experimental study. *International Journal of Evidence Based Coaching and Mentoring*, 3(2), 75–85.

Hazucha, J. F., Hezlett, S. A. & Schneider, R. J. (1993). The impact of 360-degree feedback on management skills development. *Human Resource Management*, 32(2–3), 325–351.

Hein, H. R. (1990). *Psychological type, coaching activities and coaching effectiveness in corporate and middle managers* (Doctoral dissertation). University of Bridgeport. Dissertation Abstracts International, 50 (10-A), 3293.

Heron, J. (1975). *Helping the client: A creative practical guide*. London: Sage.

Heslin, P. A. & Latham, G. P. (2004). The effect of upward feedback on managerial behaviour. *Applied Psychology: An International Review*, 53, 23–37.

Heslin, P. A., Vandewalle, D. & Latham, G. P. (2006). Keen to help? Managers' implicit person theories and their subsequent employee coaching. *Personnel Psychology*, 59(4), 871–902.

Hogan, R. & Hogan, J. (1997). *Hogan development survey manual*. Tulsa, OK: Hogan Assessment Systems.

Hooijberg, R. & Lane, N. (2009). Using multisource feedback coaching effectively in executive education. *Academy of Management Learning & Education*, 8(4), 483–493.

Horvath, A. O. & Greenberg, L. S. 1986. The development of the Working Alliance Inventory: A research handbook. In L. S. Greenberg & W. Pinsoff (Eds.), *Psychotherapeutic processes: A research handbook*. New York: Guilford Press.

Hoven, H., Ford, R., Willmot, A., Hagan, S. & Siegrist, J. (2014). Job coaching and success in gaining and sustaining employment among homeless people. *Research on Social Work Practice*, 26(6), 668–674.

Howard, A. R. (2015). Coaching to vision versus coaching to improvement needs: A preliminary investigation on the differential impacts of fostering positive and negative emotion during real time executive coaching sessions. *Frontiers in Psychology*, 6, 455.

Hsu, Y. P., Chun-Yang, P., Pi-Hui, T. & Ching-Wei, T. (2019). Managerial coaching, job performance, and team commitment: The meditating effect of psychological capital. *Advances in Management and Applied Economics*, 9(5), 101–125.

Huang, J. T. & Hsieh, H. H. (2015). Supervisors as good coaches: Influences of coaching on employees' in-role behaviors and proactive career behaviors. *The International Journal of Human Resource Management*, 26(1), 42–58.

Hui, T. Y., Lee, Y. K. & Sue-Chan, C. (2017). *The interactive effects of coaching styles on students' self-regulatory emotions and academic performance in a peer-assisted learning scheme*. Paper presented at the IEEE International Conference of Teaching.

Hui, T. Y. & Sue-Chan, C. (2018). Variations in coaching style and their impact on subordinates' work outcomes. *Journal of Organizational Behavior*, 39(5), 663–679.

Hui, T. Y., Sue-Chan, C. & Wood, R. E. (2013). The contrasting effects of coaching style on task performance: The mediating roles of subjective task complexity and self-set goal. *Human Resource Development Quarterly*, 24(4), 429–429.

Hui, T. Y., Sue-Chan, C. & Wood, R. E. (2019). Performing versus adapting: How leader's coaching style matters in Hong Kong. *The International Journal of Human Resource Management*, 1–27.

Hunt, C. M., Fielden, S. & Woolnough, H. M. (2019). The potential of online coaching to develop female entrepreneurial self-efficacy. *Gender in Management: An International Journal*, 34(8), 685–701.

Ianiro, P. M. & Kauffeld, S. (2014). Take care what you bring with you: How coaches' mood and interpersonal behaviour affect coaching success. *Consulting Psychology Journal: Practice and Research*, 66, 231–257.

Ianiro, P. M., Lehmann-Willenbrock, N. & Kauffeld, S. (2015). Coaches and clients in action: A sequential analysis of interpersonal coach and cliënt behaviour. *Journal of Business and Psychology*, 30(3), 435–456.

Ianiro, P. M., Schermuly, C. C. & Kauffeld, S. (2013). Why interpersonal dominance and affiliation matter: An interaction analysis of the coach-client relationship. *Coaching: An International Journal of Theory, Research and Practice*, 6(1), 25–46.

Jack, A. I., Boyatzis, R. E., Khawaja, M. S., Passarelli, A. M. & Leckie, R. L. (2013). Visioning in the brain: An fMRI study of inspirational coaching and mentoring. *Social Neuroscience*, 8(4), 369–384.

Jarzebowski, A., Palermo, J. & Van de Berg, R. (2012). When feedback is not enough: The impact of regulatory fit on motivation after positive feedback. *International Coaching Psychology Review*, 7(1), 14–32.

Jones, R. A., Rafferty, A. E. & Griffin, M. A. (2006). The executive coaching trend: Towards more flexible executives. *Leadership & Organization Development Journal*, 27(7), 584–596.

Jones, R. J., Woods, S. A. & Guillaume, Y. (2015). The effectiveness of workplace coaching: A meta-analysis of learning and performance outcomes from coaching. *Journal of Occupational and Organizational Psychology*, 89(2), 249–277.

Jones, R. J., Woods, S. A. & Hutchinson, E. (2014). The influence of the five factor model of personality on the perceived effectiveness of executive coaching. *International Journal of Evidence Based Coaching and Mentoring*, 12(2), 109–118.

Jones, R. J., Woods, S. A. & Zhou, Y. (2019). The effects of coachee personality and goal orientation on performance improvement following coaching: A controlled field experiment. *Applied Psychology*. doi:/abs/10.1111/apps.12218.

Jordan, S., Gessnitzer, S. & Kauffeld, S. (2016). Effects of a group coaching for the vocational orientation of secondary school pupils. *Coaching: An International Journal of Theory, Research and Practice*, 9(2), 143–157.

Jordan, S., Gessnitzer, S. & Kauffeld, S. (2017). Develop yourself, develop others? How coaches and clients benefit from train-the-coach courses. *Coaching: An International Journal of Theory, Research and Practice*, 10(2), 125–139.

Jordan, S. & Kauffeld, S. (2020). A mixed methods study of effects and antecedents of solution-focused questions in coaching. *International Journal of Evidence Based Coaching and Mentoring*, 18(1), 57–72.

Junker, S., Pömmer, M. & Traut-Mattausch, E. (2020). The impact of cognitive-behavioural stress management coaching on changes in cognitive appraisal and the stress response: A field experiment. *Coaching: An International Journal of Theory, Research and Practice, 16*, 1–18.

Kim, S. & Kuo, M. (2015). Examining the relationships among coaching, trustworthiness, and role behaviors: A social exchange perspective. *Journal of Applied Behavioral Science, 51*, 152–176.

Kines, P., Andersen, L. P. S., Spangenberg, S., Mikkelsen, K. L., Dyreborg, J. & Zohar, D. (2010). Improving construction safety through leader-based verbal safety communication. *Journal of Safety Research, 41*, 399–406.

Kiresuk, T. J. & Sherman, R. E. (1968). Goal attainment scaling: A general method for evaluating comprehensive community mental health programs. *Community Mental Health Journal, 4*, 443–453.

Klonek, F., Will, T., Ianiro-Dahm, P. & Kauffeld, S. (2020). Opening the career counseling black box: Behavioral mechanisms of empathy and working alliance. *Journal of Career Assessment, 28*(3), 363–380.

Kochanowski, S., Seifert, C. F. & Yukl, G. (2010). Using executive coaching to enhance the effects of behavioural feedback to managers. *Journal of Leadership and Organizational Studies, 17*, 363–369.

Kombarakaran, F. A., Yang, J. A., Baker, M. N. & Fernandes, P. B. (2008). Executive coaching: It works! *Consulting Psychology Journal: Practice and Research, 60*(1), 78–90.

Ladegard, G. & Gjerde, S. (2014). Leadership coaching, leader role-efficacy and trust in subordinates. A mixed methods study assessing leadership coaching as a leadership development tool. *Leadership Quarterly, 25*(4), 631–646.

Lambert, M. J. (1992). Psychotherapy outcome research: Implications for integrative and eclectical therapists. In J. C. Norcross & M. R. Goldfried (Eds.), *Handbook of psychotherapy integration* (pp. 94–129). New York: Basic Books.

Latham, G. P., Ford, R. C. & Tzabbar, D. (2012). Enhancing employee and organizational performance through coaching based on mystery shopper feedback: A quasi-experimental study. *Human Resource Management, 51*(2), 213–230.

Leary, T. (1957). *Interpersonal diagnosis of personality*. New York: The Ronald Press.

Leonard-Cross, E. (2010). Developmental coaching: Business benefit – Fact or fad? An evaluative study to explore the impact of coaching in the workplace. *International Coaching Psychology Review, 5*, 36–47.

Liu, X. & Batt, R. (2010). How supervisors influence performance: A multilevel study of coaching and group management in technology-mediated services. *Personnel Psychology, 63*, 265–298.

Losch, S., Traut-Mattausch, E., Mühlberger, M. D. & Jonas, E. (2016). Comparing the effectiveness of individual coaching, self-coaching, and group training: How leadership makes the difference. *Frontiers in Psychology, 7*, 1–17 [629].

Luthans, F. & Peterson, S. J. (2003). 360-Degree feedback with systematic coaching: Empirical analysis suggests a winning combination. *Human Resource Management, 42*(3), 243–256.

MacKie, D. (2014). The effectiveness of strength-based executive coaching in enhancing full range leadership development: A controlled study. *Consulting Psychology Journal: Theory and Research, 66*(2), 118–137.

MacKie, D. (2015). The effects of coachee readiness and core self-evaluations on leadership coaching outcomes: A controlled trial. *Coaching: An International Journal of Theory, Research and Practice, 8*(2), 120–136.

Martin, D. J., Garske, J. P. & Davis, M. K. (2000). Relation of the therapeutic alliance with outcome and other variables: A meta-analytic review. *Journal of Consulting and Clinical Psychology, 68*, 438–450.

McDermott, M., Levenson, A. & Newton, S. (2007). What coaching can and cannot do for your organization. *Human Resource Planning, 30*(2), 30–37.

McDowall, A., Freemann, K. & Marshall, K. (2014). Is feed forward the way forward? A comparison of the effects of feed forward coaching and feedback. *International Coaching Psychology Review, 9*(2), 135–146.

McGonagle, A. K., Beatty, J. E. & Joffe, R. (2014). Coaching for workers with chronic illness: Evaluating an intervention. *Journal of Occupational Health Psychology, 19*(3), 385–398.

McGonagle, A. K., Schwab, L., Yahanda, N., Duskey, H., Gertz, N., Prior, L., Roy, M. & Kriegel, G. (2020). Coaching for primary care physician well-being: A randomized trial and follow-up analysis. *Journal of Occupational Health Psychology, 25*(5), 297–314.

McGovern, J., Lindemann, M., Vergara, M., Murphy, S., Barker, L. & Warrenfeltz, R. (2001). Maximizing the impact of executive coaching: Behavioural change, organizational outcomes, and return on investment. *The Manchester Review, 6*, 1–9.

McKenna, D. D. & Davis, S. L. (2009). Hidden in plain sight: The active ingredients of executive coaching. *Industrial and Organizational Psychology: Perspectives on Science and Practice, 2*, 244–260.

Miller, D. J. (1990). The effect of managerial coaching on transfer of training. *Dissertation Abstracts International Section B, 50*(2435).

Miller, W. R., Yahne, C. E., Moyers, T. B., Martinez, J. & Pirritano, M. (2004). A randomized trial of methods to help clinicians learn motivational interviewing. *Journal of Consulting and Clinical Psychology, 72*(6), 1050–1062.

Moen, F. & Skaalvik, E. (2009). The effect from executive coaching on performance psychology. *International Journal of Evidence Based Coaching and Mentoring, 7*(2), 31–49.

Mukherjee, S. (2012). Does coaching transform coaches? A case study of internal coaching. *International Journal of Evidence Based Coaching and Mentoring, 10*(2), 76–87.

Myers, I. B., McCaulley, M. H., Quenk, N. L. & Hammer, A. L. (1998). *MBTI manual*. Palo Alto, CA: Consulting Psychologists Press.

Neipp, M. C., Beyebach, M., Nuñez, R. M. & Martínez-González, M. C. (2016). The effect of solution-focused versus problem-focused questions: A replication. *Journal of Marital and Family Therapy, 42*(3), 525–535.

Newsom, G. & Dent, E. B. (2011). A work behaviour analysis of executive coaches. *International Journal of Evidence Based Coaching and Mentoring, 9*(2), 1–22.

Nieminen, L. G., Smerek, R., Kotrba, L. & Denison, D. (2013). What does an executive coaching intervention add beyond facilitated multisource feedback? Effects on leader self-ratings and perceived effectiveness. *Human Resource Development Quarterly, 24*(2), 145–176.

Niglio de Figueiredo, M., Krippeit, L., Ihorst, G., Sattel, H., Bylund, C. L., Joos, A., Bengel, J., Lahmann, C., Fritzsche, K. & Wuensch, A. (2018). ComOn-coaching: The effect of a varied number of coaching sessions on transfer into clinical practice following communication skills training in oncology: Results of a randomized controlled trial. *PLoS One, 13*(10), e0205315.

Noer, D. M. (2005). Behaviourally based coaching: A cross-cultural case study. *International Journal of Coaching in Organizations, 3*, 14–23.

Noer, D. M., Leupold, C. R. & Valle, M. (2007). An analysis of Saudi Arabian and U.S. managerial coaching behaviours. *Journal of Managerial Issues, 19*(2), 271–287.

Norcross, J. C. (Eds.). (2011). *Psychotherapy relationships that work*, 2nd Edition. New York: Oxford University Press.

Nowack, K. M. (2003). Executive coaching: Fad or future? *California Psychologist, 26*(4), 16–17.

Oberschachtsiek, D. & Scioch, P. (2015). The outcome of coaching and training for self-employment. A statistical evaluation of outside assistance support programs for unemployed business founders in Germany. *Journal for Labour Market Research, 48*, 1–25.

O'Connor, S. & Cavanagh, M. (2013). The coaching ripple effect: The effects of developmental coaching on wellbeing across organizational networks. *Psychology of Well-Being: Theory, Research and Practice, 3*(2), 1–23.

Olivero, G., Bane, K. D. & Kopelman, R. E. (1997). Executive coaching as a transfer of training tool: Effects on productivity in a public agency. *Public Personnel Management*, 26(4), 461–469.

Orenstein, R. L. (2006). Measuring executive coaching efficacy? The answer was right here all the time. *Consulting Psychology Journal: Practice and Research*, 58(2), 106–116.

Page, N. & De Haan, E. (2014). Does coaching work . . . and if so, how? *The Psychologist*, 27(8), 582–586.

Parker-Wilkins, V. (2006). Business impact of executive coaching: Demonstrating monetary value. *Industrial and Commercial Training*, 38(3), 122–127.

Passmore, J. & Rehman, H. (2012). Coaching as a learning methodology: A mixed methods study in driver development. A randomized controlled trial and thematic analysis. *International Coaching Psychology Review*, 7(2), 166–184.

Passmore, J. & Theeboom, T. (2015). Coaching psychology: A journey of development in research. In L. E. Van Zyl, M. W. Stander, & A. Odendal (Eds.), *Coaching psychology: Meta-theoretical perspectives and applications in multi-cultural contexts*. New York: Springer.

Passmore, J. & Velez, M. J. (2012). Coaching fleet drivers: A randomized controlled trial (RCT) of short coaching' interventions to improve driver safety in fleet drivers. *The Coaching Psychologist*, 8(1), 20–26.

Peláez, M. J., Coo, C. & Salanova, M. (2019). Facilitating work engagement and performance through strengths-based micro-coaching: A controlled trial study. *Journal of Happiness Studies*, 21(4), 1265–1284.

Peláez, M. J., Salanova, M. & Martínez, I. M. (2020). Coaching-based leadership intervention program: A controlled trial study. *Frontiers in Psychology*, 10, 3066.

Perkins, R. D. (2009). How executive coaching can change leader behavior and improve meeting effectiveness: An exploratory study. *Consulting Psychology Journal: Practice and Research*, 61(4), 298–318.

Peterson, D. B. (1993). *Measuring change: A psychometric approach to evaluating individual coaching outcomes*. Presented at the annual conference of the Society for Industrial and Organizational Psychology, San Francisco.

Pittenger, D. J. (2005). Cautionary comments regarding the Myers-Briggs type indicator. *Consulting Psychology Journal: Practice and Research*, 57, 210–221.

Poepsel, M. (2011). *The impact of an online evidence-based coaching program on goal striving, subjective well-being, and level of hope* (Doctoral dissertation). Capella University. ProQuest No: 3456769.

Poluka, L. A. & Kaifi, B. A. (2015). Performance coaching within the telecommunications industry. *Journal of Applied Management and Entrepreneurship*, 20(4), 49–65.

Pousa, C. & Mathieu, A. (2014). The influence of coaching on employee performance: Results from two international quantitative studies. *Performance Improvement Quarterly*, 27(3), 75–92.

Ragins, B. R., Cotton, J. L. & Miller, J. S. (2000). Marginal mentoring: The effects of type of mentor, quality of relationship, and program design on work and career attitudes. *Academy of Management Journal*, 43(6), 1177–1194.

Rank, J. & Gray, D. E. (2017). The role of coaching for relationship satisfaction, self-reflection, and self-esteem: Coachees' self-presentation ability as a moderator. *Consulting Psychology Journal: Practice and Research*, 69(3), 187–208.

Reyes Liske, J. M. & Holladay, C. L. (2016). Evaluating coaching's effect: Competencies, career mobility and retention. *Leadership & Organization Development Journal*, 37(7), 936–948.

Roberts, B. W., Luo, J., Briley, D. A., Chow, P. I., Su, R. & Hill, P. L. (2017). A systematic review of personality trait change through intervention. *Psychological Bulletin*, 143(2), 117–141.

Safran, J. D., Muran, J. C. & Eubanks-Carter, C. (2011). Repairing alliance ruptures. *Psychotherapy*, 48(1), 80–87.

Schermuly, C. C. (2014). Negative effects of coaching for coaches: An explorative study. *International Coaching Psychology Review*, 9, 167–182.

Schermuly, C. C., Schermuly-Haupt, M. L., Schölmerich, F. & Rauterberg, H. (2014). Zu Risiken und Nebenwirkungen lesen Sie . . . – Negative Effekte von Coaching [For risks and side effects read . . . – negative effects of coaching]. *Zeitschrift für Arbeits- und Organisationspsychologie*, 58, 17–33.

Schermuly, C. C., Wach, D., Kirschbaum, C. & Wegge, J. (2020). Coaching of insolvent entrepreneurs and the change in coping resources, health, and cognitive performance. *Applied Psychology*.

Schlosser, B., Steinbrenner, D., Kumata, E. & Hunt, J. (2007). The coaching impact study: Measuring the value of executive coaching. *International Journal of Coaching in Organizations*, 5(1), 140–161.

Schwarzer, R. & Jerusalem, M. (1995). Generalized self-efficacy scale. Measures in health psychology: A user's portfolio. *Causal and Control Beliefs*, 1, 35–37.

Scoular, A. & Linley, P. A. (2006). Coaching, goal-setting and personality type: What matters? *The Coaching Psychologist*, 2, 9–11.

Scriffignano, R. S. (2011). Coaching within organizations: Examining the influence of goal orientation on leaders' professional development. *Coaching: An International Journal of Theory, Research & Practice*, 4(11), 20–31.

Seifert, C. F., Yukl, G. A. & McDonald, R. A. (2003). Effects of multisource feedback and a feedback facilitator on the influence behaviour of managers toward subordinates. *The Journal of Applied Psychology*, 88(3), 561–569.

Shanock, L. R. & Eisenberger, R. (2006). When supervisors feel supported: Relationships with subordinates' perceived supervisor support, perceived organizational support, and performance. *Journal of Applied Psychology*, 91(3), 689–695.

Singh, P., Aggarwal, R., Tahir, M., Pucher, P. H. & Darzi, A. (2015). A randomized controlled study to evaluate the role of video-based coaching in training laparoscopic skills. *Annals of surgery*, 261(5), 862–869.

Slegers, A. S., Gültuna, I., Aukes, J. A., Van Gorp, E. J. J. A. A., Blommers, F. M. N., Niehof, S. P. & Bosman, J. (2015). Coaching reduced the radiation dose of pain physicians by half during interventional procedures. *Pain Practice*, 15, 400–406.

Smith, B. W., Dalen, J., Wiggins, K., Tooley, E., Christopher, P. & Bernard, J. (2008). The brief resilience scale: Assessing the ability to bounce back. *International Journal of Behavioural Medicine*, 15(3), 194–200.

Smith, I. M. & Brummel, B. J. (2013). Investigating the role of the active ingredients in executive coaching. *Coaching: An International Journal of Theory, Research and Practice*, 6, 57–71.

Smither, J. W., London, M., Flautt, R., Vargas, Y. & Kucine, I. (2003). Can working with an executive coach improve multisource feedback ratings over time? A quasi-experimental field study. *Personnel Psychology*, 56, 23–44.

Sonesh, S. C., Coultas, C. W., Marlow, S. L., Lacerenza, C. N., Reyes, D. & Salas, E. (2015). Coaching in the wild: Identifying factors that lead to success. *Consulting Psychology Journal: Practice and Research*, 67(3), 189–217.

Spence, G. B., Cavanagh, M. J. & Grant, A. M. (2008). The integration of mindfulness training and health coaching: An exploratory study. *Coaching: An International Journal of Theory, Research and Practice*, 1, 145–163.

Spence, G. B. & Grant, A. M. (2007). Professional and peer life coaching and the enhancement of goal striving and well-being: An exploratory study. *Journal of Positive Psychology*, 2, 185–194.

Stewart, L. J., Palmer, S., Wilkin, H. & Kerrin, M. (2008). The influence of character: Does personality impact coaching success? *International Journal of Evidence Based Coaching and Mentoring*, 6(1), 32–42.

Stiles, W. B., Barkham, M., Connell, J. & Mellor-Clark, J. (2008). Responsive regulation of treatment duration in routine practice in United Kingdom primary care settings: Replication in a larger sample. *Journal of Consulting and Clinical Psychology, 76*(2), 298–305.

Stiles, W. B., Barkham, M. & Wheeler, S. (2015). Duration of psychological therapy: Relation to recovery and improvement rates in UK routine practice. *British Journal of Psychiatry, 207*(2), 115–122.

Stiles, W. B., Glick, M. J., Osatuke, K., Hardy, G. E., Shapiro, D. A., Agnew-Davies, R., Rees, A. & Barkham, M. (2004). Patterns of alliance development and the rupture-repair hypothesis: Are productive relationships U-shaped or V-shaped. *Journal of Counseling Psychology, 51,* 81–92.

Strijk, J. E., Proper, K. I., Van Mechelen, W. & Van der Beek, A. J. (2013). Effectiveness of a worksite lifestyle intervention on vitality, work engagement, productivity, and sick leave: Results of a randomized controlled trial. *Scandinavian Journal of Work, Environment & Health,* 66–75.

Sue-Chan, C. & Latham, G. P. (2004). The relative effectiveness of external, peer and self-coaches. *Applied Psychology, 53*(2), 260–278.

Sue-Chan, C., Wood, R. E. & Latham, G. P. (2012). Effect of a coach's regulatory focus and an individual's implicit person theory on individual performance. *Journal of Management, 38*(3), 809–835.

Sun, B. J., Deane, F. P., Crowe, T. P., Andresen, R. & Oades, L. G. (2013). A preliminary exploration of the working alliance and 'real relationship' in two coaching approaches with mental health workers. *International Coaching Psychology Review, 8*(2), 6–17.

Taie, E. S. (2011). Coaching as an approach to enhance performance. *The Journal for Quality and Participation, 34,* 34–38.

Taylor, L. M. (1997). *The relation between resilience, coaching, coping skills training, and perceived stress during a career threatening milestone* (Doctoral dissertation). Georgia State University, DAI-B 58/05, p. 2738.

Tee, D., Shearer, D. & Roderique-Davies, G. (2017). The client as active ingredient: 'Core self-evaluations' as predictors of coaching outcome variance. *International Coaching Psychology Review, 12*(2), 125–132.

Tee, D., Shearer, D. & Roderique-Davies, G. (2019). Goal attainment scaling and coaching client core self-evaluations. *The Coaching Psychologist, 15*(1), 47–54.

Teemant, A. (2014). A mixed-methods investigation of instructional coaching for teachers of diverse learners. *Urban Education, 49*(5), 574–604.

Telle, N. T., Moock, J., Heuchert, S., Schulte, V., Rössler, W. & Kawohl, W. (2016). Job maintenance through supported employment PLUS: A randomized controlled trial. *Frontiers in Public Health, 4,* 194.

Tennant, R., Hiller, L., Fishwick, R., Platt, S., Joseph, S., Weich, S., Parkinson, J., Secker, J. & Stewart-Brown, S. (2007). The Warwick-Edinburgh mental well-being scale (WEMWBS): Development and UK validation. *Health and Quality of Life Outcomes, 5,* 63.

Thach, L. (2002). The impact of executive coaching and 360 feedback on leadership effectiveness. *Leadership & Organization Development Journal, 23*(4), 205–214.

Theeboom, T., Beersma, B. & van Vianen, A. E. M. (2014). Does coaching work? A meta-analysis on the effects of coaching on individual level outcomes in an organizational context. *The Journal of Positive Psychology, 9*(1), 1–18.

Theeboom, T., Beersma, B. & Van Vianen, A. E. M. (2016). The differential effects of solution-focused and problem-focused coaching questions on the affect, attentional control and cognitive flexibility of undergraduate students experiencing study-related stress. *The Journal of Positive Psychology, 11*(5), 460–469.

Toegel, G. & Nicholson, N. (2005). Multisource feedback, coaching, and leadership development: Personality and homophily effects. *Sixty-Fifth Academy of Management Annual Meeting,* f1–f6.

Ungerer, C., Heinzelmann, N., Baltes, G. H. & König, M. (2019). The Effect of Business Coaching on NTBF Survival–Findings and Lessons Learned from a Randomized Controlled Trial. In *2019 IEEE International Conference on Engineering, Technology and Innovation (ICE/ITMC)* (pp. 1–10). IEEE.

Vale, M. J., Jelinek, M. V., Best, J. D., Dart, A. M., Grigg, L. E., Hare, D. L., Ho, B. P., Newman, R. W. & McNeil, J. J. (2003). Coaching patients on achieving cardiovascular health (COACH): A multicenter randomized trial in patients with coronary heart disease. *Archives of Internal Medicine, 163*(22), 2775–2783.

Vale, M. J., Jelinek, M. V., Best, J. D. & Santamaria, J. D. (2002). Coaching patients with coronary heart disease to achieve the target cholesterol: A method to bridge the gap between evidence-based medicine and the "real world" – Randomized controlled trial. *Journal of Clinical Epidemiology, 55*(3), 245–252.

Van Berkel, J., Boot, C. R., Proper, K. I., Bongers, P. M. & Van der Beek, A. J. (2014). Effectiveness of a worksite mindfulness-based multi-component intervention on lifestyle behaviors. *International Journal of Behavioral Nutrition and Physical Activity, 11*(1), 9.

Van Dun, R. (2020). *Coaching als energiebron: Wat is de samenhang tussen coaching en vitaliteit en welke rol speelt de relatie tussen coach en coachee binnen de uitkomsten van coaching?* [The link between coaching and vitality; and what role for the relationship between coach and coachee for outcomes of coaching?] (MSc thesis). Open University, Heerlen, NL.

Van Meurs, N. (2003). Negotiations between British and Dutch managers: Cultural values, approaches to conflict management, and perceived negotiation (PhD thesis). University of Sussex, Brighton.

Vande Walle, K. A., Pavuluri Quamme, S. R., Leverson, G. E., Engler, T., Dombrowski, J. C., Wiegmann, D. A., Dimick, J. B. & Greenberg, C. C. (2020). Association of personality and thinking style with effective surgical coaching. *JAMA Surgery, 155*(6), 480–485.

Vandekerckhove, L. (2010). Coaching and the Flemish medical entrance exam: Efficacy and self-selection. *Bulletin of the Transilvania University of Brasov, VII, 3*(52), 121–140.

Vidal-Salazar, M. D., Ferrón-Vílchez, V. & Cordón-Pozo, E. (2012). Coaching: An effective practice for business competitiveness. *Competitiveness Review: An International Business Journal, 22*(5), 423–433.

Viering, S., Jäger, M., Bärtsch, B., Nordt, C., Rössler, W., Warnke, I. & Kawohl, W. (2015). Supported employment for the reintegration of disability pensioners with mental illnesses: A randomized controlled trial. *Frontiers in Public Health, 3*, 237.

Wageman, R. (2001). How leaders foster self-managing team effectiveness: Design choices versus hands-on coaching. *Organization Science, 12*, 559–577.

Walker, A. & Smither, J. W. (1999). A five-year study of upward feedback: What managers do with their results matters. *Personnel Psychology, 52*(2), 393–423.

Wampold, B. E. (2001; updated 2015). *The great psychotherapy debate: Models, methods, and findings.* Mahwah, NJ: Lawrence Erlbaum.

Ward, M. K., Meade, A. W., Allred, C. M., Pappalardo, G. & Stoughton, J. W. (2017). Careless response and attrition as sources of bias in online survey assessments of personality traits and performance. *Computers in Human Behaviour, 76*, 417–430.

Wasylyshyn, K. M., Gronsky, B. & Haas, W. (2006). Tigers, stripes, and behaviour change: Survey results of a commissioned coaching program. *Consulting Psychology Journal: Practice and Research, 58*(2), 65–81.

Weer, C. H., DiRenzo, M. S. & Shipper, F. M. (2016). A holistic view of employee coaching: Longitudinal investigation of the impact of facilitative and pressure-based coaching on team effectiveness. *The Journal of Applied Behavioral Science, 52*(2), 187–214.

Will, T., Gessnitzer, S. & Kauffeld, S. (2016). You think you are an empathic coach? Maybe you should think again. The difference between perceptions of empathy vs. Empathic behaviour after a person-centred coaching training. *Coaching: An International Journal of Theory, Research and Practice, 9*(1), 53–68.

Will, T., Schulte, E. & Kauffeld, S. (2019). Coach's expressed positive supportive behaviour linked to client's interest to change: An analysis of distinct coaching phases. *Coaching Theory & Praxis, 5*, 1–10.

Williams, J. S. & Lowman, R. L. (2018). The efficacy of executive coaching: An empirical investigation of two approaches using random assignment and a switching-replications design. *Consulting Psychology Journal: Practice and Research*, 70(3), 227–249.

Willms, J.-F. (2004). *Coaching zur Umsetzung persönlicher Ziele. Entwicklung, Durchführung und Evaluation*. Universität Osnabrück: Diplomarbeit im Fachgebiet Arbeits- und Organisationspsychologie, Germany.

Wolever, R. Q., Dreusicke, M., Fikkan, J., Hawkins, T. V., Yeung, S., Wakefield, J., Duda, L., Flowers, P., Cook, C. & Skinner, E. (2010). Integrative health coaching for patients with type 2 diabetes. *The Diabetes Educator*, 36(4), 629–639.

Woo, H. R. (2017). Exploratory study examining the joint impacts of mentoring and managerial coaching on organizational commitment. *Sustainability*, 9(2), 181–196.

Yalom, I. D. & Leszcz, M. (2005). *The theory and practice of group psychotherapy*. 5th Edition. New York: Basic Books.

Zanchetta, M., Junker, S., Wolf, A. M. & Traut-Mattausch, E. (2020). "Overcoming the fear that haunts your success" – The effectiveness of interventions for reducing the impostor phenomenon. *Frontiers in Psychology*, 11, 405.

Zilcha-Mano, S. (2017). Is the alliance really therapeutic? Revisiting this question in light of recent methodological advances. *American Psychologist*, 72, 311–325.

Zilcha-Mano, S., Dinger, U., McCarthy, K. S. & Barber, J. P. (2014). Does alliance predict symptoms throughout treatment, or is it the other way around? *Journal of Consulting and Clinical Psychology*, 82, 931–935.

Zimet, G. D., Dahlem, N. W., Zimet, S. G. & Farley, G. K. (1988). The multidimensional scale of perceived social support. *Journal of Personality Assessment*, 52, 30–41.

Zimmermann, L. C. & Antoni, C. H. (2018). Problem-specific coaching interventions influence goal attainment via double-loop learning. *Zeitschrift Für Arbeits-Und Organizationspsychologie*, 62(4), 188–201.

Zimmermann, L. C. & Antoni, C. H. (2020). Activating clients' resources influences coaching satisfaction via occupational self-efficacy and satisfaction of needs. *Zeitschrift für Arbeits- und Organizationspsychologie*, 64(2), 149–169.

Subject index

attrition 20, 21, 28, 35, 60, 159, 161

causality 76, 91, 94, 98, 99, 119
cognitive dissonance 99

data slicing 3, 162
diversity 14, 45, 80, 82, 94, 106, 162, 163
dose-effect curve 31, 34, 36, 96, 97, 144, 155

false positives 3, 4, 15, 17, 21, 109, 159
file drawer problem 17, 160

gamma change 16
goal attainment 22, 29, 32, 34, 50–52, 55–57, 63, 66, 68, 69, 72, 73, 76, 77, 111, 121, 123, 132, 138
group coaching 6, 24, 25, 29, 58, 60, 61, 66, 67, 73, 121
GROW (Goal, Reality, Options, Wrap-up) coaching 31, 32, 34, 43, 52, 61, 66, 121

halo effect 45, 99, 105, 111, 114, 118, 124, 133

impostor tendencies 32, 77, 119, 123, 127, 129

longitudinal research 21, 30, 32, 55, 62, 66, 74, 77, 91, 96, 97, 99, 100, 135

manager as coach research 50, 54–56
medical model 90
mentoring research 95, 96
meta-analysis 3, 20, 95, 96, 106, 107, 123
multi-source (360 degrees) feedback 1, 18, 23, 28–30, 34, 35, 51–53, 57, 59, 60, 71, 107, 108, 112, 116–118, 123, 127, 132–134, 154
mutual idealisation 113, 121, 133–135

negative side effects 151–160
nonrepresentative samples 120, 163
null hypothesis / null result 21, 152, 158, 160, 161

objective outcomes 6, 36, 44, 49, 50, 52–56, 62, 65, 66, 76, 100, 109, 113, 114, 122, 154

perceived social support 24, 66, 80, 82, 95, 97
personality changes 33, 34, 36, 123, 124, 132
placebo 88, 99, 162
plagiarism 162, 163
positive affect 57, 58, 69, 70, 120
positive transference 133
post-hoc rationalisation 15, 20, 43, 132, 133, 145
psychological capital 33–35, 79, 82, 119, 120

qualitative research 2, 14, 134, 151, 152, 162

randomised controlled trial 18, 19, 23–36, 42, 96, 114, 120
remedial coaching 11, 29, 70, 85
research biases: central-tendency bias 144; choice-supportive bias 15, 16; common-methods bias 17, 133; Hawthorne effect 17, 18, 21, 43, 157; multiple-comparisons bias 19–21; perceptual bias 131–137, 145; publication bias 17, 21, 109, 160; response bias 21, 87, 144; same-source or self-score bias 4, 17, 29, 34–36, 44, 99, 133, 138, 144, 163; social-desirability bias 144
resilience 24, 29, 31, 34, 35, 40, 44, 50, 57, 62, 66, 79, 80, 97–100, 120, 144

self-awareness 74, 103, 127–129, 133
self-efficacy 24, 34, 40, 44, 47–50, 57–69, 79–82, 97–100, 119–121, 144
self-perceptions of coaches 131–136, 141–145
side effects see negative side effects
solution-focused coaching 40, 43, 46, 50, 67–72, 76, 77, 80, 107, 115, 116
Systems Psychodynamic coaching 43

team coaching 6, 53, 56, 78, 108, 115, 158
therapy model 90, 91

virtual coaching research 49, 72, 73

working alliance 8, 25, 44, 46–51, 63–72, 78–82, 85, 87–100, 134, 144

Author index

An overview of all first authors of the nearly two hundred peer-reviewed original quantitative studies in coaching that were extensively reviewed for this book.

Agarwal, R. 54
Allan, J. 33, 36, 108, 119
Andreanoff, J. 60, 115, 122
Anthony, A. 64, 119, 144
Aust, B. 50, 157

Baron, L. 3, 63, 66, 79, 81, 95, 99, 119
Behrendt, P. 62, 75, 76
Bonrath, E.M. 32, 113, 115, 122
Bowles, S.V. 49, 53, 120
Boyce, L.A. 63, 74, 80, 81, 90, 91, 95, 98
Bozer, G. 3, 7, 59, 74, 79, 80, 98, 157
Braunstein, K. 69, 77, 79, 107, 119
Bright, D. 58
Buljac-Samardzic, M. 53, 56, 78, 108, 111, 117, 158
Burke, D. 52, 121

Carson, J.B. 53, 78, 111, 115, 158
Cerni, T. 58, 117
Chen, G.H. 137
Chinn, A.T. 65, 80

Dahling, J.J. 20, 49, 55, 75, 106, 114, 122, 153
De Haan, E. 1, 2, 4, 13, 14, 16, 20, 24, 34–38, 43, 44, 46, 49, 62–66, 71–82, 85, 91–100, 106, 108, 110–112, 119–123, 134, 137–139, 142–145, 154, 162
Deane, F.P. 3, 68, 76, 114, 122, 158
Dello Russo, S. 8, 34, 35, 50, 112, 117, 120, 123, 135
Deviney, D.E. 28, 36, 158
Duijts, S.F.A. 3, 30, 35, 106, 116, 120
Dyrbye, L.N. 33, 120

Ebner, K. 61, 66, 111, 117, 121, 157, 158
Egan, T. 35
Ellinger, A.D. 49, 54, 112, 113, 117, 120, 122, 134, 135, 144
Emmons, K.M. 28, 159
Evers, W.J.G. 49, 57, 99, 119

Finn, F.A. 30, 117, 134, 159
Fischer, X. 73, 114, 122
Fontes, A. 34, 35, 112, 117, 120, 123
Franklin, J. 62, 77, 115, 122, 158

Gan, G.C. 52, 81
Gardiner, M. 59, 112, 115, 120
Gattellari, M. 96, 115, 122, 153
George, E.R. 54, 75, 84n2, 115, 122
Geraedts, A.S. 28, 159
Gessnitzer, S. 65, 71, 72, 76, 81, 82, 91, 92, 95, 98, 100, 107, 116, 134, 144
Goff, P. 31, 58, 64, 112, 117, 123, 134, 144
Grant, A.M. 29, 34, 35, 50, 51, 64, 68–70, 74–81, 92, 107, 119–121, 158, 159
Graßmann, C. 81, 95, 98, 153, 155–157
Gray, D.E. 52, 78, 80, 162
Green, L.S. 29, 73, 120, 159
Gregory, J.D. 54, 113, 117, 120, 122, 135, 144
Gyllensten, K. 57, 120

Hazucha, J.F. 53, 107, 116, 132
Hein, H.R. 136–138
Heslin, P.A. 55, 74, 132, 134
Hooijberg, R. 51, 76
Hoven, H. 59, 79, 116, 122
Howard, A.R. 71, 75, 77, 92, 100, 107, 116
Hsu, Y.P. 54, 113, 117, 120, 122, 135, 144
Huang, J.T. 54, 113, 117, 120, 122, 135, 144
Hui, T.Y. 3, 8, 50, 64, 68, 76–78, 80, 116, 117, 120, 122, 135, 144, 158
Hunt, C.M. 64, 119

Ianiro, P.M. 8, 71, 75–77, 107, 116, 135, 138

Jack, A.I. 70, 75, 77, 100, 107, 116
Jarzebowski, A. 67, 76, 117, 122, 135
Jones, R.A. 57, 120

Jones, R.J. 20, 66, 78, 79, 107, 112, 118, 159
Jordan, S. 60, 61, 72, 75–77, 107, 116, 121
Junker, S. 32, 120, 121, 158

Kim, S. 54, 81, 113, 120, 122
Kines, P. 58, 114, 122
Kochanowski, S. 30, 108, 112, 117, 123, 134
Kombarakaran, F.A. 51

Ladegard, G. 59, 75, 112
Latham, G.P. 55, 62, 74, 78, 113, 114, 122, 132
Leonard-Cross, E. 58, 79
Liu, X. 3, 20, 55, 82, 106, 114, 122
Losch, S. 32, 35, 77, 78, 115, 121
Luthans, F. 50, 107, 116–118, 120

MacKie, D. 3, 60, 79, 121
McDowall, A. 69, 76, 119, 121, 153
McGonagle, A.K. 31, 33, 79, 120
McGovern, J. 50
Miller, D.J. 56, 158
Miller, W.R. 29, 116
Moen, F. 3, 58, 119, 121
Mukherjee, S. 51, 121

Neipp, M.C. 69, 119
Newsom, G. 137
Nieminen, L.G. 49, 58, 107, 112, 118, 121, 123, 159
Niglio de Figueiredo, M. 18, 33, 36, 113, 115, 122
Noer, D.M. 137, 141

Oberschachtsiek, D. 60, 116, 159, 160
O'Connor, S. 52, 69, 70, 75, 77, 82, 107, 112, 113, 118, 119, 123
Olivero, G. 49, 53, 60, 77, 108, 115, 122
Orenstein, R.L. 49, 53, 107, 117

Passmore, J. 20, 31, 36, 115, 121, 122, 159
Peláez, M.J. 61, 112, 117, 120
Perkins, R.D 49, 53, 62
Peterson, D.B. 49, 53, 117
Poepsel, M. 29, 72, 120
Poluka, L.A. 60, 77, 79, 115, 122
Pousa, C. 56

Rank, J. 52, 78
Reyes Liske, J.M. 60, 115, 117, 123, 134

Schermuly, C.C. 51, 81, 153, 155–157, 159
Schlosser, B. 51, 112

Scoular, A. 61, 76, 78, 108
Scriffignano, R.S. 79
Seifert, C.F. 53, 107, 116
Shanock, L.R. 54, 113, 117, 120, 122, 135, 144
Singh, P. 32, 113, 115, 122
Slegers, A.S. 65, 115, 122
Smith, I.M. 50, 79, 80
Smither, J.W. 57, 108, 112, 117, 132, 134
Sonesh, S.C. 20, 51, 74, 79, 81, 95
Spence, G.B. 8, 29, 63, 120
Stewart, L.J. 63, 78, 79, 99, 108
Strijk, J.E. 28, 159
Sue-Chan, C. 50, 62, 64, 67, 68, 74, 76, 78, 115, 117, 120, 122, 135, 144
Sun, B.J. 3, 68, 76

Taie, E.S. 31, 77
Taylor, S.T. 29, 80, 120
Tee, D. 32, 35, 36, 65, 79, 115, 158
Teemant, A. 3, 60, 117
Telle, N.T. 30, 116, 120
Thach, L. 49, 53, 107, 112, 117
Theeboom, T. 7, 20, 69, 70, 77, 107, 115, 119
Toegel, G. 52, 80, 112, 118

Ungerer, C. 35

Van Berkel, J. 28, 159
Van Dun, R. 73
Vandekerckhove, L. 63, 73, 115, 122
Vande Walle, K.A. 3, 76, 78, 96
Vidal-Salazar, M.D. 58
Viering, S. 30, 116, 122

Wageman, R. 54, 82, 108, 111, 113, 114, 122, 158
Wasylyshyn, K.M. 51
Weer, C.H. 56, 77, 113, 117, 120, 122, 135, 144
Will, T. 72, 76, 77, 107, 116, 138, 143
Williams, J. S. 32, 68, 75, 107, 112, 118, 159
Willms, J.-F. 57, 78, 80, 120, 121
Woo, H.R. 56

Zanchetta, M. 32, 36, 77, 119, 121, 123, 158
Zimmermann, L.C. 3, 66, 75, 79, 81, 97–100, 112, 121, 144

Printed in Great Britain
by Amazon